Growing Beyond Hate

Keys to Freedom from Discord, Racism, Sexism, Political Conflict, Class Warfare, Violence, and How to Achieve Peace and Enlightenment

By

Dr. Muata Ashby
and
With Essays by
Dr. Karen Dja Ashby

Cruzian Mystic Books / Sema Institute of Yoga
P. O. Box 570459
Miami, Florida, 33257
(305) 378-6253 Fax: (305) 378-6253

The author is available for group lectures and individual counseling. For further information contact the publisher.

Ashby, Muata
Growing Beyond Hate ISBN: 1-884564-81-X

Library of Congress Cataloging in Publication Data

1 Hate 2 Race relations, 3 Egyptian Philosophy, 4 Esotericism, 5 Conflict resolution, 6 Self-Help.

Also by Muata Ashby

Egyptian Yoga: The Philosophy of Enlightenment
Initiation Into Egyptian Yoga: The Secrets of Sheti
Egyptian Proverbs: Tempt Tchaas,
Mystical Wisdom Teachings and Meditations
The Egyptian Yoga Exercise Workout Book
Mysticism of Ushet Rekhat: Worship of the Divine Mother

For more book listings see the back section.

Sema
ⳡ Institute of Yoga ⳡ

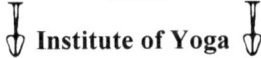

Sema (ⳡ) is an ancient Egyptian word and symbol meaning *union*. The Sema Institute is dedicated to the propagation of the universal teachings of spiritual evolution, which relate to the union of humanity and the union of all things within the universe. It is a non-denominational organization, which recognizes the unifying principles in all spiritual and religious systems of evolution throughout the world. Our primary goals are to provide the wisdom of ancient spiritual teachings in books, courses and other forms of communication. Secondly, to provide expert instruction and training in the various Sema-Yogic disciplines including Ancient Egyptian Philosophy, Christian Gnosticism, Indian Philosophy and modern science. Thirdly, to promote world peace and Universal Love.

A primary focus of our tradition is to identify and acknowledge the Sema-Yogic principles within all religions and to relate them to each other in order to promote their deeper understanding as well as to show the essential unity of purpose and the unity of all living beings and nature within the whole of existence.

The Institute is open to all who believe in the principles of peace, non-violence and spiritual emancipation regardless of sex, race, or creed.

About the authors:

Dr. Muata Abhaya Ashby

Mr. Ashby began studies in the area of religion and philosophy and achieved a doctorate degree in these areas while at the same time he began to collect his research into what would later become several books on the subject of the African History, religion and ethics, world mythology, origins of Yoga Philosophy and practice in ancient Africa (Ancient Egypt/Nubia) and also the origins of Christianity in Ancient Egypt. This was the catalyst for a successful book series on the subject called "Egyptian Yoga" begun in 1994. He has extensively studied mystical religious traditions from around the world and is an accomplished lecturer, musician, artist, poet, painter, screenwriter, playwright and author of over 50 books on yoga philosophy, religious philosophy and social philosophy based on ancient African principles. A leading advocate of the concept of the existence of advanced social and religious philosophy in ancient Africa comparable to the Eastern traditions such as Vedanta, Buddhism, Confucianism and Taoism, he has lectured and written extensively on the correlations of these with ancient African religion and philosophy.

Muata Abhaya Ashby holds a Doctor of Divinity Degree from the American Institute of Holistic Theology and a Masters degree in Liberal Arts and Religious Studies from Thomas Edison State College. He has performed extensive researched Ancient Egyptian philosophy and social order as well as Maat philosophy, the ethical foundation of Ancient Egyptian society. In recent years he has researched the world economy in the last 300 years, focusing on the United States of America and western culture in general. He is also a Teacher of Yoga Philosophy and Discipline. Dr. Ashby is an adjunct professor at the American Institute of Holistic Theology and worked as an adjunct professor at the Florida International University.

Dr. Ashby has been an independent researcher and practitioner of Egyptian Yoga, Indian Yoga, Chinese Yoga, Buddhism and mystical psychology as well as Christian Mysticism. Dr. Ashby has engaged in Post Graduate research in advanced Jnana, Bhakti and Kundalini Yogas at the Yoga Research Foundation.

Since 1999 he has researched Ancient Egyptian musical theory and created a series of musical compositions which explore this unique area of music from ancient Africa and its connection to world music. Dr.

Ashby has lectured around the United States of America, Europe and Africa.

Through his studies of the teachings of the great philosophers of the world and meeting with and studying under spiritual masters and having practiced advanced meditative disciplines, Dr. Ashby began to function in the capacity of Sebai or Spiritual Preceptor of Shetaut Neter, Ancient Egyptian Religion and also as Ethics Philosopher and Religious Studies instructor. Thus his title is Sebai and the acronym of his Kemetic and western names is MAA. He believes that it is important to understand all religious teachings in the context of human historical, cultural and social development in order to promote greater understanding and the advancement of humanity.

Dr. Karen Dja Ashby

"Dja" is the spiritual partner of Dr. Muata Ashby. She is the director of C.M. Book Publishing. She is an independent researcher, practitioner and teacher of Yoga, a Doctor in the Sciences and a Pastoral Counselor, the editor of the Egyptian Yoga Book Series. Dr. Ashby has engaged in post-graduate research in advanced Jnana, Bhakti, Karma, Raja and Kundalini Yogas at the Yoga Research Foundation. She is a certified Yoga Exercise instructor, and a teacher of health and stress management uses of Yoga for modern society, based on the Indian and/or Kemetic yogic principles. Also, she is the co-author of The Egyptian Yoga Exercise Workout Book, and author of Yoga Mystic Metaphors for Enlightenment.

TABLE OF CONTENTS

List of Tables

List of Figures

PART 1: WHAT IS HATRED?

INTRODUCTION: WHY DO WE HATE?

Hatred is one of the fundamental motivating aspects of human life; the other is desire. Desire can be of a worldly nature or of a spiritual, elevating nature. Worldly desire and hatred are like two sides of the same coin in that human life is usually swaying from one to the other; but the question is why? And is there a way to satisfy the desiring or hating mind in such a way as to find peace in life? Why do human beings go to war? Why do human beings perpetrate violence against one another? And is there a way not just to understand the phenomena but to resolve the issues that plague humanity and could lead to a more harmonious society?

Hatred is perhaps the greatest scourge of humanity in that it leads to misunderstanding, conflict and untold miseries of life and clashes between individuals, societies and nations. Therefore, the riddle of Hatred, that is, understanding the sources of it and how to confront, reduce and even eradicate it so as to bring forth the fulfillment in life and peace for society, should be a top priority for social scientists, spiritualists and philosophers.

This book is written from the perspective of spiritual philosophy based on the mystical wisdom and *sema* or yoga philosophy of the Ancient Egyptians. This philosophy, originated and based in the wisdom of *Shetaut Neter,* the Egyptian Mysteries, and *Maat,* ethical way of life in society and in spirit, contains Sema-Yogic wisdom and understanding of life s predicaments that can allow a human being of any ethnic group to understand and overcome the causes of hatred, racism, sexism, violence and disharmony in life, that plague human society.

While most religions advocate for less hatred, more understanding, peace for all humanity, etc. the world as it is today does not seem to have been helped by the efforts of world religions, which have the majority of the practitioners of religion in the world. Even though we may find some kernels of wisdom in them that could promote peace and harmony, in a real and abiding way, that has not been the active or emphasized aspect of religious practice. Also, the even higher mystical philosophy has also not been forthcoming or even acknowledged. Religions and philosophies without a mystical perspective cannot lead a human being or society to harmony and peace because the religious practice devolves into the mundaneness of ritualism and religious competitions between the religions. The higher perspective of religion, of discovering higher consciousness is thereby relegated to the fringe or even repudiated as aberrant by mainstream practitioners of the world religions. Thus, religious philosophies such as Shetaut Neter can provide the missing ingredient of spiritual philosophy that truly makes the path of *Growing Beyond Hate* possible, which requires a human being to acknowledge their kinship to humanity and effective access to higher consciousness. In secular life, supposedly enlightened government leaders espouse ideals of humanity but the societies around the world are still regularly plunged into the jaws of war due to the inability of nation states to share resources or protect the needs of their neighbors as they look out for their own welfare.

Hate can manifest in a myriad of ways; Hate speech, Hate crime, Genocide, Ethnic cleansing, Terrorism, etc. All of these manifestations have a single cause and in a higher sense, the same cure.

This volume is dedicated to the exploration of that wisdom that promotes understanding of the underlying causes of hatred, strife and discontent in life that can lead a person to resolve the important riddles of life and to create a life that is peaceful, fulfilled and enlightened. The understanding and practice of this wisdom will automatically transform the world from a place of conflict and delusion to a place of discovery, wonder and peace.

THE FRUSTRATION OF LIFE

"Indulge not thyself in the passion of Anger; it is whetting a sword to wound thine own breast, or murder thy friend."

"When sent as an emissary between people of great means, be careful to relay the true essence of the message and guard against provocative speech that angers such people. Stay with the truth. If the message was given to you with outburst, do not repeat the outburst, for maligning others is abhorred by the KA."

Ancient Egyptian Proverbs

Aristotle, a student of Ancient Egyptian philosophy, viewed hate as a desire for the annihilation of an object that is incurable by time.[1] The idea is that anger arises when an object is perceived as an obstacle to fulfilling one s desire, be it a situation or the acquisition of an object that one believes will bring happiness. But why has a person come to have that belief? And how does that belief system lead to frustration, unhappiness, anger and hate?

The Body gets older but the desires get younger.

Vedanta (Indian) Proverb

A parable is told of a man who enjoyed life. He enjoyed it so much that he began to realize that as he was growing older he would eventually not be able to do the things that he liked to do. One day he asked one of his sons to trade places with him. His son agreed because even though he was young he had studied and practiced the teachings of mystical wisdom for a long time. So the son became old and the father became young again. The father was very happy because he could once more pursue all of his desires and to attempt once more to satisfy the cravings of the body.

In time he began to grow old again and this time he became reflective. He thought within himself: I have tried for two lifetimes to satisfy all of my desires, but no sooner do I satisfy one desire than another arises, and that same desire I thought I had satisfied, I feel compelled to pursue over and over again within a very short time. What is this process of desiring and what is the end of it? It seems that no matter what I do I am never at rest. The father realized that his search to fulfill his desires by indulging in sensual pleasures of the mind and body through various activities in the world was in vain. So he resolved to study and practice the teachings

---

[1] Royzman, E. B., McCauley, C. & Rozin, P. (2005). From Plato to Putnam: Four ways to think about hate. In *The Psychology of Hate* by Sternberg, R. (Ed.).

of wisdom philosophy about life, as his son had done before, in order to end the senseless cycle of dissatisfaction, disappointment and frustration in life, leading to hatred of the things that frustrate us and cause unhappiness and finally to violence against those things. But where does this cycle of frustration begin? Why do human beings engage in activities that lead them to frustrations and ill will, to anger, hatred and violence?

This problem of the continuous cycle in which human beings, again and again, lead themselves to frustrations and conflict is called The Cycle of Vice.

Table 1: The Cycle of Vice

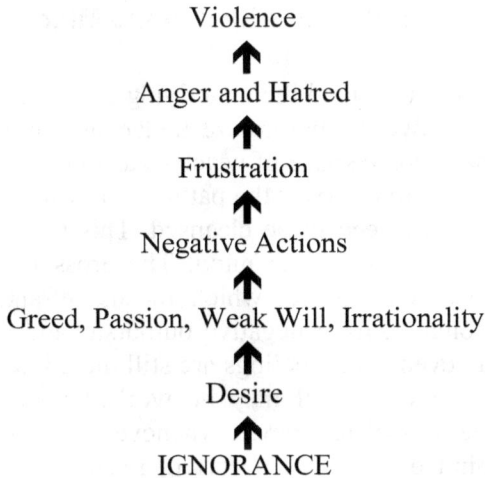

Violence

↑

Anger and Hatred

↑

Frustration

↑

Negative Actions

↑

Greed, Passion, Weak Will, Irrationality

↑

Desire

↑

IGNORANCE

How does a human being learn to feel, think and act in certain ways about the world? Of course we know about the socialization process wherein society and the experiences a human being has in it, teach them about life in that society. But the life of that society is particular to that society and not necessarily to the rest of the world or to a universal truth beyond worldly notions. Also there is something else that gives rise to the individual proclivities of a human being, their own innate understanding of life that they bring with themselves into the world when they are born and the desires that the individual s innermost feelings and thoughts lead them to. Where do those innate tendencies, preferences and understandings come from? The wisdom teaching explains that they originate from previous life experiences that left impressions in the unconscious mind that carried over into the present life experience. In Ancient Egypt this process of reincarnation and processing of desires based on previous experiences and actions [*ariu*] into a new life experience was handled by a goddess by the name of Meskhenet. These *ariu* are subtle mental impressions that cause tendencies of thought and feeling and consequently, desire in the human heart. It is those impressions that cause a human being to have individual desires, opinions and feelings based on the particular way of seeing the world that they engender in the mind of that individual. What if the mind were clear of those individuating impressions? There would be no need for desires and without desires no frustrations and without frustrations no hatred and without hatred no violence or conflict. But in order for that to be possible there must be removal of the cause for the impressions in the first place, ignorance of the knowledge of Self. So how is that accomplished?

The Cure for the Subtle Impurities of the Mind

The goal is to understand the underlying cause of hatred and that is ignorance. However, before we understand about ignorance we need to make some space of peace so as to be able to work on the hating mind. In order to discover the pathway of peace, firstly, the gross impurities of the heart need to be cleansed. This means controlling the body; next one can work on the mind. The gross impurities relate to uncontrolled ethical conscience, which means refraining from acting unrighteously, violently, from negative outbursts, and manifestations of anger and hatred even if the feelings are still there internally. If there is outer control then the internal may be worked upon. To control the external manifestations of ignorance, whenever a negative expression is arising in the mind or if it has occurred, regain control by removing yourself from the situation, go to a quiet place, alone and focus on your breath, recall this wisdom, that the present actions are due to past mental impressions, past training of the mind but now you will induce new training and in the future you will be a transformed personality.[2] Other techniques you can use to control the personality are exercise and meditation.[3] Also you should change your diet to one that promotes mental balance instead of mental agitation and also make sure you have

---

[2] For expert instruction in handling stress see the book De-Stressing 101 by Dja Ashby
[3] see the books The Postures of the Gods and goddesses by Muata Ashby and Dja Ashby, Meditation the Ancient Egyptian Path to Enlightenment by Muata Ashby

the proper nutrients the mind and body need to promote healthy and balanced thought processes.[4]

Once the gross impurities of the mind have been worked upon, it is necessary to work on the subtle impurities of the mind. For this task the disciplines of Ethical[5] culture and Wisdom philosophy was created. In order to have a mind that is capable of imbibing and making use of wisdom, the personality needs to be trained to be ethically conscious. Then the mind becomes ordered, balanced and conducive to wisdom and understanding.

In brief, there are three stages or phases in the practice of *Sema Tawi*[6] [Sema-Yoga/Egyptian Yoga] Wisdom philosophy. First the aspirant is to listen to the teachings. This stage alone is not easy if the heart is not already purified (cleansed from the gross impurities). Secondly, the task is to reflect on those teachings constantly and act in accordance with them in day to day life and understand them. Thirdly, the task now is to allow the mind to transcend the lower nature by meditating on the Higher Self.[7] When this discipline is advanced, the *ariu* or impressions from previous actions that would normally impel the individual to more egoism and ignorance, are cleansed.

Table 2: The Stages in the practice of Kemetic Wisdom Yoga to Enlighten the Mind.

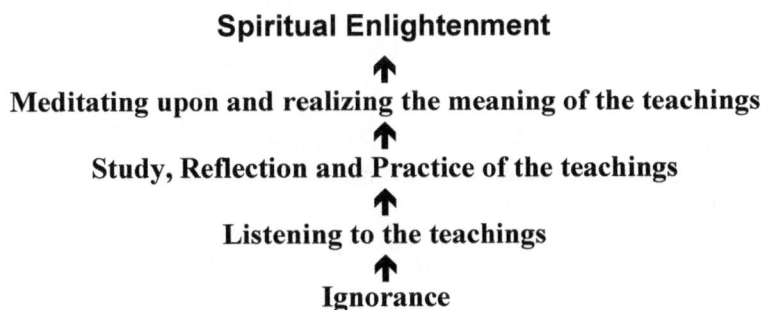

Spiritual Enlightenment
⬆
Meditating upon and realizing the meaning of the teachings
⬆
Study, Reflection and Practice of the teachings
⬆
Listening to the teachings
⬆
Ignorance

---

[4] see the book The Kemetic Diet by Muata Ashby
[5] see the book Introduction to Maat Philosophy by Muata Ashby
[6] Egyptian Yoga see the book Egyptian Yoga the Philosophy of Enlightenment by Muata Ashby
[7] For more details on the practice of Wisdom Yoga consult the book *The Wisdom of Isis* by Muata Ashby.

ATTACHMENT AND HATRED

The heart of the envious is gall and bitterness;
His tongue spits venom; the success of his neighbor breaks his rest.
He sits in his cell repining, and the good that happens to another is to him
an evil. Hatred and malice feed upon his heart, and there is no rest in
him.

Ancient Egyptian Proverb

Many people live in a state of competition, envy, jealousy and greed which causes them to resent when others prosper. It is an egoistic development which arises due to the inability to satisfy the true needs of the desiring heart. People are, in reality, not craving worldly possessions but rather inner peace, which they will never find in worldly possessions, but that belief leads them to untold degradations, resentments, hatreds and violence against themselves or others. Frustration in life arises out of ignorance of the true nature of human existence and the erroneous attachments that that ignorance leads to.

A parable is told of two men who practiced rowing for month after month because they wanted to cross a river. However, they had a problem. They did not own a boat. One evening they were drinking heavily as they walked along the shore. They became intoxicated. They saw a dinghy on the shore and so they decided to seize the opportunity and steal it right then. They jumped in and immediately began to row just as they had trained to do for so many months. They rowed for hours and as the sun began to rise they could see the shore and the people who were coming out to bathe in the river. They thought they had reached their destination after rowing all night. However, when they could see better they realized that these were people they previously knew. The people on shore began to shout, What are you doing? The two men said, We have crossed the river. What are you doing here? The people on shore replied: You fools, you were so drunk that you forgot to untie the boat. You haven't gone anywhere!

This humorous parable calls to mind the image of a hamster running feverishly in a wheel that goes nowhere; it drives home the most important teaching a spiritual aspirant needs to understand once they have advanced in the study and practice of the teachings. You can perform all of the rituals, all of the exercises, fast all you want, meditate all you want, believe all you want, learn all you want, memorize philosophy and quote all of the scriptures and still not attain wisdom or enlightenment because of one important factor. You have embarked on your journey of wisdom and self-discovery but you have forgotten to

16

untie your boat. The rowing symbolizes the rituals and outer practices of Sema-Yoga and philosophy (study of the teachings, meditation, prayer, chanting, righteous action, devotional rituals, etc.). The river symbolizes the world process (human ego with its fears, worry, illusions, ignorance, etc.) that must be traversed in order to reach the other side, the other way of life of peace, sanity, gentleness and wisdom. The boat of course symbolizes the mind and body, the vehicle you have been given for crossing the ocean of the world process. The rope tying the boat symbolizes attachments and desires. Anything you are holding on to is holding you (fettering), like a chained up animal, to the misery of human existence and is preventing you from discovering the expansion and majesty that is your true Self.

"True knowledge comes from the upward path which leads to the eternal Fire; Error, defeat and death result from following the lower path of worldly attachment."

Ancient Egyptian Proverb

The cause of human discord and racism in particular, constitutes a profound study in the nature of the human mind and the manner in which it becomes degraded to the extent of acting out of ignorance and violence. So we need to look objectively at the history of humanity as well as the nature of the mind. We will also take a closer look at the nature of human attachment.

Whenever there is partiality in the human heart there will be unrest in the mind and injustice in society. Attachment [an effect of desiring] is related to an important human factor: hatred. Both of these stem from the same source, a deep seeded ignorance[8] of the Higher Self which is the aspect of the personality most people are unaware of but that part that transcends all attachments and all hatreds. The study of the states of mind (waking and dream) offers answers to this problem of attachment and hatred. Consider that when you are asleep your dream appears real. Also consider that when you love something, you attach to it, but when you hate something, you seek to get away from it even in your dreams. However, when you wake up, both attaching and getting away from the objects of your dream becomes ridiculous. You simply dismiss everything that occurred in your dream. To achieve success in your practice of mystical spirituality you must firmly understand that like the dream world and the objects of your dream, this physical world you wake up to and the objects in it are also illusory. How is that possible? Quantum physics already demonstrates the illusoriness of the world;[9] but what does that have to do with the human mind and how can this

---

[8] Ignorance is defined here as: absence of the knowledge of the Self
[9] see the books *The Dancing Wu Li Master* and *The Tao of Physics*

knowledge be useful in discovering a pathway to peace and freedom from desire and hatred? In the state of Enlightenment, a Sage wakes up from the ego-based realities of the waking state of consciousness just as an ordinary person wakes from a dream. Further, the people in your waking dream are no different than objects in it. You have given them life and also the power to engender desire, happiness and joy in you as well as the fear and hatred in you. In reality your egoism (spiritual ignorance causing attachment to the limited personality) has allowed the world to overpower you. This translates into the various complexes, desires and fears of life. All of these stem from one source: ignorance of the knowledge of self.

Saying that the world is illusory does not mean that the world does not exist, rather, that it exists in a different form than that which can be experienced by the ordinary mind and senses. This means that the world an ordinary human being experiences is not the way the world truly is and that disparity leads human beings to think, feel and act in erroneous ways about worldly concerns; those errors lead to frustrations and conflicts. Consider that if you were to walk into a dimly lit room, you might mistake a piece of rope on the floor for a snake. However, as soon as you turn on the light in the room, it is clear that the object is only a piece of rope. Likewise, in the dimly lit mind, that is, a mind that is ignorant of its true nature, this creation appears to be a world filled with separate, individual objects. However, just as when the light is turned on in the room the snake is found to be illusory and the rope is revealed, when the light of intuitional wisdom dawns within one s consciousness, the illusion of the world disappears and the Self is revealed. And just as there was never a snake to begin with, it was always only a piece of rope, there never has really been a world process, only the manifestation of a world that was created and sustained by the ignorance that gave rise to the jealousy, envy, greed, and the desires and hatreds of life that engendered certain thoughts and feelings about the world and impelled certain actions in line with those perceptions. It was only because of ignorance as to who you really are that you allowed yourself to be duped into believing that the world as you experience it through the unenlightened mind and senses contained true sources of happiness or objects that could satisfy or fulfill your desires. However, as you work to remove the ignorance by enlightening the mind, the world and all its seemingly varied realities will have less and less hold over you, since you can see beyond the illusoriness it presents. Just like a mirage which fades when you realize that it is not real, all ego-based complexes of the mind fade, revealing the Higher Self.

The process of dealing with attachments is very subtle. Having the intellectual knowledge about what attachments are and how they affect our lives is only the beginning. A person can know something is wrong but why can t they stop themselves from doing that wrong thing? A person can feel detached but when life brings adversity such as the death of a close relative, why are the emotions overwhelmed? Why is there no intellectual capacity at that time? In practical terms, becoming wise and enlightened requires the willingness to let all attachments go and this means being unaffected by the presence or absence of people and objects as well as the things they may say or do. It means being internally established in the innermost Self and understanding as well as experiencing that everything in the universe is only a manifestation of a higher essence, just as a person manifests a dream world when they sleep. Just as objects in the mind, when one thinks thoughts, are part of the essence of the mind and are in reality not separate from the mind so too the objects of the world are part of a whole that cannot be lost or separated; therefore, desiring worldly objects is a process of trying to separate them, which is indeed an error in thought that leads to believing in the separateness of objects, people, events and concepts, like the idea that individual objects, situations or persons can bring one happiness. This erroneous thought process is the foundation of egoism, selfishness and the capacity to see others as rivals or obstacles to one s happiness. Thus, instead of continuing to be deluded into believing that objects can bring you happiness, you are to understand that the Higher Self within, is the only source of true happiness and that the little bits and pieces of happiness you experience as a result of acquiring objects is only a speck as compared to the ocean of happiness that awaits you in the state of Enlightenment. Objects have the capacity to allow you to experience happiness since they essentially are the Self. However, since your view of objects is limited, (egoistic, seeing the object as something different and separate from yourself) you will only have a limited experience of happiness through objects. Therefore, if you really want to be truly happy, stop running after objects (includes people) and instead seek to become enlightened. Ancient Egyptian Sema-Yoga[10] is a set of disciplines that promote ethical conscience, inner peace and mystical wisdom. It is part of the greater religious mystical philosophy of Ancient Egypt called Shetaut Neter. We will draw heavily from this wisdom teaching as we explore the nature of the Cycle of Vice and the means to overcome it.

Enlightenment means having woken up to the illusoriness of the dream of human life. This can only be successfully accomplished by first learning and practicing the outer teachings and then discovering and experiencing the inner Self. This experience allows the mind to let go of all illusions, fears and attachments. A person is shaken by the world because they depend on it. They believe it is the only reality. The teachings of Sema-Yoga and Mystical Spirituality show the baselessness of the world and of the egoistic human concepts. This teaching allows

---

[10] Egyptian Yoga see the books *Egyptian Yoga The Philosophy of Enlightenment* and *Initiation Into Egyptian yoga and Neterian Spirituality* by Muata Ashby

the spiritual aspirant to let go intellectually, if they have correctly understood the teachings. However, intellectual detachment alone is not the goal. The idea is to lead yourself to turn away from thinking of the world, including family, as being tied to or responsible for your experience of happiness, even as you continue to live in it, and to then attain the higher experience of life   Self Discovery. The teaching must also be practiced in daily life. And an artful way of handling the world through understanding and caring is to be developed without the burdens of attachments and hatreds.

THE SEEDS OF HATRED

Hatred originates in the consciousness of a human being as a result of ignorance of their higher nature, but how does this process work?

Ignorance

The first mental stage leading towards the development of hatred is ignorance. When the soul of a human being incarnates (associates itself with a human body and is born into a human family), an innate desire arises in the mind. This is the desire for wholeness   the wholeness which it experienced in the spirit form originally, before being born. But is it a feeling of wholeness that is not fully remembered. So the soul seeks to restore the wholeness through the prism of an ignorant mind that thinks the world holds the key to its satisfaction.

Desire

Bhagavad Gita: Chapter 16

Daivasur Sampat Vibhag Yogah--The Yoga of Division Between the Divine and Demoniac Qualities

16. Confused because of many evil desires, entangled by the snares of infatuation, intensely attached to the gratification of the senses, they fall into a foul hell.

The desire to regain the higher wholeness becomes distorted since the soul has forgotten its true immortal, eternal, blissful and peaceful nature. It identifies with the mind and body, so it thinks that the survival and prosperity of the body is its own survival and prosperity. It begins to think unconsciously: I must survive by getting food, shelter and objects which will allow ME and MY family to survive and be happy.

Most worldly-minded people believe that desires are to be satisfied whenever possible, and that this is the sole purpose of life. They believe deep down, that if this process is not possible then their life is not worth living. They come to accept the notion, reinforced by the society at large, that the pursuit of happiness means acquiring wealth and experiencing sensual pleasures. Further, people believe that the more successful (worldly success) a person is, the more possessions they have acquired, the more pleasures they are able to seek out and experience, the happier they are going to be. This is a highly incorrect notion. You need to understand that the only source of true happiness is the Higher Self which is your innermost reality and indeed connected with the universe. All happiness emanates from this source when there is understanding and experiencing of this wisdom. When people do not understand this, they believe the happiness they experienced when something happened, a situation or object they interacted with, was a result of the situation or object they acquired or experienced. They do not realize that they are merely getting a little glimpse of what is already inside of them, of their very innermost Self because the happiness was not given by the object or situation but rather opened up from inside themselves through the means of the object or situation. In other words the happiness is already there but conditioned with the idea that it needs to be allowed only when the external situation allows or elicits it. This condition renders a person a slave to the world, unable to experience happiness unless the world allows it which means a person must toil endlessly in order to promote conditions in which the world will allow them the situation or object they think brings happiness. But again, the happiness is never abiding so the cycle never ends and this is what people call the ups and downs of life or they say you have to take the bitter with the sweet , etc. A wise person does not live by those ignorant notions and does not kowtow to the vagaries or whims of the world.

The illusion that acquiring wealth and experiencing sensual pleasures is what makes people happy is based on an illusion that the media portrays with respect to materially wealthy people. However, if you were really able to peer into the day to day experiences of wealthy people, you would be able to see the shortcomings in their lives. You would see that they really are not happy, peaceful people as they may appear to be on TV or other entertainment media. Indeed, they are like everyone else except that they have the capacity to explore more egoistic desires and their wealth allows them to shield themselves from the harsher realities of life which in the end may be a worse predicament than that of an average person. The poor are also more troubled because the miseries of life put constant pressure on them and that makes reflective life difficult as well. The best condition is the one in which a person has the basic necessities of life but is neither constantly pressured by miseries nor constantly pressured by wealth to throw money at problems of life which will not be faced but in an illusory way covered over as if they do not exist. Many of them cannot even sleep without the help of drugs at night.

"It is more difficult to be well with riches, than to be at ease under the want of them. Man governs himself much easier in poverty than in abundance."
-Ancient Egyptian Proverb

A wise human being must clearly understand that true happiness and peace can only be experienced in the state of enlightenment, and cannot result from any attainment or possession in the material world, including wealth. The only way that a wealthy person can be truly happy is to become enlightened. However, even a poor person can attain this happiness and peace if they work to become enlightened. So do not become caught up in the illusion of wealth. Work to acquire wealth only to the extent that you need it to sustain your practical realities, and then use the rest of your time to pursue true happiness and peace through your practice of the disciplines of mystical spirituality.

There is no one, no matter how materially wealthy they are, that is not afflicted by adversity in life. This is because life is for spiritual growth and not just indulging in sensual pleasures. There is no corner of the world a person can go to escape their karmic destiny (effects which must manifest based on their past negative actions). Yes, sometimes people will have what appears to be a run of good luck, however; this must be put into perspective. They are merely experiencing positive fruits from seeds of action they had sowed in this area previously, either in this or past lifetimes. However, for the unenlightened, these seemingly positive effects will eventually run out, and they will have further negative experiences in the future. This is basically what life consists of, alternating experiences of pleasure and pain, with painful experiences generally predominating. Even enlightened sages experience adverse situations in their practical lives, since they too had set certain negative *ariu* (karmas/actions) in motion before they became enlightened. The difference is that an enlightened sage does not become caught up in the cycle of pain and pleasure since the sage is ever experiencing the bliss and peace of the innermost Self. A spiritual aspirant must see past the illusion that adversity in life is a bad thing. Adversity in life serves to test one s metal, just as the hardness of iron and other metals are tested by banging them with a hammer. If you see the spiritual lesson and deal with adverse situations from the perspective of becoming spiritually stronger, in faith, practice and experience, then it actually becomes prosperity. Thus, there is a spiritual saying that says, adversity is really prosperity in disguise, and prosperity is really adversity in disguise.

"Presume not in prosperity, neither despair in adversity: court not
dangers, nor meanly fly from before them."

"Adversity is the seed of well doing; it is the nurse of heroism and
boldness; who that hath enough, will endanger himself to have more?
Who that is at ease, will set their life on the hazard?
-Ancient Egyptian Proverbs

A person who operates under the philosophy that wealth, acquiring objects and indulging in sensual pleasures will bring them happiness and peace in life will always be disturbed if they cannot get what they want, and elated if they seem to get it. People think that it is good to achieve the objects they desire, but not realizing that this also leads to more entanglement, more trouble in life. When a person gets what they wanted they develop a desire for more. This is known as greed. Also, desires are addictive. After a brief period of apparent satisfaction after getting what was wanted, there emerges a craving to satisfy the same desire again and again, much like a drug addict who seeks a more potent dose each time to feel the same high. Craving may be defined as intense and uncontrolled desire. In this condition if the desires are not fulfilled, there is misery and anger. If there is a favorable situation, there is a feeling of gain. Then a longing develops to seek more opportunities to reproduce the apparently pleasurable situation. A situation of greed develops which leads to stress and anxiety. In the state of greed urges develop, to do things which you think will please others or cause others to act in your favor, or that will get you what you want, but you are disappointed when you discover that others have their own desires, feelings and goals which do not necessarily match your plans. Life does not always provide what the ego desires. You acted in a certain way expecting them to act reciprocally but were disappointed when they did not give you what you wanted, after all of your efforts. In all of this there is no peace or rest for the mind.

Therefore, the pursuit of satisfying desires in the world of human experience is not the answer to the problem of desiring just as indulging in drinking alcohol is not the answer to the problem of alcoholism. The reality is that this is an extremely dull state of mind which leads to constant mental agitation as well as untold suffering and frustration. There is never any fulfillment or contentment and without these elements the heart cannot fathom the depths of peace wherein mystical experience is to be achieved. This condition has gone on for many years, therefore, there is no guarantee that the desires will ever be fulfilled in this manner. So why not explore another way? A wise person will turn away from the ignorance and egoism which makes life miserable and enter into the intensive practice of Sema-Yoga.

There is no peace, such as that which is experienced, when there are no egoistic desires in the mind; or another way to think of it is, when the desires are all fulfilled by discovering the true source of satisfaction in life. When you realize that all occurrences in the world, good and bad, are transitory and stressful, you will turn away from the world of egoistic human activity to discover the true wellspring of happiness and peace. You will break the bonds which compelled you to act un-righteously or to act with erroneous expectations of gaining something abiding out of your activities. Then you will be beyond disappointments and frustrations. When you reach this point in your life you will realize that you can seek to advance in life but that advancement should not be seen as the source of happiness. Your inner spiritual attainment is the only true source of abiding happiness. All outer forms of pleasure are in reality only limited manifestations of your inner fullness. Therefore, as you grow spiritually, you will discover greater and greater inner peace and happiness, even though you continue to perform your duties in the world.

Frustration

The world is purposely made so there is no perfect situation in which a human being can achieve abiding happiness. Yet, human beings strive endlessly, trying to produce conditions in the world which will provide happiness, security and prosperity. Eventually this struggle becomes frustrating and agitating to the mind. This frustration with the world leads a person to feel anger towards that which they perceive as obstructing their movement towards fulfilling their desires. This may be an object, a person or a group of people. The next stage is where a person feels repulsion from that which is perceived as the source of pain and frustration. They develop dislike or hatred towards the object, situation or person. The thoughts which arise at this level are similar to: This object is preventing me from getting what I want so I don t like it. A sense of contradictions, with life, develops. Instead, one needs to realize that the world is purposely made so that there is no perfect situation to push every individual to strive for inner perfection. And one must also reflect on the law of cause and effect, and acknowledge that it is due to their own actions that this situation has developed.

Anger

Anger is an expanded feeling of frustration. It clouds the intellectual capacity of a human being. The mind rationalizes its feelings of discontent and pushes out the thoughts of understanding, compassion and sharing. The comfort and discomfort of the ego become the central issue. *ME, MY* and *"what I want"* become the focus of attention and the object of all efforts. Thus, anger is due to the inflation of the ego. The thoughts at this level have escalated to: Its ME against the world and I resent everyone who is competing with ME and MY family for jobs, food and wealth and I don t like people who come into MY neighborhood and change it with their ways; I want things MY way, etc.

Hatred

Hatred is an expanded feeling of dislike towards something and it is so powerful that it clouds the intellectual capacity of a human being. When a person constantly feeds the mind with negative thoughts and the frustrations of life accumulate, the feelings of anger grow into the emotion of hatred towards that which is perceived to be the cause of the frustration. Now a person is openly expressing animosity and dislike towards things. Hatred is an intensified form of negativity towards particular objects and people. There develops a loathing and heightened repugnance which leads a person to a state of desperation, a hopelessness, whereby the object or situation must be removed in order for the person to feel good again. Here the thoughts are: Let me devise a plan to get this person out of the way. I despise that person and I wish they would die or I must do something about this object which is preventing my happiness. Also compounding this situation is the lack of self-esteem in those who have weak personalities. Since they have little or no internal security in themselves or from the world they feel that in order to experience a measure of inner contentment and satisfaction with themselves, they must see faults in others, sometimes to the extent of making them out to be less than human; which allows them to justify atrocities and all manner of injustices against them.

Thus, sustaining thoughts of anger and hatred in the mind clouds the intellect and prevent a person from feeling empathy (identification with and understanding of another's situations, feelings, and motives.) This is a movement wherein the mind is deluded and a person creates ideas about the world and its people which do not conform to reality. Another problem compounding the negativity in a human being is the hardening of the ego which is caused by the lack of facing one s frustrations and desires as well as the prejudices that develop from these, with wisdom and understanding. Rather, an egoistic person seeks to segregate himself or herself as a means to escape the problems or deals with them from a position of attempting to exert physical control (with guns, money, rhetoric, dishonesty, etc.) instead of dealing with life or with other people on equal ground, with respect as equals. This delusion opens the door to the expression of the anger and frustration in the form of psychological and physical violence towards others.

All of the negative qualities in a human being exist as a result of obstructions in the virtuous capacity of a human being, just as on a rainy day, the darkness of the sky exists because of the obstruction of the light of the sun by clouds. This means that every person is innately virtuous. Negativity manifests in the personality due to the inability of a person to discover virtuous qualities within due to the existence of the dark clouds of ignorance, that cloud the mind as to the true nature of the Soul. For example, when a person s inability to love is distorted in the mind due to the process of desiring and coveting, it manifests as hatred. So it must be understood that no person is innately evil, but that they have fallen into a pit of darkness, called ignorance, from which they can all emerge through acquiring the light of wisdom, no matter how low they may have fallen.

Violence

Bhagavad Gita: Chapter 16

12. Bound by the fetters of numerous desires, obsessed by lust and anger, they strive for acquiring wealth by adopting unrighteous means, for the sake of gratifying the senses.

Feelings derived from thoughts of anger and hate accumulate like the pressure in a volcano, and when the pressure reaches a certain level, the volcano of the mind explodes in passionate feelings, thoughts, and words that cloud the intellect and impel a person to egoistic actions. Violence is an acting of out the negativity that is within. It is an expression of the lower nature in a human being and the lack of self-control. Many people in modern society feel that such physical strength and the ability to express that kind of strength in the world is a positive thing but in reality it is an expression of spiritual weakness and the inability to control the mind.

One of the most subtle but important forms of violence is the philosophy of ownership. People are little more than caretakers of their property (including their bodies) while they are alive and yet they develop pride and feelings of superiority towards others in proportion to the objects which they own. They hoard resources and, due to greed, refuse to share with others equally. This lack of understanding and harmony leads to strife and conflict often ending in wars and other forms of dispute and animosity. Modern technology could feed every person on earth and yet the resources are hoarded unjustly. By creating societies where minorities of people gain most of the wealth, people create unnecessary pain and anguish for others and an atmosphere of animosity

26

between the haves and the have-nots while professing the philosophy of the survival of the fittest. Some promote the notion that people should get out and do what they did to succeed and so on, not thinking of the barriers to advancement which those in power have set up and are supporting. Generally speaking, when people become rich they feel justified in looking down on others, and when they become poor they feel lost and inferior as well as resentful of others who move ahead. Poor people sometimes look up to the rich with admiration even if they are unrighteous and aspire to be like them, even if it means losing one s health, perspective on life or friendships. All of these situations, the superiority and the inferiority, are related to the weakness of the mind due to spiritual ignorance. In the end both wealth and poverty are illusory conditions of life since a person must leave all their material possessions behind at the time of the death of the body. Further, they are relative, based on the particular culture. If a person leads their life based on the standards of society they will be endlessly driven to struggle in the rat race of life, ending in disease and death without having achieved a higher purpose in life, like discovering the meaning of life and the path to true abiding happiness. Thus, Sema-Yoga philosophy education is a most effective way to remove animosity and improve understanding among peoples.

Another important factor about anger and violence is that they do not get a person what they want. Even though many people are not aware of it, everyone is seeking to be peaceful and happy, even when they are making themselves or others suffer. Can you think of one thought you have or one action you perform through which you are not trying to derive happiness and peace? Yet the egoism distorts the efforts and they often turn out as actions that have the consequences of acted out anger and frustration. Anger and violence only intensify the internal anxieties and create mental agitation, which prevent a person from experiencing real peace of mind and true connections with humanity and the universe. Peace of mind and awareness of the Divine in one s life is the only kind of true wealth which is real and eternal. Yet, people put all of their energies into achieving social status, gaining material riches or control over their environment or other people.

Thus, hatred of others is caused by deficiencies in the personality of the hater. Hatred may manifest as disputes over race, sex, religion, class, money, resources, ideology, etc., but the source of all hatred is the same: Ignorance of the knowledge of the Self and the understanding of the unity of all human beings in the Self. So it must be understood that when one hates others, one is hating oneself and from a higher perspective, when one is hating others or oneself, one is hating God, that divine essence within every human being. Would a person in their right mind do such a thing? If you answer no then you must also understand that those who hate are suffering from the mental disease of spiritual ignorance and this disease must be cured with the medicine of real disciplines of mind and body which will lead a person to discover true intellectual insight, psychological peace and spiritual awakening. People act with hatred due to ignorance and greed. Consider that a medical doctor does not hate patients because they are sick. Rather, the doctor tries to help them.

It must be understood that greed is a form of violence because it leads to inordinate hoarding of wealth and opportunities that prevent the people who have not hoarded wealth to pursue the necessities of life including health care, proper nutrition, educational opportunities and proper employment or commercial opportunities. This disparity causes untold miseries and early deaths due to malnutrition, disease and stress that also lead to higher rates of crime, immorality, miseducation and general degradation in society. So, egoism, which leads to greed and the resulting mass social violence of the wealthy against entire populations and even nations, is the source of the great burden of pain and suffering for society.

The Key to Understanding and Growing Beyond Hate

A person who wants to overcome hatred needs to understand that those who hate are suffering from the disease of hatred which is caused by ignorance, greed, desire, frustration and anger. They are really to be pitied. As a response, person who wants to overcome hatred should cultivate understanding and feelings of compassion towards people who promote such egoistic sentiments (hatred, racism, sexism, etc.).

The bottom line is this. The work to overcome hatred, whether at the level of the individual or between groups or societies will never reach it s fullest potential without the striving to discover the nature of the higher Self. Any efforts, no matter how well intentioned or how seemingly enlightened they may be, to move beyond hatred, will fall short if there is no movement towards discovering the essential nature of humanity and everyone s equal claim to human existence, humane treatment and opportunity to progress. This is because only the movement towards self-discovery affords a human being the opportunity to move beyond egoistic desires and selfish acts, to not only intellectually understand the underlying unity of humanity but the inexorable innate and reciprocal quality of all existence. What we speak of here is a wholistic vision not born of wishful thinking but of in the moment experiencing. Those human beings who have not been conditioned by their societies to feel and think bias do not do so. Those human beings who have experienced the oneness of humanity would not perpetrate racism, sexism or any other ism on any member of humanity. Or we may conclude that just as a person has been taught to hate they can be taught to love, if not appreciate the other. This would mean that neither love nor hate is endemic in the human personality. Rather, we could conclude that the deeper normal state is peace, which neither runs towards (desire) or runs away from (repudiation, hated) the other. We therefore could also conclude that bias, selfishness, inhumanity and hate are aberrations of the human personality, like disease.

If you were presented with someone who had a cancer of the brain, and even if they cursed you or said weird things you found distasteful, you would no doubt treat them with compassion; why, because they do not mean to be hurtful because they are suffering from an illness. You would not hate them, but pity them. Likewise, hatred is no different than a cancer of the mind which is destroying the person s ability to connect with their deeper spiritual essence and also eats away at a person s capacity to experience connections in ordinary life with other people and with nature. It begins with a seed of ignorance and grows to the cancer of hatred. That hatred not only hurts the person hated but also the hater. Anger and hatred have been shown to cause physiological damage to the body and of course the stress of hating makes one feel the discomfort one wishes on the other who is hated.

Meat Eating as a Cause of Hate

Cancer is most frequent where carnivorous habits prevail.
-Scientific American, 1892 A.C.E.

Stress is an important aspect of mental capacity and propensity to aggressiveness and violence. Health and environmental issues are great stressors that often lead people to varied degrees of mental and physical anguish that in turn promotes intensified egoism, dislikes, frustrations and ultimately hatreds. It has been documented, at least since the late 19th century A.C.E., that people that eat meat are more prone to diseases such as cancer. It has also been established that people who are vegetarians are less aggressive and less prone to violence than people who are meat eaters. Meat eating introduces to the body not only carcinogenic elements but also chemicals that affect the mind. Persons that consume the meat of animals, beef, poultry, fish, etc. have more cancers and more mental agitations; they are more sexually active and have a more active greater sex drive. Vegetarianism can sustain the human body since the human body is designed for vegetarianism. Meat eating only became fashionable and available to human beings in the last several hundred years; prior to that time humanity was mostly vegetarian. The capacity for mass production and the association of meat with status as high class as well as the addictiveness of meat, caused meat eating to become a mainstay of the diet of the developed and developing nations. It has been found that when people that live in less developed nations that do not have meat as a staple of their diet move to countries where meat eating and processed foods are the main part of the diet, those people who previously were vegetarians and suffered less diseases including cancer start to have the same incidence of disease as the country with the high meat and processed food consumption.[11] Therefore, for health reasons and for the purpose of promoting freedom from hate, it is important to consider that in promoting non-violence, peace and understanding, vegetarianism should be promoted.[12]

What is true happiness and how can it be attained?

A simile is given of a lake. When a lake is calm, it easily reflects the trees, sun and other objects around it. However, when the wind is blowing and the water becomes agitated and rippled, the images become obscure. They appear to be broken up. The more ripples are present on the surface of the water, the more broken up the images will appear. Likewise, when the mind is calm, the Higher Self is easily able to reflect in your personality, allowing you to experience peace and happiness. However, when the ripples of the desires and thoughts are stirring up the lake of the mind, the reflection of the Self becomes obstructed, and a person experiences mental and physical restlessness, unhappiness and dissatisfaction with life. Instead of understanding that the reason they are experiencing happiness when they acquire objects or situations they consider to be good is because the feeling they have of being fulfilled allows the stress from the desires of the mind to subside for a brief period allowing the Higher Self to more accurately reflect in their personality, most people relate their experience of happiness to the object or situation they acquired. So, when they desire to experience the feeling of happiness, instead of quieting the mind, they further agitate it by chasing after objects and situations similar to those which they previously related with the experience of happiness. In reality, happiness comes from mental peace and the inner feeling of fulfillment that comes from discovering freedom from the pressures of egoistic desires [that can never be fulfilled in the world because the world is always changing and situations are always temporary].

Therefore, to experience true happiness, happiness that does not fade as a result of various external happenings in the world, one should seek to learn and practice ways of controlling and calming the mind, of controlling the desires and thoughts that keep the mind in a state of

---

[11] For more details on the vegetarian diet see the book *The Kemetic Diet: Food for Body, Mind and Spirit* by Muata Ashby
[12] See the book *De-Stressing 101: Tools for Living a Stress-Free Life* by Dr. Karen Dja Ashby

restlessness and agitation. Those who have become wise do not accept the transient and faulty nature of the happiness and do not credit objects of the world for the experience. Those people who credit the objects or situations of the world for their happiness cannot maintain the object or situation in the same condition all the time, so they will cease to be happy when the object deteriorates or the situation changes, as they inevitably will at some point in the future. Again, not understanding the object or situation was not the source of their happiness, they blame the external conditions that deprive them of the object or situation that they associated with the feeling of happiness, for their loss of the experience of happiness, and run to acquire a new object or situation in an effort to be happy again. Thus, this pattern of chasing objects to be happy becomes a vicious cycle. The majority of people in this world are caught up in this vicious cycle and will continue to be caught up in it again in the future, until finally, they become introspective and reflective. If only they could realize that the only source of happiness is right in their very heart (consciousness) and is not dependent on worldly occurrences to be experienced, they could have the peace and relaxation experience at this very moment by simply relaxing the desires and thoughts of their minds. Developing this profound ability to relax the mind in order to experience this profound and abiding peace and happiness is the goal of the disciplines of Sema-Yoga.

When people do not understand this most profound point, they look for happiness in the world. They expect other people or some situation or object to make them happy. As a result, they are always in conflict with other people who they perceive are in competition for the same person, situation, resources or object. People actually come to believe that, just as people and objects can make them happy, so to they can make them unhappy; so it is someone else s fault that they are unhappy. Consequently, they develop anger, hatred, envy, jealousy, fear, insecurity, covetousness and other negative egoistic sentiments towards others, blaming others for their thwarted desires. This becomes a basis for racism, sexism and every other -ism that exists in society. Racism, like the other negative isms of society, is essentially a form of spiritual ignorance (egoism), ignorance of one s (and consequently others) spiritual basis.

SEXISM

Sexism may be thought of as distinctions in society dedicated to seeing differences between men and women and especially causing the male to be dominant over the female. Another way of understanding sexism is in terms of gender and sexual violence, as a systematic and institutionalized effort to subjugate women. In effect, sexism is a form of slavery that is born of the same ignorance that causes other forms of injustice and inhumanity of one human being on another, in this case male on female. The treatment for the problem of sexism is the same as that for racism, intolerance and other forms or derivatives of hate which emanate from the root cause of ignorance of self, which has caused such degradation in a human being as to render them incapable of feeling a kinship connection with others, sometimes even to the level of taking delight and pleasure in the suffering of others. Sexism may take the form of rape on the individual level, as domestic violence at the family level, and as social disenfranchisement on a national. Sexism can also occur when women disrespect the humanity of men.

It is important to understand that the depravities that manifest in the mistreatment of one gender of another are a result of the pain, fear and psychosis of a life led in darkness; that darkness is the place within where the negative imaginings and delusions of the heart can grow to overwhelm the personality and allow or even compel it to acts or cause others to acts of degradation and atrocity upon themselves or on others.

Figure 1: Picture of the entrance of the National Association Opposed To Woman Suffrage's headquarters.

Figure 2: US Army Private Lynndie England holding a leash attached to a prisoner collapsed on the floor in the Abu Ghraib prison. England was convicted by a US Army court martial for abusing prison detainees

RACISM

The American Heritage Dictionary defines racism as:

1. The belief that some races are inherently better than others.
2. Racial prejudice or discrimination.

The study of mystical spirituality illuminates the ignorance about race and ethnicity. Before we begin this essay it is important to understand that the definition above is incorrect. It is incorrect because it falsely accepts the notion of race itself as a fact when in reality it is illusory. Since there is no such thing as races there can be no such thing as racism . So what is going on? Where does the trouble come from that seems to manifest as conflicts between groups of people? All human beings have an eternal soul which transcends all outer appearances. All human beings originate from the same source and are all related. So where did the notion of differences come from? The notion of individuality and separate groups is based on a lack of knowledge or learning, greed, hatred, feelings of inadequacy or other failings which cause a person to act out of fear of others or think of ways to hurt or steal from others.

Racism is no different than any other form of dislike. People often want to see differences in things and thereby they attach to the good and try to get away from what they perceive as bad. But these perceptions are like those of a person having a dream and hating someone in the dream when everything in the dream is a manifestation of their own consciousness. The answer to the person dreaming is to wake up and not to hate the dream personalities or objects that seem to cause happiness or unhappiness. Yet, most people do not want to wake up from the egoistic notions they have about themselves and the world they live in. The answer to racism from the individual spiritual aspirant s perspective is the same as the answer to unhappiness, fear, egoism and all other maladies of life to wake up to your higher spiritual reality. You need to understand that you are not a body, not a black, white, red, yellow, etc., person, and that the deeper you is free of this world of human desire, frustrations, and ignorance. In a manner of speaking, these are your dream identifications due to spiritual ignorance. You are much more than that. As you study and practice the wisdom teachings you will discover this. Though your body may have some relations in the world, it is not the essence of WHO you are but only WHAT you are manifesting as temporarily. So the enjoyments or sufferings of the personality are also temporary but in the grand scheme of things also meaningless. What is more important is the WHO as in Who am I? This is the important question of life that if answered all other questions, issues, or struggles of life would be resolved.

Figure 3: An African-American man climbs stairs to a theater's "colored" entrance, Mississippi, 1939. The door on the ground level is marked "white men only".

It is important to understand that the mind that differentiates and assigns value judgments based on the egoistic notions is the problem. Also, it is important to understand that, from a philosophical perspective, desiring the good is as troubling to the mind as hating what is bad because both agitate the mind and lead one away from discovering the peace that comes from discovering the underlying essential nature of all realities. Think of your life, family and friends. From a higher philosophical perspective, if you are attached to these because you perceive them as being good it is no different than hating racists because you perceive them as being bad. This may seem hard to understand at first but when you reflect upon it deeply you will see the wisdom of this teaching. This is not to say that there are no positive and negative people in the world but loving and hating does cloud the mind to the possibilities that transcend worldly likes and dislikes, of experiencing inner peace and thereby tapping into higher powers that actually could enable a person to promote more peace, understanding and harmony in the world. This is the kind of power that great personalities throughout history, such as Mahatma Gandhi, Martin Luther King, Akhenaton, Imhotep and others have accessed in the past. Thus, the net effect of desire and or hatred on your mind is the same. Your mind is being agitated by both of these factors that which you love and that which you hate. Either way you are holding onto the illusion of body consciousness, that is to say, the idea of yourself only as an individual, as an ego, separate from others and disconnected from your higher reality as a universal being. Spiritual practice leading to enlightenment does not mean leaving the world to get away from attachments and hatreds. It means rising so high in understanding and inner experience that you transcend attachments and hatreds. You let them go internally and live life free of any restrictions and limitations of the world. It does not mean not having likes and dislikes but being indifferent to their presence or absence and being immune to their effects on the mind, essentially, being able to remain balanced and at peace whether or not a desire is fulfilled or a negative situation is experienced. This process necessitates study and reflection through instruction and coaching by authentic spiritual teachers because the mind can so easily fool itself into misapplying the teachings. The spiritual teaching does not negate the practical reality. It does however allow you to understand it and deal with it in perfect balance of mind (Maat-righteous living). This is the highest form of Maat philosophy practice to act without attachment, fear, hatred, greed, etc., but instead, from the higher divine feeling directed towards the good of all.

> "Be chief of the mysteries at festivals, know your mouth,
> come in Hetep (peace), enjoy life on earth but do not
> become attached to it, it is transitory."
> Ancient Egyptian Proverb

Many people want to go to heaven but they do not want to die. In the same way a person cannot promote qualitative peace in the world or propose to attain enlightenment and also hold onto the egoism of the world not to any part of it (good or bad). In fact a person s concepts of good and evil are egoistic concepts and the higher aspect of Maat goes beyond these. In Ancient Egyptian mysticism, Maat was a spiritual philosophy of life presided over by the goddess of cosmic order (Maat). Maat knows nothing of good and evil; she only knows of duty, correctness and truth. If you have a dream and in the dream you receive a pot of gold you may consider this good, but when you wake up it vanishes. The same thing happens in real life. A person can become rich overnight and become a pauper the next day. So, as far as the discovery of abiding happiness is concerned, the good is as illusory as the bad. The answer is to understand the nature of the world and then to rise above these concepts and their entanglements. This is accomplished through the art of detachment and dispassion born of knowledge and experience which develop into wisdom.

As an aspirant to the wisdom teaching, you must live in the world but not allow it to taint your mind with sentimentality or illusions of any kind. Patience is important; this is a discipline to be practiced and achieved over time. When a person turns away from the world it is then possible for them to discover that the attachments and hatreds of the world were preventing them from discovering the higher fulfillment of all desires. The love of ordinary human beings of other human beings and of objects of the world is a limited expression of a greater love and happiness which is possible. This is why the teachings lead an aspirant to transform attachments and desires for the world into attachments and desires for the Higher Self. When you love someone, you love only that person, but when you love the Higher Self, you love all persons. So, though seemingly a selfish venture, having to turn away from the world by developing detachment and dispassion, enlightenment is the most unselfish task anyone can undertake, because as you overcome anger, hate greed and other vices from within yourself. As you become a more understanding, compassionate, peaceful an internally happy person, the world automatically becomes a better place to live in, for yourself as well as for others. All humanity will be benefited by your attainment. This is the essence of all spiritual traditions but few people are prepared to give up their notions, their opinionated ways of thinking, about the world and their prejudices and intolerances and inability to understand and accept others in order to fully pursue the highest goal of life the wisdom of Self. They do not realize the impossibility of finding what they are looking for   true happiness and peace which does not fade away   in the world. The egoism becomes projected onto religious ideas and those are held as attainments that would produce happiness for the people that practice those religions, if only all people converted to my religion then there would be peace on earth and I would be happy , etc. Would you look for a tree in the sky? No! To look for a tree in the sky or a cloud in the mud would be irrational, yet you continue to look for true happiness and peace in the world where you can NEVER find them.

"Searching for one's self in the world is the pursuit of an illusion."
-Ancient Egyptian Proverb

This deficiency in understanding has degraded humanity to such a degree that, for the most part, religion is practiced in name only and, for the most part, the ultimate goal of religion, to discover God, is never discussed or promoted as the ideal. Rather, faith in God is touted as the higher ideal; but attaining wisdom and even experiencing God, which would seem to be higher attainments, are often repudiated by practitioners of orthodox religion. When great souls incarnate, gifted people who are versed in providing spiritual insights and urge active methods to pursue the higher ideals of religion, the popular culture often brands them as insane , radical or as fanatical. On the other hand, many ordinary people, who live in the world and intrinsically know there is a better way for all, do not change the world since they to are infected by the disease of attachments and hatreds, albeit at a lesser degree. Yet those attachments and hatreds support the world in which those people who experience these, negative aspects of human egoism, to the extreme, can lead the world to dire negative conditions. There are also sincere spiritual seekers who hurt themselves because they have gone to extremes in their search for freedom from the world due to inadequate preceptorship. True spiritual practice does advocate increasing intensity in the spiritual practice but does not advocate extremes of any kind. It is a natural movement of increasing devotion to the Divine and increasing knowledge and experience of the Divine.

There are many people who, in an ignorant search for explaining the differences among people and supporting their own delusions about people, cultures or societies, seek to prove through some scientific means that some people are different than others, stronger, more beautiful, more intelligent, etc. This fallacy can be found in all groups. Some may seek to prove some genetic difference and others may seek to prove that it is based on glands or pigmentation or any number of notions. However, when authentic science is turned towards these theories they would be quickly debunked. Even though they are often exposed for their fallacious nature, still people cling to them due to their inability to face the truth and to liberate themselves from the ignorance of looking for methods to prove superiority or inferiority. If the theories of superiority or inferiority were true, they should hold up to the test of science and time. They should be true all of the time without exception. If one group was supposed to be intrinsically superior to another, why is it that people with physical, psychological, ethical, and spiritual deficiencies can be found in all groups? If one group is supposed to be demoniac why is it possible to find people who act and encourage others to act in a saintly manner within that group? If one group is supposed to be more spiritual than another, why is it possible to find criminals who commit heinous crimes within that group regardless of their genetics or level of pigmentation?

Nature is set up in such a way that the soul may encounter all manner of different human personalities from which it can derive different human experiences. This is the underlying reason for the differences in strength, stamina, intelligence, etc. However, since every person has the same origin and fundamental genetics in common, they also have the same potential to evolve with the right circumstances and education; all have the potential, working through purified mind and wisdom, to overcome obstacles in the world. The struggle to overcome these obstacles is the process by which the soul raises itself up from degradation and illusion to discover its true, supreme nature in the Higher Self. All human beings have an innate potential to achieve great heights in their own way. Sages and saints are found in all so-called ethnic and racial groups. So there is no need to seek proof that one group is superior or inferior to another. That idea is illusory and therefore false. When you are ready to face the truth and to find happiness and fulfillment within yourself by discovering your true Self, then you will not be interested in supporting your illusions and personal feelings of inadequacy and fear by denigrating, exploiting or otherwise hurting others. Sometimes people s hatred clouds the mind to the extent that they gossip about others to enjoy hearing about the problems of others or make up stories about others to make them seem something they are not (ugly, sick, evil, subhuman, etc.). The denigration of others can originate from a political source; a political leader may denigrate others to create hatred in a group so that the political agenda against the group that is the intended target of the hatred can be achieved by manipulating the egoism of the members of the group. Posters with dehumanizing images of supposed enemies, depicting them as hideous animals, and sometimes depicting them as sexual threats to white women were common forms of propaganda. Dehumanizing epithets or slogans reflecting stereotypes of "black" people and others such as dirty Japs , gooks , sambo , towel head and a myriad of other words that can be made into slogans or may be used in unmixed company have the effect of dehumanizing the intended victim(s) in the minds of the users so as to facilitate their feelings of opposition and hatred against the victims and thereby justify their suffering and the perpetration of unrighteousness against them by the haters. When you realize the error you are promoting you will not want to become involved in these degraded human activities. You will not need to seek illusory sciences which are only helping to cloud the issue of the underlying unity among all humanity.

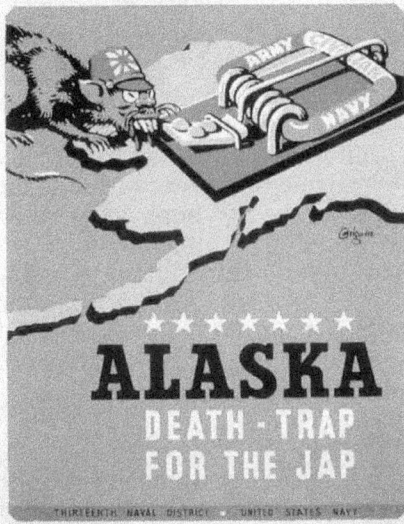

Figure 4: Poster for Thirteenth Naval District, United States Navy, showing a Japanese soldier as a rat representing Japan, approaching a mousetrap labeled "Army, Navy, Civilian," on a background map of the Alaska Territory.

In order to discover a pathway from the ignorance of dehumanization and denigration of others that degrades both the hater and the hated we need to look to the wisdom which renders such ideas powerless. In other Ancient Egyptian spiritual texts, Aset {Isis} informs Heru {Horus} that *sex is a thing of bodies and not of souls,* and elsewhere we are instructed that *the body belongs to the earth and the soul to heaven.* Therefore, we are to understand that the task of the mysteries of Sema-Yoga involve relearning our conscious identification from the body to the soul essence. Again, the question should be asked Who am I? but also the question should be asked Who is that other?

39

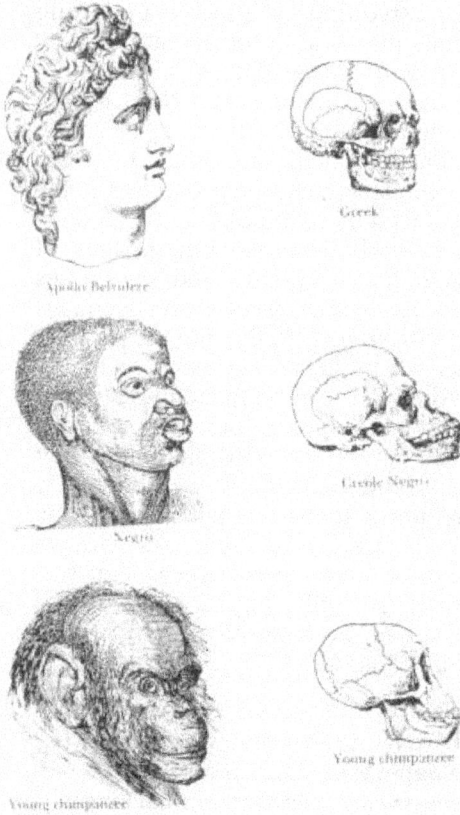

Figure 5: "A scientific demonstration from 1868 that the Negro is as distinct from the Caucasian as the Chimpanzee. Josiah Nott was a polygenist (as opposed to the slightly stronger monogenist school) - he believed that the "races" of man had always been separat e. Later he came to accept Darwinism, at least publically, whilst continuing to hold theories of inherent Caucasian superiority, and enjoying putting a contrary view to "parsons". This was not from a piece of fringe racist literature, but one of the key scientific texts on race of its day: Josiah Clark Nott and George Robert Gliddon, Indigenous races of the earth (First published 1857).

When a person is asked, Who are you? they usually point to their body and say This is me. I am right here! But to whom is this I really referring to? Is it referring to the physical body? Is it the mind, a combination of the psychophysical (mind and body) personality, or is it the body, mind and spirit? What is this spirit anyway and what is its relationship to the body? If I am the body which part of the body am I the head, the arm, the heart? If I am the arm, how can I survive without an arm? If I am the heart how can I survive without my heart, such as if I were to receive an artificial heart or a heart transplant? If I am not the body what am I and where am I?

All of these questions have to be understood well if a person hopes to succeed on the path of wisdom which leads to enlightenment. The teachings of Sema-Yoga state emphatically that the true identity of a human being is not the body. There is a deeper essence within and the objective of mystical spirituality is to allow a person to discover their true essential being. This is the true meaning of the teaching *"Know Thyself."*

The Ancient Egyptians recognized that all human beings are related and that all are expressions of the Divine. However, this raises the question of why do some people act in anger, violence, etc. and what is the cause of hatred? These questions were discussed in an Ancient Egyptian wisdom teaching referred to as,

The Instruction to Meri-ka-ra.

DURING the ninth dynasty, 3000 B.C.E., before the first Eurasian invasion of Egypt by the Hyksos, a Pharaoh passed on to his heir the following wisdom:

"Lo the miserable Asiatic, he is wretched because of the place he's in, short of water, bare of wood. Its paths are many and painful because of mountains. He does not dwell in one place. Food propels his legs. He fights since the time of Horus."

From: The Instruction to Meri-ka-ra.

The concept of the *"Miserable Asiatic"* was also given in the Ancient Egyptian teaching of *"The Land of Heru and the Land of Set."* Heru is the god of the greenery, life, righteousness, the Higher Self and Set is the god of parched land, killing, unrighteousness, egoism, the lower self. Since Set is the God of the desert, the Asiatics, who dwelt in the desert lands, became identified with Set and therefore, Setian behavior (impulsiveness, selfishness, brute force, demoniac behavior, etc.). Since Heru is the god of righteousness and truth, the dichotomy of the two opposing characters (violence and peacefulness) became identified with Set and Heru, respectively.

The message of the teaching is to beware of your environment and of the surroundings which you live in because this will have an effect on your thinking, your emotions and your concept of life. A green, healthy environment would tend to produce a different personality from that which would arise from a dry, miserable environment. A parable is given that if one were to walk into a room filled with soot, one would undoubtedly get some soot on one s clothes, no matter how careful one tried to be. Likewise, spending time in a negative environment, where one is exposing oneself to negative thoughts and feelings or violence, drugs, crookedness and other types of vices is going to have a detrimental effect on one s mind, unless one s mind is highly advanced and purified.

Harshness in the surroundings and general environment can cause negative stress which could lead to an unsettled mind. An unsettled mind is difficult to control. A mind that is uncontrollable will have difficulty in concentrating. Poor concentration will not allow for reflection. Reflection is necessary to make sense of one's situation and to gain intellectual understanding. An non-reflective, confused or "wrong thinking" mind will have difficulty meditating. A non-meditating mind will have difficulty in transcending the world of apparent dualities. It will have difficulty in seeing other people as friends. It will be more inclined to see them as rivals who are to be enslaved, conquered or destroyed in order to satisfy its desires. One will be endlessly pulled into the "world" and the apparent thoughts going on in the mind. As the mind will be caught up in the endless waves of joys and sorrows, it will be unable to find peace. A mind filled with too much joy or too much sorrow due to its experiences in the world will be equally agitated and one will have difficulty concentrating and calming down and understanding others or promoting peace.

THE APPARENT DIFFERENCES AMONG HUMAN BEINGS

> *43. Thou art Temu, who didst create beings endowed with reason; thou makest the color of the skin of one race to be different from that of another, but, however many may be the varieties of mankind, it is thou (God) that makest them all to live.*
> Ancient Egyptian Hymns of Amun verse 43

The passage above from Ancient Egyptian Sema-Yoga wisdom proclaims that all names and forms, and all human beings, regardless of their skin coloration, are in reality expressions of the same divine force which underlies all living beings and which causes them to live. This verse is referring to Amun (God, the Supreme Self) in the aspect of Khnum, the potter, and a deity who fashions the bodies of individuals. Therefore, this statement acknowledges the divine essence of all human beings. Thus, even the Ancient Egyptians discovered that although it appears that there are different races or ethnicities of human beings, the source and underlying essence of all human beings is one and the same: The Supreme Self.

> Thou settest every person in his place. Thou providest their daily food, every man having the portion allotted to him; [thou] dost compute the duration of his life. Their tongues are different in speech, their characteristics (or forms), and likewise their skins (in color), giving distinguishing marks to the dwellers in foreign lands   Thou makest the life of all remote lands.
> **—Hymns to Aton (by Sage Pharaoh Akhenaton)**

The same God has created all peoples, all nations and countries and has appointed each person s country of residence, language and even their ethnicity and physical appearance or features. So all people, including those of foreign lands, have the same Creator and owe their continued existence to the same Divine Being.

The idea of race is one of the biggest misconceptions of all time but there is also a related component that it has been promoted for political and economic reasons. Race implies some innate difference between people, like apples and oranges but modern genetic science proves that people are virtually the same in all respects. In fact, all people are the same and the apparent differences are not differences but rather variations of the same thing! This means that physical appearance is only a fa ade of diversity but rather, it is only an appearance of difference and not a manifestation of substantive differentiation. This is why people from one corner of the earth can mate with other people from the other side of the world and produce offspring. This capacity is proof that human beings are compatible and therefore equal with each other regardless of how distinguishable from each other they may appear to be. From the perspective of wisdom, the higher truth is the abiding issue of the compatibility and not the variable reality of the changing outward appearances. So to a sage all human beings have the same worth and potential; thus a sage appreciates peoples from varied ethnicities that manifest variations of worldly and spiritual realities, the study of which helps lead to understanding the world process and the means to freedom from the ignorance of self. From the perspective of those who are ego driven, the outward appearances mean all and that leads to personal likes and dislikes, degraded mind, as well as prejudices and injustices against one group from another. Can cats and dogs mate and produce offspring? These are different races or a better word would be species [13]. The human race cannot be subdivided into varieties, races, breeds, or subspecies, etc. Human beings do not exist as races just as they do not constitute a conglomeration of different species. The human race is one specie . Therefore, looking down on others as different is a factor of human ignorance (spiritual immaturity). In other words, the desire to segregate human beings is an advanced expression of intense ignorance and egoism, or we may consider this the thought and or desire of a deluded or even deranges, or psychotic mind. In reality there is no validity to the notion of race and racial differences except in the mental concepts of some people. Those who adhere to these concepts are not only expressing their ignorance but are leading themselves to negative

---

[13] Biology. the major subdivision of a genus or subgenus, regarded as the basic category of biological classification, composed of related individuals that resemble one another, are able to breed among themselves, but are not able to breed with members of another species. species. (n.d.). *Dictionary.com Unabridged (v 1.1)*. Retrieved March 11, 2009, from Dictionary.com website: http://dictionary.reference.com/browse/species

future experiences while alive and after death as well. There is only one race, the human race! Any differences are only of appearance.

Ancient Egyptians and Nubians depicted in the Tomb of Rameses III

Egyptian   Libyan   Nubian   Asiatic
                                            [Asia Minor]

There are several Ancient Egyptian reliefs depicting the known groups of people of the ancient world. Modern historians refer to these as ethnographies or the racial classifications of ancient times. The first description, ethnographies , is the correct one.   It is important to understand that the Ancient Egyptians did not practice racism of any kind and that any animosity they might have felt against other peoples was due to disputes over territory and politics stemming from the unrighteous attempts of some peoples to conquer the land of Egypt. Also, they did not classify people as racial types . This idea of racial types is a modern European (Western Culture) notion. Some scholars (Egyptologists) in modern times speak of the disputes between the Ancient Egyptians and the Ancient Nubians as   racial disputes. Confusing the issue in Ancient Egypt is the fact that in ancient times (>1500 B.C.E.) the Ancient Egyptians and Nubians looked the same and many times dressed the same. But in later times (<1500 B.C.E.) they depicted themselves differently in order to be able to differentiate themselves in artistic and religious expressions. This is shown in the ancient reliefs.[14] However, over time the mixing of the Ancient Egyptians with the lighter skinned Asiatic peoples led to changes in appearance of some of the population which saw itself ethnically as Egyptian.   Thus, the later Egyptians came to be seen as a multicultural group comprised of people with mixed ancestry, but always acknowledging their African roots while at the same time accepting those of other ethnicities (Asiatics, Libyans, Europeans (Greeks)) into their homes and in marriage.

---

[14] see the book *The Black Ancient Egyptians* by Muata Ashby

44

Motivated by the desire to reinforce negative racial stereotypes some people have engaged in a common, if not concerted, effort to misrepresent as well as cloud the understanding that all peoples, including Native Americans, Asians and Africans, have achieved greatness at one time or another. While the peoples that lived in Europe were still only starting their civilization, Ancient Egypt and Nubia has already entered into their golden ages. In the later period when the Arabs, Greeks and Romans conquered the land of Egypt (c.500-30 B.C.E.), the lighter skinned conquerors reproduced their own images in the monuments and documents proclaiming themselves as Egyptians. This is the form of appearance that many modern Egyptologists, and Hollywood movie producers, and others, have focused on as supposedly representative of all Ancient Egyptians in ancient times.

Photo of bust of Cleopatra queen of Ptolemaic Egypt

This error has caused much confusion related to the understanding that the people who created the Pyramids and Temples as well as the high mystical philosophy of Ancient Egypt were innately African people with the same capacity to create as all other human beings. This fact was acknowledged by several Greek scholars who were students of the Ancient Egyptians.[15]

The Ethiopians and Egyptians are very black

Aristotle

The Egyptians and Nubians have thick lips, broad noses, woolly hair and burnt skin....

Herodotus

In fact, Ethiopia[16] was the birthplace of the early Egyptians and all three groups, the Ethiopians, Egyptians and Indians appeared the same to Herodotus, the Greek historian, at the time of his travels through those

---

[15] see the book *The Black Ancient Egyptians* by Muata Ashby
[16] The ancient Ethiopia referred to by the ancient Greeks, known as *Kash* [Kush] to the Ancient Egyptians, is today called Sudan.

countries. Thus, the picture shows that the Ancient Egyptians looked no different from other Africans in the interior of Africa.

> *"And upon his return to Greece, they gathered around and asked, "tell us about this great land of the Blacks called Ethiopia." And Herodotus said, "There are two great Ethiopian nations, one in Sind (India) and the other in Egypt."*
>
> Herodotus (c. 484-425 B.C.E.)

Those who engage in the deception about the race of the Ancient Egyptians, which denies the accomplishments of African peoples, as well as those who are deluded by it suffer the consequences due to the limitations that these ideas impose on people. Those who espouse, support or even enforce racial differences limit themselves because they trap themselves in their own ideas of superiority and those who are controlled by the racially biased ideas are limited in their ability to explore the higher possibilities of life in society as well as internally. Thus, the egoism in both groups is intensified, and consequently the level of spiritual ignorance is also intensified. This will lead to greater animosity, fear, attachments, anger, hatreds and violence. They both limit themselves to the narrow concepts of themselves and in the process negate the higher reality and promote disharmony and suffering for each other.

If the individual ego becomes hardened, concentrated on itself, and does not expand, then feelings of gross egoism emerge such as anger, jealousy, hate, greed, lust, envy, fear, etc., which inevitably lead to the experience of mental unrest, conflict, disappointment, sorrow, mental anguish, etc. At the group level, these translate into wars, genocide, the raping and pillaging of entire nations, etc. Anger, jealousy, hatred, hypocrisy, vanity, pride, ignorance, greed, lust, etc., are to be seen as advanced forms of mental illness, aberrations from the higher reality, which is living in accordance with a delusion instead of truth and therefore this is rightly considered as a degree of insanity.

Overcoming hatreds and animosities and ignorance which lead to strife through understanding

Here we will look at overcoming hatreds and animosities and ignorance which lead to strife through understanding the ignorance about race and its perpetuation by the ignorant. On the cover of this book there is a signpost with three words: *hate, love* and *wisdom*. From an ordinary perspective, people think of love and hate as being opposites but that is not correct in that we see in the world that many times, the things that people love, sometimes they end up hating and the things they hate are seldom loved later on. From a romantic perspective love is supposed to be caring for another in an unselfish way but most people do not care in an unselfish way because they are burdened with egoism. It is important to understand that from a higher perspective, the opposite of hate is not love, as most people think; the opposite of hate is passion if we define passion as *an infatuation with form and relationship,* that is the form of objects and a person s perceived relationship to them as something desirable that could bring them fulfillment, pleasure and or happiness. It is therefore important to develop dispassion and dispassion comes with detachment and wisdom. But wisdom occurs when there is understanding and understanding comes when knowledge, such as the teaching being imparted here, is taken to heart and applied in life so that a person may experience the results and thereby adjusts their life to be more in line with the higher truths of life instead of the falsehoods of life that lead to ignorant desires, frustrations, anguish, animosities, hatreds and violence, which are in reality forms of suffering. In any case, the signpost signifies that there are two directions one can go in; downward with hate, a more positive and elevated way with love, but truly up and away from either love or hate, with wisdom. Both love and hate lead to worldliness, the same general direction, while wisdom leads to transcendence, peace and freedom from worldliness and the burdens of the lower nature.

The animosity and hatred of modern times, caused by the ignorance of the high wisdom of life, has led to a situation where social problems have rendered practitioners of religion incapable of reaching a higher level of spiritual understanding. In other words, this error thwarts human spiritual progress. Many people in modern society are caught up in the degraded level of human social interaction, of disputes and wars, in an attempt to support ideas in reference to the doctrines of religion, which are in reality absurd and destructive.

One important key of high wisdom is understanding the nature of humanity and it s origins. The inability to accept and live out of this reality is a cornerstone of the chaos in and perversion of society as it allows the existence of the negative concepts of class, privilege, and of races which degrades society through its sociopolitical application racism . Ironically, the inability of non-secular leaders in the church, mosque, synagogue or secular society to accept the truth about the origins of humanity sometimes comes from their fear of losing control over their followers. Now that modern science is showing that all human beings originated from the same source, in Africa, and that racial distinctions are at best questionable and misleading falsehoods, it means that those who have perpetrated and sustained racism can no longer use science or biblical teachings to support their ignorant or evil [if perpetrated with malice of forethought] designs. In other words, they have no leg to stand on.

The following exert was taken from Encarta Encyclopedia 1994, and was typical of the modern scientific understanding of the question of human genetics and race issues at that time.

> The concept of race has often been misapplied. One of the most telling arguments against classifying people into races is that persons in various cultures have often mistakenly acted as if one race were superior to another. Although, with social disadvantages eliminated, it is possible that one human group or another might have some genetic advantages in response to such factors as climate, altitude, and specific food availability, these differences are small. There are no differences in native intelligence or mental capacity that cannot be explained by environmental circumstances. Rather than using racial classifications to study human variability, anthropologists today define geographic or social groups by geographic or social criteria. They then study the nature of the genetic attributes of these groups and seek to understand the causes of changes in their genetic makeup. Contributed by: Gabriel W. Laser Races, Classification of, Microsoft (R) Encarta. Copyright (c) 1994

One of the major problems in society is that the teachings and scientific evidence presented here has not been taught to the world population at large. Most people grow up accepting the ignorance of their parents who received the erroneous information from their own parents, and so on, which plays into the natural fears and prejudices of the ignorant mind. Racism, sexism and other scourges of society are not genetically transmitted. They are transmitted by ignorant or evil secular and non-secular leaders, or ignorant family members who pass on their prejudices and bigotries to their children, and so on down through the generations; thus it is a sociopolitical disease. The cycle of ignorance and strife is thus carried on from one generation to another. Government leaders most often do not enforce or support this understanding beyond agreement in speeches, which are not followed up with concrete policies that could affect people s lives in a serious way. A child cannot live in a family and believe in a certain way and act in a certain way if the parents do not allow it. In the same way, the masses of people are like children and the church and government leaders are like the parents. If racism, sexism and other injustices exist, it is because the leaders are not making a sufficient effort to lead the masses towards truth and righteousness and effort is also lacking in enforcement of righteous laws to prevent and redress injustices while at the same time proactively educating the masses and rehabilitating offenders of society s laws. Religious leaders can lead in three ways, by example, moral words and by spiritual influence. Secular leaders can lead in three ways, by example, by ethical words and by influence through principled legislation, impartial law enforcement, argument and persuasion based on appeals to reason, with the intent to arrive at the best course for humanity and not just for a select few. When secular and non-secular leaders fall in their leadership duties, be it purposefully or due to incompetence and or due to ignorance, corruptions and or vice, the society also descends into ignorance, vice and delusions. The values of truth and righteousness must be part of every aspect of teaching and leadership in order to have an ethical and mentally well adjusted society, otherwise, there will be a deficit of ethical leaders and society will go astray. The leaders of society as well as the leaders of the church must make a concerted effort to engage the struggle against misunderstanding and unrighteousness. Then they will be able to lead society to an enlightened way of relating to other ethnic groups and thereby provide real hope of creating harmony in the human community. Through this harmony it would be easier to cope with the struggles of life and thereby achieve greater insight into the mystical teachings of philosophy or any religious path. Anger, hatred, greed and animosity have an adverse effect on the mind. Therefore, those who engage in racism as well as those who do not know how to deal with racists will have a much more difficult time in trying to achieve the kind of mental control and peace which is necessary to progress on the spiritual path. Those who consider themselves to be followers of truth are admonished to take control of one s egoistic tendencies and to practice humility instead of thinking of oneself as superior to others. Instead one must learn to look at others as having been given the same spark of divinity and therefore, all human beings deserve equal treatment, love and compassion. This teaching applies directly to those who try to impose themselves on others (racists, sexists, tyrants, capitalists, etc.). Those who have enough courage to face their fears, prejudices and to approach life with honesty instead of delusions of superiority and greed will discover forgiveness and inner peace, as well as the true meaning of the wisdom teachings.

Human Skin on the Move[17]

THE EARLIEST MEMBERS of *Homo sapiens,* or modern humans, evolved in Africa between 120,000 and 100,000 years ago and had darkly pigmented skin adapted to the conditions of UV radiation and heat that existed near the equator. As modern humans began to venture out of the tropics, however, they encountered environments in which they received significantly less UV radiation during the year. Under these conditions their high concentrations of natural sunscreen probably proved detrimental. Dark skin contains so much melanin that very little UV radiation, and specifically very little of the shorter-wavelength UVB radiation, can penetrate the skin. Although most of the effects of UVB are harmful, the rays perform one indispensable function: initiating the formation of vitamin D in the skin. Darkskinned people living in the tropics generally receive sufficient UV radiation during the year for UVB to penetrate the skin and allow them to make vitamin D. Outside the tropics this is not the case. The solution, across evolutionary time, has been for migrants to northern latitudes to lose skin pigmentation. The connection between the evolution of lightly pigmented skin and vitamin D synthesis was elaborated by W. Farnsworth Loomis of Brandeis University in 1967. He established the importance of vitamin D to reproductive success because of its role in enabling calcium absorption by the intestines, which in turn makes possible the normal development of the skeleton and the maintenance of a healthy immune system. Research led by Michael Holick of the Boston University School of Medicine has, over the past 20 years, further cemented the significance of vitamin D in development and immunity. His team also showed that not all sunlight contains enough UVB to stimulate vitamin D production. In Boston, for instance, which is located at about

[17] *SKIN DEEP* -COPYRIGHT 2002 SCIENTIFIC AMERICAN, INC.

42 degrees north latitude, human skin cells begin to produce vitamin
D only after mid-March. In the wintertime there isn t
enough UVB to do the job. We realized that this was another
piece of evidence essential to the skin color story.

DNA and The Spirit

The term DNA is an abbreviation for Deoxyribonucleic acid. It is a complex giant molecule that contains the information needed for every cell of a living creature to create its physical features (hair, skin, bones, eyes, legs, etc., as well as their texture, coloration, their efficient functioning, etc.). All of this is contained in a chemically coded form. The Life Force of the Soul or Spirit engenders the impetus in the DNA to function. This in turn leads to the creation of the physical aspect of all living beings (human beings, animals, plants, insects, microorganisms, etc.).

The DNA is what determines if two living beings are compatible with each other for the purpose of mating and producing offspring. If they are not compatible, then they are considered to be different species, different beings. However, if two beings have different DNA and cannot mate this does not mean that one necessarily deserves a status of inferior or the other superior ; it simply means that they are different life forms. All human beings are compatible with each other, therefore, they are members of a single species, i.e. one human race. In other words, the so called variations in skin colorations of human beings are not evidence of difference but are actually the natural mode of expression of the single human race in the same way that a single human being can manifest different shades of skin color on one body; so too, the human race is one body of humanity that displays apparently different shades of skin color depending on the location on earth where that part of humanity may be located.

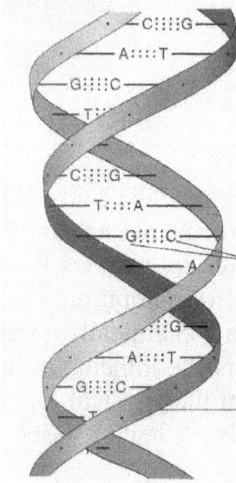

Figure 6: Image of DNA

From the point of view of religion or mystic spirituality, DNA is an instrument of the Spirit, which it uses to create the body and thereby avail itself of physical existence and experiences. According to mystical philosophy, the soul chooses the particular world, country, and family in which to incarnate in order to have the kind of experiences it wants to experience. This is all expressed in the physical plane through the miracle of DNA.

Figure 7: The origin of the Variety in the Human 'race' from Africa

The image below illustrates that ALL human beings alive today [modern Africans, modern Europeans, modern Asians, and modern Australians (Aborigines)] are descendants from ancestors who first lived in Africa over 100,000 years ago.

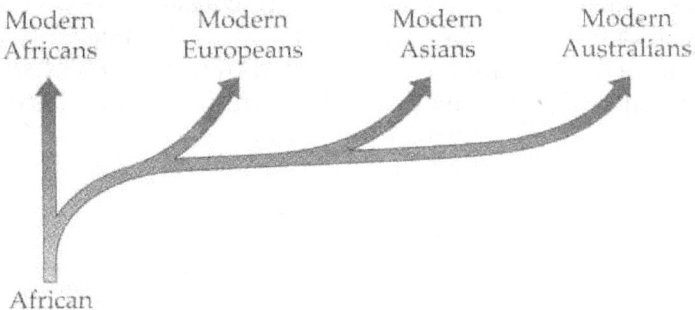

The reader may have noticed that since the premise of the findings of this book call for the constant acknowledgement of the fact that the concepts of race are illusory, false and destructive, the words multiracial , multicultural , multiethnic , white , black , brown , race , racism , latino , etc. throughout this book have been enclosed by grammatical marks . This was done for the purpose of denoting the idea that they are not being used in a conventional popular cultural sense but with the higher understanding being espoused throughout this volume. Even though these terms may be used in the text to discuss the social issues their use is not to be taken as an acknowledgement by this author of their legitimacy but rather as a practical necessity until the language evolves out of the use of false terminologies and divisive unscientific socio-political designations for human beings.

Geography and Hatred

The researcher Jarrod Diamond[18] postulated that up until recently in human history, the world s populations were about even in terms of their ability to wage war and control the environment. However, the nations of the Eurasian region were able to make use of technologies that allowed them to gain control of the world before other nations could. In Diamond s view, the technological advantage, gained by taking discoveries from far off lands and ingeniously using those to construct war implements, is what spawned longstanding wars amongst European countries and led to the ideal of creating empires by dominating as many nations as possible. Some prime examples of the move to dominate other nations and create modern empires are the colonization of the New World (The Americas) and the Scramble for Africa. [19] History does not present non north Eurasian or Asiatic examples of megalomania.[20] In other words, in the tropical regions of the world there is no record in history of Alexander The Great-type, Caesar-type, Genghis Khan- type, Attila-the-Hun- type, or Napoleon- type personalities, or personalities that have exhibited the desire to extend their power and dominion to encompass the known world.

bar·bar·i·an   *n.*

1. A member of a people considered by those of another nation or group to have a primitive civilization.
2. A fierce, brutal, or cruel person.
3. An insensitive, uncultured person; a boor.

Those people who exhibit disregard for human life, who seek to amass great wealth and power, to rule over their known world, who are brutal and cruel, and may have little regard for other cultures may be considered as barbarians regardless of the amount of technological advancement they may have achieved. Under this definition, the

---

18 Guns, Germs, and Steel by Jared Diamond

19 From Wikipedia, the free encyclopedia. Retrieved from

http://en.wikipedia.org/wiki/Scramble_for_Africa

20 1. a delusional mental disorder that is marked by infantile feelings of personal omnipotence and grandeur Source: *Merriam-Webster's Medical Dictionary, © 2002 Merriam-Webster, Inc.* 2. A psychopathological condition characterized by delusional fantasies of wealth, power, or omnipotence. *The American Heritage® Dictionary of the English Language, Fourth Edition Copyright © 2000 by Houghton Mifflin Company.*

personalities above are included as examples of barbarian leaders throughout history. Furthermore, the people that support those leaders may be considered as barbarians as well. This extended definition includes the Popes who instigated the Crusades and the Arab Islamists who sought to conquer and destroy African and Indian cultures in the way that the present day Sudanese government is doing now and others have done, off and on, since the first conquest of North Africa within 100 years after the death of Muhammad.

Figure 8: Left: Genghis Khan. "With Heaven's aid I have conquered for you a huge empire. But my life was too short to achieve the conquest of the world. That task is left for you." -Genghis Khan, to his sons at the end of his life.

There are some evidences that indicate that those peoples who come from the northern hemisphere of the planet earth, especially those above latitude 30 to the Arctic Circle, are more aggressive, militaristic and stressed than those below latitude 30 , especially those between the Tropic of Cancer and the Tropic of Capricorn. For example, the colonization of North America by Europeans was easier in South America because the Native Americans there were not as aggressive as those in North America.[21]

An example of the general peaceful culture that prevailed in Native American culture in the tropical zones is presented by Bartolome De Las Casas, who was an eye witness to the European discovery of the western hemisphere. He speaks here specifically of the peoples that were found there and their existing culture and atrocities committed by the Spaniards on the Island of Hispa ola [today Santo Domingo {Dominican Republic} and Haiti]. The same occurred in Puerto Rico.

> The Indies were discovered in the year one thousand four
> hundred and ninety two. In the following year a great many
> Spaniards went there with the intention of settling the land.
> Thus, forty-nine years have passed since the first settlers

---

[21] The Western Tradition by Ugen Webber, Professor of History, UCLA

penetrated the land, the first so-claimed being the large and most happy isle called Hispa ola, which is six hundred leagues in circumference.

... And of all the infinite universe of humanity, these people are the most guileless, the most devoid of wickedness and duplicity, the most obedient and faithful to their native masters and to the Spanish Christians whom they serve. They are by nature the most humble, patient, and peaceable, holding no grudges, free from embroilments, neither excitable nor quarrelsome. These people are the most devoid of rancors, hatreds, or desire for vengeance of any people in the world. And because they are so weak and complaisant, they are less able to endure heavy labor and soon die of no matter what malady.[22]

Similarly, the peoples of Africa (which are mostly located within the tropics), were and continue to be less aggressive in terms of initiating and instituting aggressive and warlike cultures, and social institutions. It is notable, however, that people in the tropics can be made to adopt aggression as a way of life but they did not initiate it or perpetuate it. There are no great historical barbarians in the area of the tropics or in the southern hemisphere of the earth, for that matter. From Genghis Khan and Tamerlane in East Asia to Attila and the Huns in Central Asia, to Alexander, Caesar and the Vandals, Goths, Visigoths, Gauls, Vikings and Crusaders, Muslim Conquerors, followed by Napoleon and the British empire in Eurasia, and the conquest of the Americas and subsequent creation of the United States of America empire, there have been scores of barbarian would be conquerors who pretended to the destiny of world domination [megalomania] and in the process wrought untold death, misery and destruction throughout history.[23]

---

[22] Bartolome De Las Casas - The Devastation of the Indies: A Brief Account (1542)

[23] A psychopathological condition characterized by delusional fantasies of wealth, power, or omnipotence. a delusion (common in paranoia) that you are much greater and more powerful and influential than you really are. An extremely inflated view of one's own significance and abilities. This may take on a delusional quality in which, for example, the individual may believe himself to be Jesus Christ. In this situation the description of the thoughts is referred to as *delusions of grandeur*.

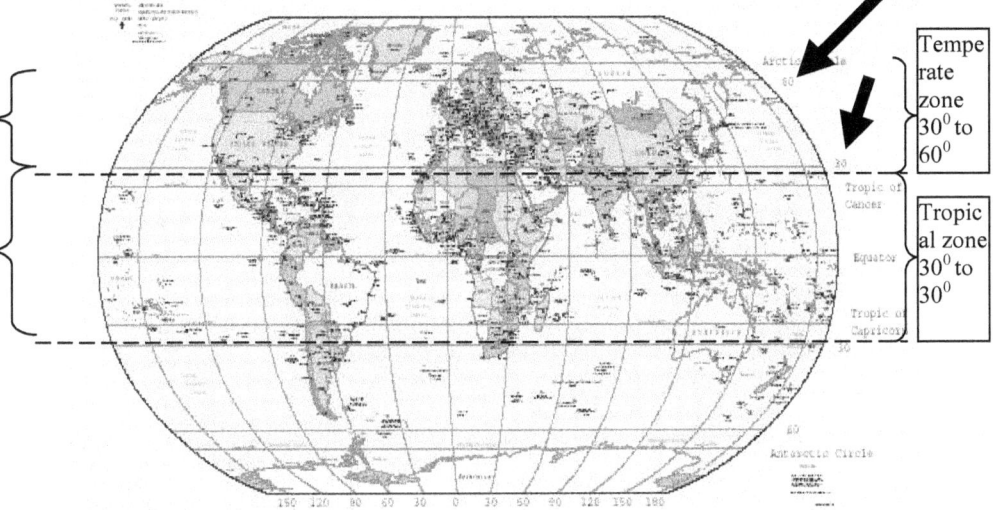

One common factor that generally affected the development of the cultures of the barbarians is the form of climate in the regions of their nations. Scientific studies have documented that changing weather conditions affect moods.[24] Weather changes also affect the immune system and health which is a contributing factor as to why many people contract colds at the beginning of the winter flu season. One of the more prominent well documented ailments based on changing seasons is *Seasonal affective disorder*, or **S.A.D.**, which is found to affect many people year-round in latitudes of 30 North and higher or 30 South and lower. One important factor which produces less vitality and mental capacity is the nature of sunlight in the affected areas. Only at latitudes between the Tropics is it possible for the sun to be at the zenith. The Tropic of Cancer (cancer (♋) is Latin for *crab*), is the farthest northern latitude at which the sun can appear directly overhead. The reduced amount of sunlight coupled with the constant changes in seasons can lead to changes in the personality. The vegetation as well as the availability of foods is different in the northern hemisphere. People tend to eat more meat products in those geographical areas. Consequently it has also been demonstrated and documented that higher consumption of meat decreases life expectancy,[25] increases diseases such as cancer,[26]

---

[24] Seasonal affective disorder, or SAD, is an affective, or mood disorder. Most SAD sufferers experience normal mental health throughout most of the year, but experience depressive symptoms in the winter. SAD is rare, if existent at all, in the tropics, but is measurably present at latitudes of 30 N (or S) and higher.

[25] Singh PN. Does low meat consumption contribute to greater longevity? In: Sabat J, ed. Vegetarian nutrition. Boca Raton, FL: CRC Press, 2001:135 70.

[26] Gottlieb S. Evidence grows that eating red meat increases cancer risk.

diabetes,[27] and produces aggressive behavior[28], which leads to lower life expectancy due to wars and the negative effects of war, like famine, contamination, stress, etc.

Perils of Recent Migrations[29]

DESPITE GREAT IMPROVEMENTS in overall human health in the past century, some diseases have appeared or reemerged in populations that had previously been little affected by them. One of these is skin cancer, especially basal and squamous cell carcinomas, among light-skinned peoples. Another is rickets, brought about by severe vitamin D deficiency, in dark-skinned peoples. Why are we seeing these conditions?
As people move from an area with one pattern of UV radiation to another region, biological and cultural adaptations have not been able to keep pace. The light-skinned people of northern European origin who bask in the sun of Florida or northern Australia increasingly pay the price in the form of premature aging of the skin and skin cancers, not to mention the unknown cost in human life of folate depletion. Conversely, a number of dark-skinned people of southern Asian and African origin now living in the northern U.K., northern Europe or the northeastern U.S. suffer from a lack of UV radiation and vitamin D, an insidious problem that manifests itself in high rates of rickets and other diseases related to vitamin D deficiency.
The ability of skin color to adapt over long periods to the various environments to which humans have moved reflects the importance of skin color to our survival. But its unstable nature also makes it one of the least useful characteristics in determining the evolutionary relations between human groups.
Early Western scientists used skin color improperly to delineate human races, but the beauty of science is that it can and does correct itself. Our current knowledge of the evolution of human skin indicates that variations in skin color, like most of our physical attributes, can be explained by adaptation to the environment through natural selection. We look ahead to the day when the vestiges of old scientific mistakes will be erased and replaced by a better understanding of human origins and diversity. Our variation in skin color should be celebrated as one of the most visible manifestations of our evolution as a species.

BMJ. 2005 Jan 15;330(7483):111. No abstract available. PMID: 15649914 [PubMed - as supplied by publisher]
[27] Fung TT, Schulze M, Manson JE, Willett WC, Hu FB. Dietary patterns, meat intake, and the risk of type 2 diabetes in women. Arch Intern Med. 2004 Nov 8;164(20):2235-40. PMID: 15534160 [PubMed - indexed for MEDLINE]
[28] *The Kemetic Diet*- by Muata Ashby
[29] *SKIN DEEP* -COPYRIGHT 2002 SCIENTIFIC AMERICAN, INC

Another emerging threat to the environment is Global Dimming this phenomenon is caused by pollution containing small particles that cause water particles to form on them than thereby produced reflective clouds in the environment. Airplane vapor trails are an example of this occurrence. The sunlight is reflected away and the world has become dimmed. Global Dimming counters the problem of global warming to some degree but if the dimming is reduced, the way it has in the last years, the warming effect will increase more rapidly. Since sunlight affects moods there are some indications that the reason why the seasonal affective disorder syndrome has increased in the past years is related to the Global Dimming problem. Another complication that may be expected is health problems due to vitamin "D deficiency. Those people who live in colder regions need to cover their bodies more so they do not receive as much sunlight touching their bodies. Direct sunlight stimulates vitamin D production in the body. It is necessary for proper nutrition. Its deficiency can cause a myriad of health issues that can add to the stress and anxiety of living in those areas.

All of the stresses related to disease exacerbate the problems due to weather and climate changes. Normal "winter blues" can usually be dampened or extinguished by exercise and increased outdoor activity, particularly on sunny days, resulting in increased solar exposure.[30] The stresses of living in the temperate zones[31] seem to produce rational anxieties [due to the harshness of the environment and the difficulty of making a living there] but also irrational anxieties that are not perceived consciously due to feelings of fear of loss of resources and worry about survival issues. In a sense, the desire to maraud, plunder, pillage, etc., may be thought of as a misguided but cathartic desire to dispel the depression caused by the weather and relieve the anxiety of a precarious existence due to scarce resources. If that activity were directed in positive ways the society could cope with the problem. However, the best solution would be to reproduce the conditions of the lower hemisphere as authentically as possible including the diet, solar exposure, etc. It is sobering to realize that the problem of major conflicts in the world due to aggressive, intolerant, dogmatic philosophies and religions may be in part or mostly due to climate and the indiscriminate migration of human beings out of Africa [where the weather and climate changes are more harmonious -less abrupt and less severe and there is greater availability of fruits and vegetables [year-round] without the need for excessive preparation as is necessary for living in other parts of the world. Thus, the climate syndrome should not be thought of as just an ancient or prehistoric issue that changed people in the northern

---

[30] From Wikipedia, the free encyclopedia
[31] In geography, temperate latitudes of the globe lie between the tropics and the polar circles. From Wikipedia, the free encyclopedia

hemisphere but one that continually affects them even today by stressing the immune system, the mind and personality. As it is impractical for the population of the northern hemisphere to relocate to the south, health strategies including changes in diet, and solar exposure, as well as the practice of meditation, and classes in conflict resolution could mitigate the situation. Therefore, peacefulness and reduced stress can be chosen if the problem is made known in this context and the proper actions are taken; all those in the northern hemisphere can be helped to better cope with the issue of weather in order to lead them towards balance, and peace.

HATRED AND THE BOND OF ARI

One most important point related to human interaction is the bond of *ari*. Here, the term *ari* refers to the philosophy of *ariu* and *Meskhenet* of Ancient Egypt. It refers to the situations of life, the conditions of existence which one finds oneself in through one's thoughts, ideas associations and actions. When a soul incarnates into human form and forgets its higher nature, it believes that the body and all of its realities are the only truth. Thus, when a person grows up and learns to identify with a particular group, it sees this as truth, being unaware of the higher reality of the spirit. This belief in the world, in ethnic differences, in social status, likes and dislikes, etc., is what keeps the soul entangled in the web of the illusions of life. This entanglement is what drives the ignorance and mental agitation in the human mind and it is the force which prevents people from living in internal harmony as well as societal harmony. However, this does not only have an effect in life but in death as well. This was explained thousands of years ago in the philosophy of *ari* of Ancient Egypt.

Figure 9: Vignette from Chapter 33 of Papyrus Ani.

Judgment of the Soul. In Ancient Egyptian wisdom, the fate of the soul was depicted in the image of an aspirant who hopes to go to heaven and become one with God by living righteously. This righteousness was explained through the aspects of the personality that operate at the judgment of the heart of a human being. The weighing of the heart is a test of the virtue which can allow a person to successfully attain the goal of life, enlightenment, or suffer hellish conditions, reincarnate and experience life over again. Far left, Ani enters the hall of Judgment. His heart (conscience) is being weighed by Anpu while the Divine principals *Shai, Rennenet and Meskhenet* look on. Ani's soul and his destiny also look on while Anubis measures Ani's heart against the feather of Maat.

At far right Deputy records the result while the Monster Ammit, the Devourer of the unjust, awaits the answer. Djehuty is the god of reason, intellect. The hands of Deputy are "Shai" and "Rennenet. The implication is that we reap (harvest) the result of our state of mind (heart). Our state of mind, including our subconscious feelings and desires, is weighed against cosmic order, Maat. If found to be at peace (Hetep) and therefore in accord with cosmic order (Maat) it will be allowed to join with the cosmos (Asar). Otherwise it will suffer the fate as dictated by its own contents (mental state of unrest due to lingering desires), which will lead it to Ammit who will devour the ego-personality. That soul will experience torments from demons until it learns the lessons of life or becomes strong enough through wisdom to know itself. Demons may be understood as negative cosmic energies which it has allowed itself to indulge in, in the form of mental anguish and torments people put themselves through, due to their own ignorance. Self-torment may be regret over some action or inaction while alive or a reluctance to leave the physical realm because of a lingering desire to experience more earthly pleasure. Therefore, one controls one s own fate according to one s own level of wisdom or reasoning capacity.

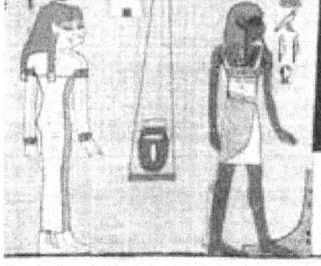

Figure 10: Above (left): the goddesses Rennet and Meskhenet, right- Shai (From the Papyrus of Ani-see Chapter 33)

The hands of Deputy (God of wisdom) are the God "Shai" which means "destiny" and the Goddess "Rennet" which means "Fortune and Harvest." The implication is that we reap (harvest) the result of our actions (destiny) according to our level of wisdom. Deputy, one s own wisdom capacity through higher intellectual understanding, bestows control over one's Shai (Fortune) and Rennet (ability to reap one's fortune) and therefore one's Meskhenet (Destiny - Karma). Therefore, one's karmic destiny depends on one's reasoning capacity, i.e. *intellect*.

Underlying the principles of Shai and Rennet is goddess "Meskhenet." She is the one who determines where the next birth (karmic fate) of the soul will take place. Therefore, the teachings of Ari (Karma) and reincarnation are an integral part of Kemetic Philosophy.

Figure 11: Above: Goddess Meskhenet as the "birthing block" overlooking the karmic scales of Maat in the Judgment scene of Papyrus Ani.

Meskhenet presides over the birth circumstances and life experiences of every individual. She is the one who carries out the decree which has been ordained by Deputy after the judgment of the heart in the hall of Maat. It is Deputy who records the deeds (actions) or *ariu* of every individual and then decrees the proper Shai (destiny) and Rennenet (harvest or fortune) which are fitting for that particular individual.

Figure 12: Above: The "Ab" heart-container being weighed in the karmic scales of Maat in the Judgment scene of Papyrus Ani.

The Ancient Egyptian hieroglyphic symbol of the heart is a heart shaped vase, ⟨♡⟩, referred to as the *ab*. The vase is a container which may be used for holding water, beer, wine, milk, etc. Likewise, the human heart is seen as a vessel which contains thoughts, feelings, desires and unconscious memories. In mystical terms, the heart is a metaphor of the human mind including the conscious, subconscious and unconscious levels. The mind is the reservoir of all of your ideas, convictions and feelings. Therefore, just as these factors direct the path of your life, so too they are the elements which are judged in the Hall of Maati by the two goddesses, Aset and Nebethet, along with Asar. The heart then is the sum total of your experiences, actions and aspirations, your conscience or *ari* (karma), and these are judged in the balance against the feather of Maat, order, balance and truth; so one is .

Thus, ari or karma should be thought of as the total effect of a person's actions and conduct during the successive phases of {his/her} existence. But how does this effect operate? How do the past actions affect the present and the future? Your experiences from the present life or from previous lifetimes cause unconscious impressions which stay with the Soul even after death. These unconscious impressions are what constitute the emerging thoughts, desires, and aspirations of every individual. These impressions are not exactly like memories, however, they work like memories. For example, if you had a fear in a previous lifetime or the childhood of your present lifetime, you may not remember the event that caused the fear, but you may experience certain phobias when you come into contact with certain objects or certain people. These feelings are caused by the unconscious impressions which are coming up to the surface of the conscious mind. It is this conglomerate of unconscious impressions which are judged in the Hall of Maat and determine where the soul will go to next in the spiritual journey toward evolution or devolution, also known as the cycle of birth and death or reincarnation, as well as the experiences of heaven or hell. The following segment from the Ancient Egyptian "Instruction to Meri-ka-Ra" explains this point.

> *"You know that they are not merciful the day when they judge the miserable one..... Do not count on the passage of the years; they consider a lifetime as but an hour. After death man remains in existence and his actions accumulate beside him. Life in the other world is eternal, but he who arrives without doing wrong, before the Judge of the Dead, he will be there as a neter and he will walk freely as do the masters of eternity."*

The reference above to <u>his acts accumulate beside him</u> alludes to the unconscious impressions which are formed as a result of one s actions while still alive. These impressions can be either positive or negative. Positive impressions are developed through positive actions by living a life of righteousness (Maat) and virtue. This implies living according to the precepts of mystical wisdom or being a follower of Heru (*Shemsu Heru*) and Aset. These actions draw one closer to harmony and peace, thus paving the way to discover the Self within. The negative impressions are developed through actions that are based on ignorance of the knowledge of self [egoism, untruth]. They are related to mental agitation, disharmony and restlessness. This implies acts based on anger, fear, desire, greed, depression, gloom, etc. These actions draw one into the outer world of human desires. They distract the mind and do not allow the intellect (*Saa*) to function. Thus, existence at this level is closer to an animal, being based on animal instincts and desires of the body (selfishness), rather than to a spiritually mature human being, based on reason, selflessness, compassion, etc.

How does this relate to a person s egoistic desires, preferences and prejudices? When a person is alive they associate with those whom they feel a kinship and disassociate from those who they dislike. In a mysterious way whatever a person feels strongly about they draw that thing towards themselves. This means that if you love something you draw yourself to it, first mentally and then physically. Also, when you hate something you also draw yourself to it as well. When a person hates something the thought of it is close in the mind as a thought of repudiation; then the object is pushed away. Either way, loving or hating, the objects are kept in mind as impressions of desire or hatred. The objects are tied to the mind through the feelings of desire and attachment or hatred and repulsion. These thoughts color the mind and lead to thoughts and actions based on desiring or repudiating those objects. This is what is referred to as the ego-personality and its likes and dislikes. It is those thoughts and actions that create a person s circumstances in life; this is why it is said that a person is the architect of their own destiny. According to mystic philosophy, these likes and dislikes, if unresolved through wisdom, impel a person to actions in life but also carry over after death and form the basis of after death experiences [heavenly or hellish] in the same way they form the basis of everyday dreams or nightmares during sleep. This is the bond of ari which people create for themselves during their many lifetimes, which can be experienced in different cultures and in the form of different ethnicities. For example, if a Chinese person and a Mongolian person hate each other, and if they do not resolve their issues while they are still alive, their souls will be drawn to each other after death and they may even be reborn in the other s ethnic group. When they reincarnate in some future lifetime, they may become part of the same family of the other person and adopt the other s culture and nationality. In other words, the Chinese person may reincarnate as a Mongolian and vise versa. This process points out the illusoriness of ethnicity and culture and the false ideal of any particular culture or ethnic group as being an abiding reality or superior or inferior to the other. If it is so changeable, it cannot be true because it is variable; it is only a practical reality to be contended with for a certain amount of time; so ethnicity and culture are only relative realities and not absolute truth. This process is engendered by the ignorance in the personality that led to the likes and dislikes sustained by a person s *ariu* [karma] so that a person may be able to resolve their mental [conscious, sub-conscious and unconscious] and emotional complexes, hatreds and desires.

When a person speaks out of ignorance and delusion they are operating from the mental impressions of individuality, duality, the negative emotions and qualities (anger, hatred, greed, etc.) and all ideas that are in contradiction with the truth of mystical reality. This contradiction with the innate nature of a human being leads to endless internal unrest. It is in effect going against one s own conscience and thereby one dooms oneself to experience discontent no matter what fame, fortune or status is attained in life or how much a person convinces themselves that they are happy.

Hatred is an impediment to physical well-being and spiritual evolution and the process of reincarnation requires that people should confront the objects which are blocking their spiritual growth. So if you hate another person and curse them saying I hope you go to hell, you are also condemning yourself to go there with them to witness their hell and in the process you will also experience it. Therefore, hate in all its forms needs to be eradicated in the heart of haters and the hated through forgiveness, understanding and love. In this manner society will become a positive force to promote the evolution of the soul and the world will become a better place for all souls to live.

Many people practice racism openly but many more practice it in subtle forms. Many people profess to be religious and yet practice segregating themselves and their families from others. Many say that racism is wrong but support it by agreeing with racial classifications such as Black, White, Hispanic, Native American, etc. The moment a person submits to a racial classification they are in effect saying, I agree with your system, I am of this particular group and I am different from those others. You cannot profess to be against racism and then uphold racial classifications. You are first and foremost the Universal Self, then an individual soul, then a human being and perhaps then a member of an ethnic group, but never a racial being. Furthermore, even the differentiation into an individual soul and a human being are only for practical purposes. Essentially you are only the Higher Self. The description of being a soul or a human being is like comparing a wave to the ocean. Essentially the basis of every wave is the ocean. Essentially there is no difference between the waves and the ocean, even though each wave is different from every other wave. Likewise, the basis of every individual soul and human being is the ocean-like Divine Self.

Many people subscribe to the idea that they are the body. They believe they are descendents from earlier patriarchs in their own ethnic group and that they are carrying on the traditions of their culture for the next generation. They also believe that their children will carry on the legacy and uphold the traditions. People also believe that they have nothing to do and have never had anything to do with other ethnic groups. It must be clearly understood that the history and evolution of the body is not the same as the evolution of the soul. Genetic evolution of the body does occur but this is separate from the spiritual evolution of the soul. Your soul may have incarnated in a physical body thousands of years ago to experience the life of that time with the human bodies and cultures that had evolved up to that time. If you do not end the cycle of birth and death (*uhm-ankh,* reincarnation) through Sema-Yoga you will reincarnate in the future and may experience the life that can be had with future human bodies. Further, you have not only been in human bodies; you have existed as animals, insects and other forms of matter as well. Thus you must understand that you are not related to the body except to the extent that your soul uses it to derive experiences it needs in order to evolve towards spiritual evolution. You must understand that it is only a tool (vehicle), like a boat, to take you across the ocean of the world process to attain Enlightenment. And just like a vehicle you expected to take you someplace important, you should take care of it, but should not think that the vehicle is you. You must strive to see your nature beyond the physical body. To do this, you must start to look at yourself and the world around you with your spiritual eye. Otherwise life becomes a degraded process through ignorance and manifold delusions.

THE DEGRADATION OF THE SOUL

According to the philosophy of reincarnation, when the soul degrades itself by acting with anger, hatred, greed, etc, it sets a process in motion which leads it to experience hellish conditions during life and after death. This is called negative *ari* or more popularly known as karma. If the *ari* is bad enough the soul will reincarnate in a lower form of life such as an animal. Further deleterious *ari* will result in reincarnation into the body of a plant, insect, etc. Then the soul must wait its turn again for a time when it will be able to incarnate into higher forms of life until it once again reaches human embodiment. The human embodiment will afford the chance again for enlightenment. This is why human life is so precious. It is in the human embodiment that the soul can use the mind to reason and discover its own nature and end the cycle of reincarnation and thereby attain enlightenment. Therefore, it is foolish to waste precious time hating things or people, desiring and longing after objects which are perishable and living in ignorance of the higher reality, thinking that human life is the only and highest achievement.

The Issue of Hate and the Importance of Culture to the Survival of a People

As a spiritual leader and professor of the Humanities (African Religion, African Philosophy and Culture) I have thought it appropriate to write this essay outlining the meaning of my work in reconstructing Ancient African religion in the context of the redemption of African culture. In this capacity I would like to make some suggestions and bring up some ideas that are important in the consideration of how to bring about peace between peoples of different cultures. Here we will begin by defining what culture is and then we will look at how culture can become an instrument of Hate and what to do about it. For a more detailed analysis of Culture in a sociological context see the book: *Comparative Mythology* by Muata Ashby. Here we will look at culture within the context of negative or unhealthy social interactions such as hate and racism.

What is Culture?

The following definitions and principles are offered as a standard to use, within the context of this discussion, for understanding what culture is, how it manifests in the world, and how that manifestation affects other cultures.

> **cul·ture** (kŭl′chər) *n.* **1.a.** The totality of
> socially transmitted behavior patterns,
> arts, beliefs, institutions, and all other
> products of human work and thought.
> -American Heritage Dictionary

Purpose of Culture:

- Culture is a people's window on whatever they perceive as reality (to understand the world around them) and their concept of self.

- Culture is a conditioning process, necessary for the early development of a human being.

68

- Culture defines the agenda of a society (government, economics, religion). Religion is the most powerful force driving culture.

- Culture is a manifestation of a people s ideas about themselves and their realities through customs, language, art, entertainments, religion, philosophy, clothing, tools, legends and other artifacts that are unique to the society.

If culture may be seen as a development of a people s experiences, knowledge and relation to the world around them, what form of culture would be most ideal to promote a people s beneficial existence and development?

Principles of a Healthy Culture

- A Healthy Culture allows a people to develop as human beings in the context of their own reality and the universal reality.

- A Healthy Culture allows a people to thrive in their own social structure without the need to subjugate other cultures.

- A Healthy Culture allows a people to discover the higher perspective of life beyond the conflicts and miseries of life. The philosophy of balance (Maat, Dharma, Tao, Beatitudes) promotes cooperation instead of competition, and humility instead of pride.

- A Healthy Culture is guided by a universal philosophy of reality as opposed to an exclusive ethnocentric model.

- A Healthy Culture views the ethnocentric model in the context of a community of complementary ethnic or cultural groups and not as an exclusive and or superior factor in culture.

- A Healthy Culture is based on a spiritual concept of existence, i.e. that all is a manifestation of the same ultimate reality and is therefore worthy of respect. This is the mystic, ecumenical, universal spiritual model of religion.

The Importance of Nationality in the Cultural Development of a People

Homeland + Belonging + Common History + Heritage + Legacy = <u>*Support System*</u>

From a developmental standpoint, all human beings begin life needing to be able to feel a sense of having a homeland, a physical country to which they can say they belong. This sense of belonging, coupled with the comradely that is developed with other people who have a common history and heritage is what allows a people to pass on a legacy to their descendants. People need this type of support system so that they may be able to develop and learn, that is to be socialized and thereby develop healthy egos. Nationalism is therefore a legitimate and natural aspect of culture to the extent that it is a banding together of people who have a common culture for the advancement of their lives, however, there is a caution, because it can become degraded into a concept of self-importance and endemic hubris wherein people develop arrogance with their own customs and ideas, and a lack of consideration or respect for that of others. A person with a healthy ego is a person who is well adjusted, and who has meaning and fulfillment in life without the need to hurt or otherwise diminish others. Sometimes it happens that entire societies become egoistic and thereby develop ideas which are detrimental to the people of the same culture and that of others. This is Cultural Egocentrism.

Danger of Culture as a tool for projecting a political or economic agenda.

- If culture becomes egocentric, its manifestations become imbued with pride, conceit, segregation and a will to control or subjugate other cultures [cultural and military imperialism].

- Egocentrism is a symptom of orthodox religion or introverted cultural patterns of thinking.

- Egocentrism is not found in cultures which espouse a universal, mystical, ecumenical or universal pattern of thinking.

✓ <u>Cultural Egocentrism leads to</u>: cultural bias (discrimination, segregation, aggression) against other cultures. The concept of Manifest Destiny is a stark example of cultural egocentrism. The term Manifest Destiny has come to be regarded by many scholars as a term used to describe statements by a culture that justify certain actions. This concept furnishes the culture with a self-given right to subjugate another culture by force (violence, killing, destruction)

✓ Members of the ethnocentric culture become: prideful, arrogant and conceited. This leads to the belief that one s ethnic group is different and or better than other groups.

Historical Examples of Cultural Egocentrism

➔Ex. United States right to expand west and annex Texas and California (manifest destiny) 19th century A.C.E.

➔Ex. European treatment of Africans (during the African slave trade) as an inferior race (culture) Europeans had the right to enslave them because they were not Christians and or advanced culturally. 15th century A.C.E.

➔Ex. Roman emperor Theodosius edict to outlaw and close all non-Roman Christian religions and other Christian sects (4th century A.C.E.) labeling them as the inferior religions.

➔Ex. The right to decimate Native Americans and the take of the New World by Europeans. 15th century A.C.E.

➔Ex. The right of the Jewish people to oust the Canaanites and establish a homeland in Palestine by divine right. 8th century B.C.E.

→ Ex. The right of Alexander, Caesar, Attila, Genghis Khan, Hitler, the illuminati, the Superpower governments (United States-USSR) to establish a New World Order.

→ Ex. The right of Moslems to conquer India and Africa and enslave those people while converting them to Islam. 7th-13th century A.C.E.

→ Ex. The right of Israelis to conquer Palestine and usurp the land and subjugate the Palestinian people. [1949 A.C.E. present]

→ Ex. The right of the United States to set up over 700 bases around the world to conquer territory and control world commerce [1776 A.C.E. to present]

The Confusion of Religion and Ethnicity

Many people make the mistake of confusing culture, religion, ethnicity and nationalism. This error is expressed in phrases like Palestinians and Jews . The term Palestinians refers to an ethnic and perhaps political affiliation and the term Jew relates to a religious affiliation. So if the statement is referring to the conflict between to nationalities it is incorrect because even if we wanted to refer to Israel as a Jewish state , even though its politics may be dominated by religious fundamentalists or others who may use religious grounds to promote certain policies, it is actually a secular state composed of people who may be Jews and also followers of other religions. In any case, in order to be a Jewish state it would have to have its governmental institutions and legal system completely based on Jewish religious tenets. So it is important to distinguish between the varied forms of human interaction while at the same time not generalizing relationships or conflicts that muddle the pathways to understanding human relationships and the means to resolve conflicts.

Culture Studies for Philosophers and Mystics

While this book is primarily about sociology, psychology, ethics and philosophy, it is also about spirituality. The idea of culture and its trappings can sometimes pose a conflict for people following the mystical paths of spirituality. Many times people on the path of mysticism develop the idea that it is wrong to feel part of a particular culture or another because they want to feel universal or all-embracing. They have learned that the pursuit of the mystical experience requires a letting go of the trappings of cultural identity as well as gender identity and ultimately ego identity. All of that is true; however, how is it to be applied in order to grow spiritually in an integrated, psychologically well adjusted manner? Cultural, gender and ego identity are seen as varying forms of ignorance that lesser evolved people uphold. Now, the question may be asked of those same mystics, how did they become mystics in the first place? Were they born and immediately taken from the hospital, when they were born, to an initiation by a sage and they instantaneously assumed a spot among the Sages? Can we ask a child to give up the toys before they are outgrown, before the child has a chance to grow up and see a higher perspective in life? Of course not, and so too lesser evolved human beings need to have the toys, so to speak, until they are transcended. But how is this process to proceed if they are not led to that higher perspective and who will do the leading? Children playing with toys cannot lead other children to go beyond the toys. Also, it is important to not let children play with dangerous toys that can be a danger to others or themselves. In the same way human beings need evolved beings who, while working with the toys can show people to grow beyond them. In other words, sages work with people at their level and while the sages themselves have outgrown the trappings of culture, racial determinations, creeds, religious tenets, etc. the sages use these to lead people to higher wisdom and thereby to the higher realizations of the mystical experience. Therefore, what is needed is for those on the mystical path to practice detachment and dispassion when relating in the world so that they may assist others while at the same time out-stepping the traps of worldly entanglements. This means that people who want to follow the African path of mysticism (Shetaut Neter) can safely do so while at the same time considering themselves as African in culture, ethnicity or consciousness just as a person following the path of Indian mysticism, Vedanta, can see him/herself as an Indian, culturally, but mystically as a transcendental and universal human being.

In this way, the mystic learns to transcend culture and worldliness through increasing dispassion and detachment while at the same time work, using cultural traditions, histories, language, etc. to assist others who are coming along in the next generation, thereby keeping the mystic tradition alive for future generations, as a deeper aspect of the culture. The work in the world of time and space within a culture can actually be a vehicle to a higher mystical realization, *IF* it is handled in the correct manner. This is the path of Maat, being the actionless actor, acting with peace and contentment, i.e. not being caught up in the action and not expecting rewards or praises from it either. Actually, just as a person is not fit for the teaching of ordinary education unless they grow from childhood into adulthood and become balanced and grounded in their personality as a mature human being, so too an aspirant is not fit for the teaching as long as they deny the cultural perspective from which they come and set out to work through it and transcend it and not just avoid or sidestep it. This error will lead them to suppress aspects of their personality and their evolution will be stunted due to not confronting the issues that bind them to the world of time and space. In other words, for example, a French person who starts on the path of self-discovery saying I am not French, I am a human being, a spirit! I will study Sema-Yoga and forget my western culture! is denying an aspect of their personality. If they have not worked through the complexes of their culture they will not raise their own consciousness beyond a certain level and they will not raise the consciousness of their own culture either. This will make for a degraded culture in which the practice of the teachings will become more difficult. Whenever there is a scarcity of authentic wise personalities in a culture or when a culture becomes so degraded that it drowns out the voices of wisdom, that culture becomes deluded, greedy and destructive. High spiritual attainments in a society are supported by a healthy culture just as a human being cannot be sane without a healthy ego. The ego is not contradictory to a positive spiritual movement unless it is degraded, egoistic. In the same manner, culture is not detrimental to a society s positive evolution if it is not devoid of virtue. When a culture is guided by sages, or at least, wise leaders, it can be actually an enhancer to the spiritual evolution of the entire population. This is part of the secular duty of initiates and sages as part of their responsibility is to help humanity.

Finally, the sages of Ancient Kamit [Egypt] had no compunction in admitting they were Kamitans but they also affirmed their Asarian (higher) nature that is transcendental, beyond worldly designations. They managed the society even while writing about the glories of the Divine and the means to attain spiritual enlightenment. Many people are ashamed of their culture or of their past, etc. and they seek to deny or forget about it and this is not the higher way. Authentic aspirants will deal with the darkness of the past or their lower nature, and purify it and then move on to serve all humanity everywhere instead of running around the world helping others when one needs emergency attention to understand, resolve and work through egoistic complexes that are culturally related. How would it be if a medical doctor went to a hospital across town when her own hospital has patients who need her because the hospital is broken down and the one across town looks modern and pretty? However, once those patients are taken care of in her own hospital there is no problem in going across town and helping there as well. In this way, her own hospital provides a needed service and if she performs that service without egoism, she will grow from it instead of following the illusion of the other hospital. Her service will lead to the eventual uplifting of that hospital that is run down, that community that is run down and in the process she attains a higher fulfillment through the higher wisdom awareness that it is not the running away but the accepting and transcending of one s condition that leads to the numinous attainment that is sought. This should not be taken to mean that it is wrong to seek better conditions but if one can improve one s conditions where one is that should be seen as a viable venue for spiritual evolution until better situations may arise where one can do better. So egoistic running away from situations of dislike will not provide as much satisfaction and evolutionary opportunity as confronting the present with as much composure as possible, realizing that all situations are temporary and letting time bring forth the next opportunity to move on, when the lessons of the current condition/situation are learned. When this discipline is adopted the actions, the culture and the ego, become spiritualized tools for the skilled mystic that lead him/her to the mystical experience.

Ethnicity, Illusion, Conflict and Hatred

Ethnicity
noun
an ethnic quality or affiliation resulting from racial or
cultural ties; "ethnicity has a strong influence on
community status relations"
WordNet   3.0,   2006 by Princeton University.

----

ethnicity [(eth-nis-uh-tee)]

Identity with or membership in a particular racial,
national, or cultural group and observance of that group's
customs, beliefs, and language.

The American Heritage   New Dictionary of Cultural
Literacy, Third Edition
Copyright   2005 by Houghton Mifflin Company.
Published by Houghton Mifflin Company. All rights
reserved.

----

eth · nic · i · ty [eth-nis-i-tee] noun, plural -ties.
ethnic traits, background, allegiance, or association

Origin:
1765 75, for earlier sense; ETHNIC + -ITY
Dictionary.com Unabridged
Based on the Random House Dictionary,   Random
House, Inc. 2006.

The American Heritage Dictionary defines ethnicity as:

  Of or pertaining to a group of people recognized as a class on the
basis of certain distinctive characteristics, such as religion,
language, ancestry, culture, or national origin.

In the definitions above the common themes are brought forth in the following words: *affiliation, identity with or membership, allegiance, or association.* These words defining the concept of ethnicity do not denote any real or abiding differences between people. They do not mean real, intrinsic differences amongst people. They do not necessarily relate to a person s so called race though it can relate to the person s racial identity, the race they think they are and or belong to. They do in fact mean that a person s ethnicity relates to their upbringing and social associations. This can be expanded to include the association with or belief in or allegiance with the ideas and belief systems, traditions and customs of a society. In other words, the term ethnicity may be further defined simply as a person s cultural association . For example, there are many peoples of varying hues of skin that practice Islam; we may say that Islam is a religion but it also relates to Arab culture so persons of different races may have an allegiance with Arab culture and or ethnicity.

Oftentimes, due to ignorance and a low state of social and spiritual development, people focus on ethnicity as a basis for separation and divisions among peoples. There can also be additional issues such as Class differences even within the same ethnic group. Due to greed, anger, hatred, etc. these divisions degrade into the notion of race, racism and sexism. Essentially, the primary condition of these various negative -isms of society is ignorance of the source of all happiness and peace, the Higher Self. When people do not understand that it is the Self reflecting in their personality that allows them the experience of happiness and peace and not the objects of the world, they seek to experience happiness by acquiring objects.

To what ethnic group do two boys who were born as twins and who were separated at birth and one grew up with his Chinese mother who was Christian and lived in the United States, speaks English and who likes rock music and American Idol, while the other grew up with his Indian Hindu father in Brazil and speaks Portuguese and likes samba music? Clearly, the example above demonstrates the fallacy of conflating ethnicity with race or assigning particular ethnic associations based on outward appearance. This example also highlights the error of considering ethnicity as a real and abiding feature of human existence that can be used as a legitimate means to brand a person s existence. The erroneous use of ethnicity colors a person s reality, blinding them to the wider world beyond by causing them to believe that their own ethnicity is somehow superior or inferior to that of others. Ethnicity is the cultural association a person can grow into through socialization or associations a person can choose but in and of themselves they have no innate value except perhaps if the customs and traditions of the ethnic group can provide advantages in survival or progress in life. If an ethnic group were to develop knowledge and resources to promote the welfare of the group that ethnic group would develop a feature that would help it s perpetuation. Any ethnic group can do that. If an ethnic group were to formulate ideas of superiority, and to create belief systems and institutions to discriminate, segregate and subjugate others that superiority would not be due to an intrinsic superiority of the underlying components of the ethnic group [race , knowledge, customs, geography, etc.] but rather a result of the association of its individuals with the ideas [in this case, egoistic (negative) ideas], that when acted upon collectively, achieve the power not only to be manifested in the world but also the effect of self-delusional narcissism wherein the ethnic group projects those ideals, for their own consumption and that of others, through the media, arts, and in speech as well as institutions that reflect the illusion of superiority of the ethnicity for it s adherents to admire, feel pride in and or aspire to.

Yet, all the while, ethnicity in and of itself is merely a vehicle of social association to allow adherents of a particular culture to associate, band together and see each other in an ethnic light; the question is how is this ethnic vision used by a people? In other words, from an egoistic perspective, ethnicity is a way of describing the process of individuation wherein a person becomes fragmented in their ideals of human existence, from a wholistic being at birth to a segregated, prejudicial, individualistically self-aware human being who can see him or her self as separate from other individuals, groups, societies and nations while adhering to a particular cultural point of view, which is itself a larger group. So the individual is part of a collective and as such the individuality is lost in the association, thereby rendering that person apparently free as an individual but in reality bound, caught up in the illusion of the larger group identity. Nationality in this context may be seen as the most powerful form of ethnic delusion as it envisions a particular group as being separately originated in a country with it s own culture, identity and rights, separate from the rest of humanity. It is consequently the most dangerous form of egoism since it can amass enough deluded individuals to produce ideals and war instruments to allow the egoistic differences, which manifest as ethnic animosities to erupt in large scale conflicts that end in mass death and mass destruction.

The error of conflating race and ethnicity is starkly evident in human history. For example, some Egyptologists and scholars of history are fond of considering the rivalry between the Ancient Egyptians and Nubians as racial , labeling the Nubians as black Africans and the Egyptians as either a separate race, or as Asians or even as Europeans. The conflicts between the Ancient Egyptians and the Nubians were ethnic conflicts and not racial conflicts because the Ancient Egyptians and the Ancient Nubians were kinfolk. The same is true of the ancient Hebrews and Canaanites, the forerunners of the modern day Palestinians and Israelis [though in the 19th and 20th century, Jews from Europe introduced European ethnic ideals to Asia Minor]. The conflicts between the French and Germans and the English during World War Two were ethnic conflicts and not racial ones since they all belonged to the same so called race and so were committing genocide against themselves. The conflict between the Sunni Muslims and Shia Muslims of Iraq, after the invasion of their country by the United States in 2003, was also an ethnic (religious beliefs) conflict and not racial since they all belonged to the same so called race and so were committing genocide against themselves. The conflict between the Tutsi and Hutus of Rwanda was also an ethnic conflict and not racial since they all belonged to the same so called race and so were committing genocide against themselves. The Rwanda case is interesting because peoples were pitted against each other, who lived with and in many cases married each other but who harbored ethnic individuality which was brought to the surface, manipulated by unethical and ignorant leaders to foment conflict, not unlike the leaders of countries such as the United States of America, foment intra-national divisions by exploiting sub-ethnic differences within the national culture; rich are pitted against the poor, Protestants against Jews, white against black , latinos [32] against black , white against latinos , etc.

---

[32] the use of the term latino should not be taken as an assignation of people who speak Spanish or who come from Hispanic related countries as being part of a separate racial group. There is no such thing as a latino race . The term latino relates to a culture which can have people of European descent, Native American descent, people of African descent, etc. within the context of the illusory and bogus racial discourse, the phrase Africans and latinos is incorrect because the former is a racial designation and the latter is a cultural designation.

Figure 13: Skulls of victims in Rwandan Genocide museum.

Human beings may be classified in a triune format. This is derived from the virtually universal understanding of cultures around the world of a Trinity or three-fold mode of expression of Creation. There are people who are wise, people who are dull and people who are mixed. The dull people tend to follow negative human ideals, and endeavors; the mixed may follow a righteous path with ethics and progressive ideals if all is well but when provoked or frustrated they may follow a negative path in life. The mixed personality is not disposed to crime but is disposed to pursuing the perceived sources of pleasure and the values of the society [the ethnic group]. These pursuits of worldly ideals weaken the capacity of the mixed personality to follow a righteous path. This makes them susceptible to the persuasions of the dull, fundamentalists, ideologies and other strong personalities who know how to manipulate the masses. Even if they do not participate in illegal or immoral activities they may acquiesce to the desires of the strong personalities or allow themselves to benefit from the unrighteous actions of the few corrupt individuals; which makes them accomplices and supporters of the unrighteousness. The wise follow a path of truth instead of delusion, regardless of the provocations or temptations of life. In times of trouble the mixed and dull are blind followers of demagogues and charlatans. This gives rise to great followings of the ignorant, violent and megalomaniac and or imperialist personalities of the world like religious Pontiffs, or Emperors like the leaders of the Roman Empire, the British Empire, the Islamic Empire, the United States of America Empire or colonialists, capitalists, dictators and despots like Hitler, Attila the Hun, Genghis Khan, War Presidents, Prime Ministers and others. Ethnicity, like other elements of culture, such as religion, can be a tool to be manipulated by unscrupulous leaders, who prey on the ignorance and blindness of the weak elements of humanity [the dull and mixed personalities].

Figure 14: Khoisan man from Southern Africa

The country Botswana and its policies on the indigenous peoples (Khoisan) is an example of discrimination, abuse and mistreatment of one group against another that is not composed of white members. One of the groups of peoples that remained in Africa after the spread of humanity (to the rest of the world out of Africa), most recently developed into what cultural anthropologists refer to as Bantu Speaking peoples. The **Bantu** refer to over 400 different ethnic groups in Africa, from Cameroon to South Africa, united by a common language family, the Bantu languages, and in many cases common customs. The scholarly consensus is that the Bantu speaking peoples of Africa were located generally in the area of present day Nigeria and then spread south throughout the area that was inhabited exclusively by the Khoisan or San (indigenous tribal population-also referred to as Bushmen). The Bantu expanded to encompass southern Africa but there was separation between themselves and the Bushmen. To this day there is segregation as the two peoples hold separate values but also their respective cultures were affected by the ravages of racism that was imposed by European colonists. We may consider that the Bantu and the Khoisan have certain physical differences, just as Bantus look somewhat differently from African peoples of Nubia, but are two groups of black people albeit with different ethnic affiliations. Today, the rift is wide enough to the extent that the government of Botswana, now controlled by descendants of the Bantu, after achieving liberation from European [white] rule, actively imposes similar kinds of discriminative tactics against the Bushmen to dispossess them of their lands as were used on them all by the European colonists. Botswana is a landlocked nation in Southern Africa. It was formerly the British protectorate of Bechuanaland. Botswana adopted its new name after becoming independent from British rule on September 30, 1966. The openness and fairness of the political system is credited for the flourishing economy. With its proven record of good economic governance, Botswana was ranked as Africa's least corrupt country by Transparency International in 2004, ahead of many European and Asian countries. The World Economic Forum rates Botswana as one of the two most economically competitive nations in Africa. In 2004 Botswana was once again assigned "A" grade credit ratings by Moody's Investors Service and Standard & Poor's. This ranks Botswana as by far the best credit risk in Africa and puts it on par or above many countries in central Europe, East Asia, and Latin America. However, one area of struggle for improvement in the Botswana political system is that there has been ongoing debate about the political, social, and economic marginalization of the San The unequal treatment of the majority Bantu population and economic interests versus the government's policies for the Basarwa (San) and other remote area dwellers continue to spark controversy.

On the island of Dominica, an example of freed African slaves mistreating the native population is found. The Commonwealth of Dominica, is also popularly known as Dominica. Dominica is an island nation in the Caribbean Sea. Dominica should not be confused with the Dominican Republic, which is another Caribbean nation. The pre-Columbian name of Dominica' is *Wai'tu kubuli*, which means "Tall is her body." Dominica was first sighted by Christopher Columbus, and other Europeans in 1493 ACE. There they encountered the Caribs, the indigenous peoples. [Native Americans] Remarkably, when they immediately attempted to enslave the Caribs the Caribs fought them fiercely and defeated the Spaniards so the Spaniards left the island. The island was settled by the British and by the year 1838, Dominica became the first British colony in the Caribbean to have a Black-controlled legislature. However, even though the Caribs still resided on the island, the Black-controlled legislature did not include substantial participation of the Caribs and later and even into the present the Black [descendants of the former African slave population] has attempted to diminish the rights and marginalize the descendants of the Caribs, about

3,000 of whom live on the island's east coast in their own territory. In 1896 ACE, the United Kingdom re-took governmental control of Dominica and turned it into a crown colony.

The situation between Bantu Africans and the Bushmen Africans [Native Africans] in Africa and the situation between the African freed slaves and the Native Americans in Dominica raises important human issues related to the age old question of nature versus nurture. If we are to accept, based on the solid evidence of examples throughout history, that the peoples of the temperate zones are more aggressive than those of the tropical zones how do we explain the fact that when the culture of peoples of tropical zones are negatively affected by the peoples of the temperate zones, and when the oppression from the peoples of the temperate zones is lifted, why is it that the oppression on the native populations is continued by the peoples of African descent who are now the dominant population? Why is it that great dictators and tyrants emerge in such populations as occurred in Africa during the neo-colonial period?

We may conclude that ethnic affiliations, even when not affected by temperate zone interventions, are prone to developments of discrimination and segregation. Furthermore, when a people s culture is damaged or destroyed, that people s future is in danger because culture is needed to give direction and a sense of purpose in life; absent that direction and purpose a people can adopt the values of others and act accordingly. Culture is not the absolute and ultimate determiner of a person s fate but it is the necessary infrastructure the personality needs to derive its sense of community, ethics and self-concept as a human being. However, that culture should not be a source of hubris, or exclusion, it should be open and ethical. Therefore, it is possible to re-program people to act in different ways if their culture is manipulated (disrupted), that is, if their language, traditions, relationships etc. are taken away or replaced with other cultural elements and values.

These examples point to the need to grow beyond the false categorizations of race but also the illusory categories of ethnicity and culture. It is important to see these as manifestations of social custom and traditions with no intrinsic superiority but which may have aesthetic and intellectual wisdom value as well as spiritual value if they lead to ways of understanding history through the eyes of cultural wisdom and freedom from stereotypes, prejudices and closed mindedness. Otherwise they lead to resentments, jealousies, conflicts, and social clashes. If we consider that segregation, oppression or other injustices directed at particular groups can cause those groups to develop into ethnicities we are again confronted with the idea that ethnicity is not an abiding reality but rather a construct for social survival, a means for its adherents to cope with and or meet the challenges of life as they see it, by means of the coagulation of a perceived need to which a shared belief is ascribed value and associated with. The challenge is to use the ethnic crutch but only until it is possible to grow into a more abiding and truly universal human awareness essentially, becoming a mature human being. Few icons encapsulate the ideal and illusion of nationalism as a national flag, which is often used by politicians to promote the idea of their own patriotism or the lack of patriotism of their opponents. Ignorant allegiance to national causes, anthems, flags and slogans has been used successfully to delude people into believing they are supporting everyone s interests [national interests] but in reality they are supporting the interests of those who benefit by segregation and discrimination as well as war. Powerful national artifacts, such as flags, can be used to promote ethics and civic at seemingly innocent venues such as sports meetings and just as easily, at social or political gatherings, can be turned to promote separateness, exclusivism, intolerance [even of citizens who disagree or criticize the policies] national hubris, a sense of entitlement and war. This means not buying into flag waving, believing in the innate superiority of one s own culture and nationality or harboring mindless hope in the rhetoric of ethnic leaders but rather in the higher truth that recognizes the kinship of humanity and the lofty ideal of ethical environmental stewardship and universal progressive social humanitarianism, in other words, *globalism*, the attitude or policy of placing the interests of the entire world above those of individual nations. It is important to understand that national egoism is an exacerbation of the individual egos that it is composed of. Therefore, nationalism, like egoism, racism, sexism and the other negative isms that plague humanity, are to be considered social pathologies that are to be cured by the sincere and effective practice of high wisdom philosophy; until this is done, the efforts of politicians, religious leaders, and other well meaning social activists will be limited and the underlying causes of social conflict, unrest and ignorance of the true nature of humanity and the self, will not be resolved leading to more conflicts, and wars.

Figure 15: Image of the pledge of allegiance to the flag and what it supposedly stands for, using a Nazi like salute before it was changed.

Finally, what is a healthy cultural ego? A healthy cultural ego is one wherein the people that adhere to the culture are aware of their history, and their worth as human beings as part of the family of humanity who are worthy to partake in the rights and benefits of civilized world culture and to demand the same respect as other members of humanity. For example, in the case of African peoples, due to colonialism, neocolonialism, the misrepresentations of history by various scholars and the prejudices of some white people, most people of African descent [African ethnicity] and others of other ethnicities, have developed the idea that African peoples did not contribute to humanity in such areas as technology, art, literature, music, civilization, etc. In order to redress that imbalance and counteract that erroneous notion, many have sought to bolster the African mind through education formats such as history classes, Africentrism and even nationalistic movements. If these efforts cause peoples who adhere to African ethnicity to develop the correct notion about their culture, that is, realizations like, hey, our people had technology, art, literature, music, civilization, etc. just like other peoples around the world and we are just as worthy as other peoples around the world then the cultural ego may be considered healthy. If the realizations above are led to thoughts like hey, our people had technology, art, literature, music, civilization, etc. just like other peoples around the world and we are just as worthy as other peoples around the world and in fact we did greater things than others and we are naturally superior and others should look up to us and others should be our slaves because we are the chosen ones, etc. then the cultural ego may be considered not only unhealthy and egoistic but also deluded, dangerous and destructive. A healthy cultural ego allows its people to affirm their own value while also validating the right of other culture to express their values and respect the values of others even while not necessarily agreeing with them, yet understanding that others may feel the same way about one s own values. This kind of allowance goes beyond tolerance because in tolerance one accepts the values of others until they can be stopped; here there is no real acceptance or respect. In the allowance born of respect and understanding there is the capacity to seek common ground and view the variations as explorations of the realities of life based on the perspectives of others which may or may not contain valuable insights and contributions to the betterment of humanity. Through respect and understanding it is possible to promote great advancement and progress, whereas the opposite holds back the progress of humanity, a social process that may be considered illogical if not pathological [holding back one s own progress due to the inability to receive good advice, technologies, or other ideas from other ethnic groups due to one s own ignorance, prejudices, or other failings of individual and or cultural egoism.

Cultural Identity V.S. Mystical Spirituality

Cultural identity is not in contradiction with Mystical Spirituality. To say that All is One, and the goal of spirituality is to go beyond ordinary human experience, the great truths of mysticism, which were affirmed by the great African Sages of Ancient Egypt, does not mean that culture is bogus or that culture cannot coexist with mysticism. How can this ideal work? Culture, government, and social institutions are supposed to be tools through which the leaders of society lead the masses to evolve. They are not realities in and of themselves. Human beings are the realities who make up cultures. A person can evolve by growing closer to the understanding of his or her own higher spiritual reality by working through and then transcending the realities presented by their culture, discovering it s wisdom and expanding to discover universal wisdom. Part of that growth process is the manner [egoistic, non-egoistic] in which that person learns from their culture and the manner in which intercultural relations are conducted. The issue is how productive and vibrant, as a member of society is that person, and how are they learning to grow professionally and spiritually through their culture. Culture is an expression (one of a numerous number) of universal consciousness, which expresses in the form of human activity. The human spirit manifests through the myriad of dazzling colors, sounds, and forms of the cultures of all peoples. Since each expression of life [human, animal, spiritual] desires to exist and discover the fullness of life, each expression is equally legitimate to the extent it does not harm life and or nature. Culture also has the important role of allowing a people to understand their role in the world and their relationship to other cultures and to nature.

People without Culture are easy prey for conquerors

Cicero

Human society has to have culture just as the spirit needs to have a body in order to interact in the world and to have experiences. The question should therefore be asked is the culture based on truth and righteousness or on destruction, delusion and unrighteousness? If it is based on truth its fruit will be nonviolence, sharing, and a spirit of camaraderie with all peoples. The people of such a culture could discover contentment and peace and that would give rise to cultural empathy, sympathy, and compassion; cultures would care about the well-being of other cultures and would not seek to pit themselves against other cultures and vie for supremacy or control of resources at the expense of the other culture. When people are able to feel empathy, sympathy and compassion there naturally develops a feeling towards service to humanity wherein people desire to assist others and improve their condition; they actually feel good about helping others and helping others achieve higher living conditions, to experience a higher standard of living the way the empathic, sympathetic and compassionate person has experienced. In such a culture there would be no need for intra-cultural conflicts and competitions [white vs. black, black vs. brown , brown vs. yellow , young vs. old, men vs. women, southerners vs. northerners, rich vs. poor, etc.]. If it does not, it s fruit will be the bitter pain of stress and strife, divisiveness, dissent and conflict.

Culture and ethnicity were never thought of as separating factors until the advent of nationalism, despotism and racism emerged in government and societies. In reality the culture of every group in humanity should be seen as an integral part of the greater society of human beings on earth as a collective. Think of a garden. In a garden there can be many types of flowers, geraniums, roses, lilies, daisies, etc. All of these various types of flowers create the marvelous collective ambiance of the garden through the beauty brought forth from the endless variety and the combinations, which are possible even though the individual glowers exist in distinct forms. Indeed, variety is the spice of life but notions that include the ignorance of thinking that the variations are real and abiding differences is like a body with a cancerous growth that will eventually kill it. The variety of human expressions has come to be thought of as a great evil by those who out of ignorance and fear, seek to separate themselves and thereby maintain themselves as a distinct class, ethnic group or culture on to themselves, promoting their own agendas for their own benefit.

Obviously, it is easier to maintain notions of separation or even superiority if there is an apparent distinctive culture that supremacists can point to, a distinct culture for people to feel part of or adhere to [ethnicity]. However, just having a cultural ego is not enough for negative cultural manifestations to be possible. Without the egoistic cultural ego such notions are unsustainable. The bases of the egoistic cultural ego are ignorant and weak personalities lacking the ethics of self-worth, and possessing fear of the other. We may consider such a personality that is so weak that it needs to feel secure in it s identity by constantly affirming its superiority and or by affirming its different-ness from the rest of humanity as a socially dysfunctional [pathological] personality. Such a diseased mind needs to be helped and not despised, shown compassion and not insensitivity. This is the way to heal the insanity, not by hatred, animosity and violence. They who heal with peace grow to heaven while those who meet hatred with hatred go to hell with the haters.

This philosophy of anger and hatred is in contravention with the very basis of human existence and this is why there are many people in all ethnic groups who strenuously object to this negative philosophy, meeting anger with anger, hatred with hatred, violence with violence, etc. On the other hand however, complacency and acquiescence is equally undesirable. One may go into a closed room and then say that the sun does not exist. The sun shines on regardless, despite that person s delusion (inability to accept and live by truth). If that person stays away from the sun long enough they will die from lack of vitamin D and Life Force Energy among other things. Likewise, a person or a group of people (ethnic or nationalistic) who stay away from truth, affirming ignorant notions such as narcissism, exceptionalism, racism, nationalism, sexism, etc. will also be frustrated and ultimately their lives, communities and social systems will decay, dragging along with them those (including their victims who do not know how to forgive) who adhere to the negative philosophy.

Even if you are a victim of someone else s wrongdoing you also suffer their malady or the insanity which caused their attack on you, if you agree with their insane philosophy. For example, if you were robbed, raped or maimed by someone and then you too begin to hate, despise and vilify them and wish them, or others, ill you are in effect suffering from the same illness that was the cause of the original attack. This applies to individuals as well as to groups, nations and cultures. Why, because human beings who commit acts of anger, hatred or violence are acting out of the illness of egoism and spiritual ignorance. Anger, hatred and greed are only outer symptoms of the deeper problem. They are so far away from the reality of their own spirit that they can see others as separate beings and not as part of themselves or at least as part of the same reality that all human beings share and therefore have a legitimate right to participate in. Can you hurt your own arm, or your own leg? Can you cut your hand off or burn yourself? Some people are so distraught and depressed or psychotic that they do commit self-mutilation or harm themselves in other ways and this is to be considered insanity. Likewise when one human being hurts another, in fact when one human being hurts nature (animals, trees, the environment, etc.) they are suffering the same insanity, the same disease of self-mutilation but the disease is being projected outwardly instead of inwardly.

In any case, the outward unrighteous actions of a person have an internal physiological and subconscious effect and this will always lead to internal tension, frustration, and eventually self-destruction, in the form of drugs, alcohol, stress, disease, and any number of self-destructive lifestyles which render a person incapable of experiencing true [abiding, based on truth] happiness, peace and joy in life. So there is a real suffering for the perpetrator of unrighteousness. Should the victim suffer doubly? This is what happens when a victim becomes angry, hateful, and bitter towards the attacker and towards the culture of the attacker, or towards anyone or anything else as a result of unresolved trauma from the hurt. The attacker injures them and then they injure themselves with the degrading mental cancers of hatred and revenge, passing on the legacy by poisoning their children with the same feelings and justifying their own actions in the same manner. An example of this effect on a society is the Israeli culture wherein the suffering of a people through massacres, discrimination and widespread abuse developed into a state that perceives reality through the prism of that victimization wherein their conclusion, that that should never happen again, translates into the victimization of others, namely the Palestinians, at any cost, even living as if in a state of perpetual siege and even if it means depriving others of basic human rights, including their lives. While there are many individuals who feel otherwise, as a culture the Israeli nation is unable to trust others or feel empathy, sympathy and compassion for other peoples and to lead a shared existence with their environment. They are not an exclusive example of this problem in humanity but a starkly representative one for the purposes of this study. That lack of feeling allows them to, as a state, maintain the ideal of segregation and entitlement above others and to, with the help and support of the Unites States of America, perpetrate war crimes and social indignities on their neighbors, especially the Palestinians.[33] It also has developed into manipulations of and spying on their supposed allies in order to provoke the support of their supposed allies for their war crimes [purposeful killing women and children in Lebanon, and Palestine, taking annexing lands and occupying their lands], essentially the same kinds of unrighteous acts as was perpetrated upon their own people in the past.

Nevertheless, whole societies may have an unrighteous effect but that does not mean that individuals or subgroups do not oppose the agendas of the majority. Just as one bad apple does not spoil a whole bunch, one should recall the understanding that individuals who perpetrate injustice or violence do not represent the group as a whole even if hey do gain political control and direct the culture towards unrighteous behavior. In all cultures there are righteous and unrighteous people but this is no excuse for allowing unrighteous leaders to control the direction of culture. Therefore, the deeper struggle is not one of nationalism or even culturalism but a question of righteousness versus unrighteousness. When two siblings are fighting it is the job of the parent (if they are righteous) to mediate and make peace. But how can an unrighteous parent mediate if they themselves do not know what is right and wrong or if they have a personal stake in the process? How can leaders of societies (who are like parents to society) bring peace and justice if their own lives are based on ignorance, greed, lust, bigotry, and discrimination?

Degraded Culture, Neo-colonialism and the Redemption of African Religion

Africa and peoples of African descent as well as peoples of other cultures, are beset with continuing problems of social injustice, economic enslavement, malnutrition, miseducation, disease and other maladies. What is the source and nature of these maladies, how did they come into being and how should the solutions to them be pursued? Also, what should the role of spirituality be in such an endeavor?

---

[33] **Massive US Arms Sale to Israel Disclosed**

Amnesty International has revealed that the United States has sent a massive new shipment of arms to Israel despite evidence that US weapons were misused against civilians in the Gaza attacks.
Amnesty said a German cargo ship carrying about 14,000 tons of arms docked in late March at the Israeli port of Ashdod, about twenty-five miles north of Gaza. The ship left for Israel on December 20, a week before the start of Israel s attacks on Gaza. *Democracynow.org,* Headlines for April 06, 2009

Movements in Africa such as the Mau Mau and in the African Diaspora, such as Rastafari, Africentrism and the Marcus Garvey movements have resisted neo-colonialism[34] but have achieved only limited success in promoting not only the end of sociopolitical and economic colonialism but also the elimination of cultural oppression. Neo-colonialism is a continuing problem for African nations as well as other developing countries around the world but in the late 20th century the stronger instrument for domination evolved into economic tyranny, otherwise referred to as globalization. While it appears that the colonial powers of Europe withdrew from developing nations, after sometimes hundreds of years of colonization, under the guise of bringing civilization to native peoples, but in reality usurping their natural resources and denigrating their humanity in order to make them pliable personalities for exploitation, the lasting effects of colonialism are still being felt in many cultures around the world. Cultural oppression involves forcing cultural changes on an indigenous population such as forcing the use of clothing, changes in language, changes in religion, etc. Colonialism involves cultural oppression but also involves exploitation of the labor of indigenous peoples as well as extraction of raw materials from another country without proper compensation and subjugation of the native population through the imposition of slavery or meager wages (tantamount to slavery). It may seem that a given country is free from colonialism when the ruling country seems to remove its governing population and army from a colony but this is only a withdrawal of direct forms of control such as governors and foreign armed forces. Upon their withdrawal they leave in place another system of control called neo-colonialism. Neo-colonialism makes use of economic dependency and political manipulation of the elite of an indigenous population to retain control over a country after the society has been fully disrupted, the culture destabilized and the religion has been disrupted by missionaries and or interrupted by occupation or war. The ruling country s rulers rationalize their right to control other countries and people by saying they are giving them civilization and they are better off by being subjugated and exploited. One means to organize a neo-colonial system is by leaving a privileged class of natives in ruling positions, that may be in direct collusion and sharing profits with the elites of the conqueror culture, to keep the local population dominated and to do the bidding of the foreign power. Another means is to cripple the economy of the developing country through usurious[35] loans initially given with the stated purpose of providing development capital for the country. Since the country is ruled by dictators and or a corrupt ruling class, the moneys

---

[34] A policy whereby a major power uses economic and political means to perpetuate or extend its influence over underdeveloped nations or areas.

[35] The practice of lending money and charging the borrower interest, especially at an exorbitant or illegally high rate. An excessive or illegally high rate of interest charged on borrowed money.

are appropriated by these peoples and the country languishes in poverty and despair while the armies of the dictators impose harsh and brutal tactics, which are supported by the ruling foreign powers, to help the local, unpopular government, retain control and impose policies favorable to the foreign country. The weakness of the populace, due to irresolution by following divergent religions and the pursuit of un-virtuous lifestyles and worldly goals, renders them as submissive followers of government [free market capitalism, consumerism] and or religious [foreign religion is true religion, indigenous religion is heathenish] propaganda and or the government and or religious fundamentalism of the foreign culture. This condition renders their efforts at freedom, weak and ineffectual even if they seem to have a revolution that eliminates the native ruling class and foreign control; that is because the ignorance due to lack of knowledge of self remains and the damaged, degraded culture, after years of destabilization through war, colonialism or neocolonialism, has lost its way in promoting a higher perspective for its people. The society thus moves on in a mediocre state or may descend to lower levels of corruption and degradation, such as failed states, civil wars and other negative social conditions.

Colonialism can affect people in their country or the same people in the country of the conqueror culture. An example of this is the situation of Africans who were enslaved in the Americas. The descendants of the original Africans have experienced hundreds of years of colonization through subjugation by and immersion in the conqueror culture (Europeans that enslaved African peoples and brought them to the Americas). For the most part those people see themselves not as Africans but as Americans (whether they come from South America, Central America, North America or the Caribbean). In this way they have adopted the culture of the Americas even though they may, in appearance, look like descendants of Africans, albeit, many with genetic traits of Europeans, who raped their ancestors. Nevertheless, the point is that the cultural perspective is of the Americas and not African or we may refer to it as a subculture, applying the definition of culture as a belief system, activities and artifacts that make a group of people distinctive, though in the case of the Americas most people are not completely distinct since they are part of a larger dominant culture; therefore, the designation of subculture is more appropriate than culture , for most people of African descent living in the Americas.

An interesting issue of note is the tendency of many African American black and brown people from countries other than the United States of America and other non- white peoples to look down upon African Americans of the United States of America, somehow believing that they are better than [pretentious, proud, snobbish] the African Americans of the United States of America. Presumably this may be because African Americans of other countries did not experience the intensity of colonization, identity destruction, and degradation that was experienced by African Americans of the United States of America. In any case, for the purposes of this essay, the idea to be brought forth is that it is remarkable that even though their ancestors experienced the same origins and even though the African Americans of the United States of America could even be related to the African Americans of, say, the Caribbean, Brazil or other parts of the Americas, that feelings of animosity, resentments, disdain, scorn, or otherwise hold them in contempt, could develop, causing rifts and deep social differences. The differences are not of origins or genetics since those are the same; the differences are due to divergence in culture, in other words, ethnicity. Beyond the trappings of ethnicity there is an inexorable commonality between these groups. Growing beyond the illusion of ethnicity is therefore a necessary and integral part of promoting unity among natural allies who could come together to counter the ignorance of racism. Growing beyond the illusion of ethnicity, and considering that race, a common means used to automatically and ignorantly assign ethnic affiliations to people [without taking into account their culture of upbringing] is a necessity for discovering the deeper essence of people that may project a particular appearance due to their hue, name, physiognomy or other external features. When this is done, the illusoriness and perhaps also the ridiculousness of ethnic distinctions will become evident.

There are some who assign the title black culture to the ideas followed by many blacks that being smart is "uncool" and makes them like the white people, which is tantamount to being like the oppressor, the enslaver. Another cultural idea is that black people, especially young black males should walk around in public without shoe laces or belts, without shirts and with pants hanging around the thighs so as to show the exposed buttocks and underwear. The look, as relates to the laces and belts, has been likened to the prison policy of not allowing inmates to have shoe laces or belts for fear they might commit suicide or harm others, which causes them to walk around with untied shoes and pants falling down. This signals the internalization and adoption of the trauma of over-imprisonment wherein black males have been imprisoned in higher rates than whites even though whites form a majority of the population. The internalization and adoption of the prison culture has been possible due to the same mechanism that caused African peoples to lose their religions, traditions, languages, and other values, the process of enslavement, socialization into western culture over many generations and the systematic exclusion of them from the mainstream social, economic and political life of the mainstream culture, which is why they may be considered to have a sub-culture [which has its own proclivities, values and traditions (not necessarily derived from Africa) but which also includes some aspects of the mainstream culture. The internalization and adoption has been accepted by some as a rite of passage, to have experienced imprisonment as a sign of manhood . The display of underwear has been explained by a black psychiatrist[36] as stunted mental growth due to the trauma of slavery and racism in an environment of poor male role models that has caused them to revert to a childlike mental state. This may be likened to a young child who is unable to fasten his/her pants and is even oblivious to the problem. If this is the model for black men then the so called black culture has become self-destructive and detrimental to the people who adopt it. The expression of these internalized social pathologies can express as self-destructive behavior such as overindulgence in junk foods, self-dumbing-down [purposely not studying in school], drug abuse, and promiscuity, increased anger and violence towards other members of the community and general apathy towards the search for a higher perspective in life due to atrophied intellect and impure feeling.

Hate, Fundamentalism and Neocolonialism

Fundamentalism may be defined as a movement or point of view characterized by rigid adherence to fundamental or basic principles [this definition does not imply correct principles]. Fundamentalism is the practice of religion by those who are incapable of formulating and practicing religion based on their own higher understanding. Due to mental weakness, produced by war, colonialism, neocolonialism, government corruption, poverty, ignorance and indulgence in vices (oftentimes supported and provided by the government to devitalize the will [drugs, alcohol, entertainments]), many in the population feel they must adhere to fundamentals, dogma and blind faith in their practice of religion since ignorance and authoritarian government foment the development of an acquiescent population, since they are not able to work out the higher meaning of the religious tenets and how to practice these in the context of a tolerant, ecumenical or universal perspective. Believing only the literal interpretation of their scriptures, fundamentalists do not rise beyond the lower levels of religious practice

---

[36] Dr. Frances Cress Welsing

[myth-ritual] and thereby enter into conflicts with themselves and with other fundamentalists given that all fundamentalist religions are exclusive and dogmatic, and it is these qualities that produce a fertile ground for animosities between religions and cultures.

This formula of neo-colonialism, control over other countries through surrogates, financial subjugation or destabilizing the social, economic and political order of other countries, has existed throughout history but was started in earnest in the late 19th century and perfected in the 20th, thereby affording foreign countries (almost all European, United States and later including the Soviet Union) the capacity to retain control of other countries through financial coercion for the benefit of business interests without openly appearing as imperialists.[37] Sometimes neocolonialism begins under the auspices of missionary work, wherein missionaries move to a country and help usher in the following of western ways and values, making the place welcome for USA corporations and populations that gradually take over the government of the country by controlling the economy and buying off government leaders or supporting dissident movements that may not have even existed previously by enticing individuals or families to form parties or factions opposing the traditional government system, for their own financial benefit [at the expense of the rest of the population-this explains the origins of many oligarchies around the developing world.]. This situation has occurred several times in history. Some examples of the colonial and neo-colonial problem are all countries in Africa, Hawaii, South America, Puerto Rico, India, China, Guam, American Samoa, and others.

Oftentimes, there develops within a society the following of culture that has been affected by a colonial process. Here colonialism should not just be thought of as a political or economic process but also a mental process. The colonized mind has been forced to forget or distort its indigenous culture in favor of the ideals and values of the dominant culture which can include prejudices, propensity for pleasure seeking, greed, irreverence towards life and or apathetic or uncaring values towards nature. There are many who don the colors of African textiles but who do not follow the philosophy of African High culture (for example, Maat Philosophy, Ubuntu or other similar teachings). Some who, in an effort to revive culture, promote culturally based religious practices, often produce other problems in society.

It is important to understand that Culture-based religions tend to exclude other cultures and points of view, fomenting unrest and

---

[37] The policy of extending a nation's authority by territorial acquisition or by the establishment of economic and political hegemony over other nations.

divisiveness between peoples of different backgrounds if the tradition does not contain the enlightening teachings that embrace all humanity. This emphasis on culture, history and tradition forces the practitioners of the orthodox culture-based religions to keep out and even ostracize others that are from different cultural backgrounds. Even though it is laudable that people of African descent and others who have been enslaved, are striving to raise themselves up from the scourge of slavery, racism and unhealthy dietary practices due to adoption of western cultural dietary practices that are known to cause more cancer and disease than the native diets of other countries, it must be understood that true liberation cannot come from culture-based religion itself because this form of religious practice ties people to cultures, rituals, and worldly concepts which are in the end, egoistic ideals as opposed to mystic ideals. Cultural trappings such as special clothing, personal markings, ways of wearing hair, coverings, and other traditions actually are beneficial for sustaining culture by causing the followers of the culture to look in a distinctive manner but that also serves to exclude others and set them apart from others; but most importantly it is a way of reinforcing the egoistic ideal I am part of this culture and tradition which is special and different. So, in this example, people come to feel different and separate and special in a worldly sense, which may also lead them to develop notions of being privileged, entitled and superior, which are negative [egoistic] aspects of culture. Note that we are referring here not just to a religion that exhibits distinct cultural values, traditions or customs but one that exhibits distinct cultural values, traditions or customs and assigns to these the status of absolute and true while assigning the religions of others the status of untrue, primitive, pagan, etc. which lead to notions of high self worth and low esteem of others since they are not following the true way ; and since they do not follow the true way the followers of the true way can rationalize that their lives are of lesser value since they are going to hell anyway or are otherwise wasting their lives, in which case it is permissible to exploit or abuse them. This practice of religion or culture wherein the people come to believe they are special, exceptional, and correct while others are wrong, etc. may be referred to as orthodox and or exceptionalist and should be considered as being based on parochial and egoistic values as opposed to universal wisdom.[38] All religions need to incorporate ALL levels of religious practice especially *Mysticism,* and in so doing a practitioner will be able to rise above cultural limitations and culture differences and thereby the cultural aspects of religion are also transcended to a level where all human beings from any tradition can meet to discover the universality of life in spirit. A practitioner of this

---

[38] , very limited or narrow in scope or outlook; provincial: parochial views; a *parochial mentality.* (n.d.). *Dictionary.com Unabridged (v 1.1).* Retrieved February 27, 2009, from Dictionary.com website: http://dictionary.reference.com/browse/parochial

ideal will truly become a source for uplifting all peoples, regardless of their religion or ethnicity. This is why Sema-Yoga can help all religions. Though originated in Ancient Egypt, it is universal in scope and therefore, can be practiced by anyone, anywhere in the world. If peoples of all religions were to emphasize the higher mystical principles within their respective religions there would be an automatic movement towards ecumenism among all faiths.[39] And that would be a powerful force away from Hate and towards understanding and peace. This should be one of the most important ideas to be learned from this book.

There are two major obstacles to the realization of the ecumenical[40] nature of all religions. Firstly, most religions are not practiced in their advanced levels or in a way that leads to a mystical realization, a path that would necessarily lead to the recognition of the common yearning and destiny of humanity, promoting peace and understanding among peoples who seem to come from different perspectives but are in reality seeking for the same ultimate higher way of life and in the mean time experiencing the same human quest for higher consciousness. Rather, they are practiced in a limited way which perpetuates the practice of rituals and upholding dogmatic, exclusive and reactionary aspects of the religion. In this way people cannot grow to realize that the goal of all religions is the same, a higher spiritual experience and not a political or exclusivist end. Secondly, the sacred scriptures of western religions especially, are beset with statements that preclude the acceptance of an ecumenical approach. They contain statements that necessarily promote an exclusive idea about God and religion and often this idea goes hand in hand with nationalism and so people lead themselves to struggles that are mixed with political, economic and religious implications. When a religion contains exclusivist (accepting their own religion and excluding others as legitimate), dogmatic (rigid and narrow), self-important (seeing their own culture and religion above that of others) statements like ours is the only true way, this is the truth, our book contains the true revealed word of God, those who came before were not the true prophets, we have the true prophet, God is with us, we are true believers, others are unbelievers, we are God s special people, etc., these statements unavoidably set people at odds with each other. All of these statements have been uttered by those practicing orthodox religions, the mainstream versions of religion and not the mystical level. The orthodox practitioners of the major world religions of the West have

---

[39] A movement promoting worldwide unity among religions through greater cooperation and improved understanding.

[40] Of worldwide scope or applicability; universal.

been the principal perpetrators of the dogmatism/exclusivism problem and this has led to more wars atrocities and injustice in the world than from any other source. Further, the practice of orthodox religion cannot lead to a peaceful and well adjusted society because the orthodox practice cannot lead a human being to higher self-discovery and without self-discovery, inner peace, tolerance in society and understanding of others or an ecumenical vision for religion are next to impossible. Further, complicating the issue are the problems of the oversexed and undernourished level of overall human life in the ego-centric culture and the vices of society. The overindulgence in sex promotes debilitation in the mind and personality in general. The addiction to pleasure-seeking, coupled with the overindulgence in over processed and synthetic [inorganic, man-made, and unnatural] foods promote disease and mental disturbance leading to stress and psychological imbalance. The vices promoted by worldly society are the persistent pressures, both imposed by society and accepted by individuals (as addicted) to pursue the worldly values: sexuality, which leads to lust, greed and gluttony which lead to corruption and other base emotions such as anger, which leads to hatred, covetousness and envy, which lead to stealing, and pride which leads to egoism and orthodox and dogmatic behavior. Through orthodoxy, religious fanaticism and fundamentalism, the ordinary worldly mind can be easily manipulated by unscrupulous leaders and foreign powers to pit peoples against each other and it is always the poor, common folk who suffer the brunt of the ravages of human degradation in the form of war, famine, atrocities, rape, plunder, etc.

Thus, a reevaluation of the role of religion and other cultural values is necessary if culture is to be redeemed and revitalized. Africans and all peoples of the world who recognize their original African ancestry as well as the universal principles of righteousness, justice and truth need to reassess the role of religion as a force for spiritual enlightenment and as a force for cultural upliftment. If these goals are to be pursued, the religion that is practice must be in harmony with the higher principles of spirituality and this includes a philosophy of social order and justice. This applies to the masses, the population of conqueror cultures as well as the peoples of the weaker controlled country. The natives of the developed country are as affected as the populations of the countries being conquered or occupied. The religious standards along with standards of beauty, propriety, economics, politics, etc. affect all who are exposed.

In order to be redeemed a nation needs a system of spirituality that is in line with its culture and this process is disrupted due to the religions introduced by colonial powers into developing nations. Under the control of foreign religions the indigenous people s affected turn attention towards the values of the foreign cultures and this weakens the native culture in its goals, values and social order. It is a wonder that a religion can be imposed on a colonized people and that even when those people are liberated and after they learn the truth about their own heritage and the damaged and deviation caused by their enslavement or colonial past, they still continue to worship in a foreign way and in a foreign language and continue supporting the traditions, values and ideals of the previously colonial culture. All of this occurs when people are forcibly prevented, over generations, from practicing their own religion and culture and this process occurred throughout history when one culture conquered or oppressed others and over time caused other peoples to adopt the elements of the conquering culture such as when the Arabs conquered western India and caused many people there to convert to Islam. This process was evident during the European colonial period in Africa and Asia where large numbers of people in those areas converted to western religions and during the European/American slave trade where the majority of the descendants of the original people who were enslaved converted to the western religions. Out of ignorance and fear people go along with the rulers of the conquering culture which asserts its dominance through suppressing the native practice of language, religion and other cultural values while imposing their cultural values, traditions and ideals on the oppressed culture with the incentive of profit [those who convert to the values of the oppressing culture can partake in the economy of the new order set by the oppressing culture]. While this condition of colonized cultural values continues there will be no true liberation or peace for oppressed peoples, because the deficient practice of religion has rendered them spiritually bankrupt and intellectually weak. Those people caught up in the effects of cultural colonization are fit only to serve the master and stand in the way of others who are trying to raise themselves up.

Many people currently are searching for the source of religion and they have moved towards native religions and native peoples. However, this movement is thwarted by the fact that the traditions and legacies of most native peoples has been damaged or interrupted and the limited or total lack of scriptural records, coupled with the discontinuity of the initiatic system in those cultures (process of teacher-disciple relationship) has caused a situation in which the practitioners of those native systems have lost or forgotten the higher mystical aspects of their native religion. What is left is a disorganized and limited practice of religion that only rises to fragmented knowledge, rituals and myths; not the high science of mystical awakening which gave rise to the great civilizations of the past. Oftentimes corruption of the religion due to ignorance is compounded by corruption due to greed and many charlatans emerge because there is no central authority to establish a righteous leadership for the religious orders and the government of society. In this environment, of ignorance many other people cling to the popular world religions sometimes because they have been indoctrinated since birth with the idea that this is the true religion of their family or culture and that the indigenous religion is primitive and incorrect. Fear of being outside the norms of their family which is practicing the adopted culture [not the native culture], people follow the values of the adopted culture such as the tenets of the imposed religion, without seriously questioning or challenging these and so they are led to a myriad of conflicts within themselves, due to the inherent contradictions within their own religion, and conflicts with others who follow other faiths blindly also.

In order to overcome the limitations of the adopted culture and the damage to the original native culture what is needed is a movement to the source of wisdom and not a holding onto dogmas since concepts are not truth and faith is not truth. Only the mystical experience is truth and a serious aspirant is never satisfied to live with platitudes and slogans or dogmatic and authoritarian statements of faith in religion or in secular government. Faith alone did not build the pyramids and the great civilization of Ancient Egypt that lasted for thousands of years nor were they built with a philosophy of disharmony and greed, capitalism or pleasure-seeking, pride or atheism. Rather, a movement to the true source of spiritual power needs to be undertaken. Only this power can counteract the forces of ignorance and greed which have devastated the entire planet. The authentic practice of religion and high wisdom philosophy contains all of the necessary elements needed to revive positive culture and spirituality. These elements of High Culture, not limited, dogmatic or degraded culture, can lead not only to the reconstruction of real human civilization but also to world harmony, since as long as the prevailing world order, based on greed, dogmatism, faith-based religion, capitalism, globalization, etc. remains, humanity will continue in a degraded state, racked by wars, famines, disease and instability.

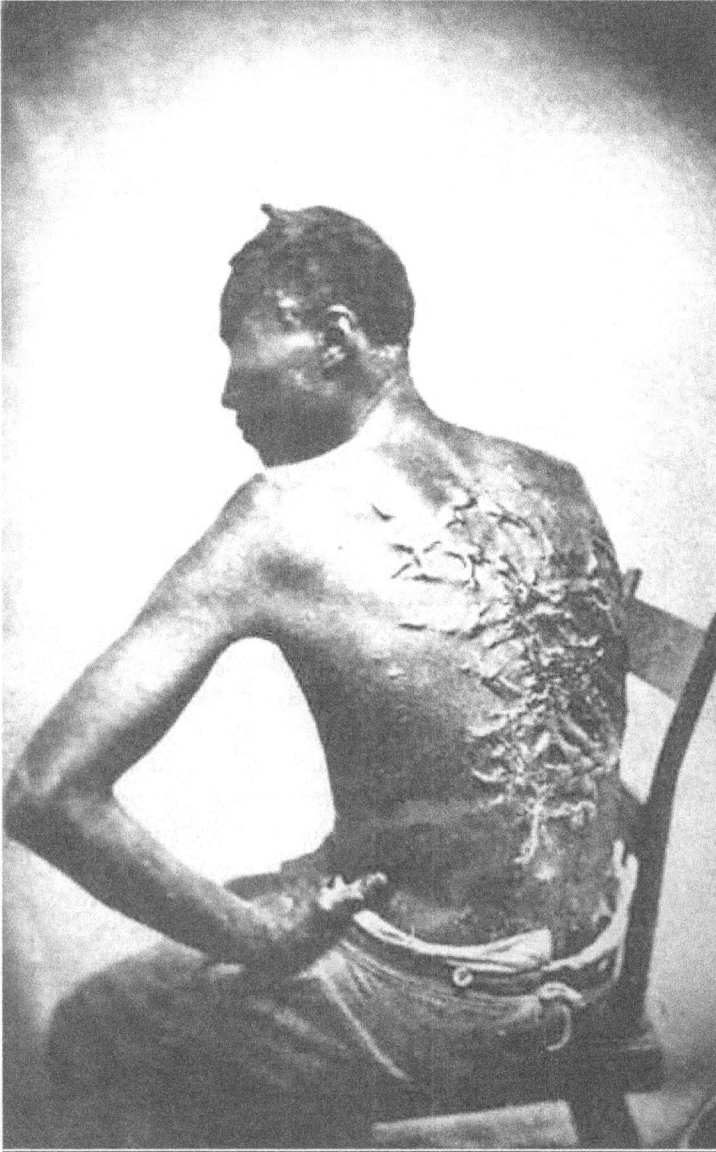

Figure 16: Scars of a whipped slave (April 2, 1863, Baton Rouge, Louisiana, USA.

Original caption: "Overseer Artayou Carrier whipped me. I was two months in bed sore from the whipping. My master come after I was whipped; he discharged the overseer. The very words of poor Peter, taken as he sat for his picture."

An example of neocolonialism with racial implications is the country known as Haiti. From the time of its independence from France, the political and economic leaders of the United States of America feared that the Haitian revolution that freed the African slaves in Haiti would spread to the U.S.A. but even after slavery was supposedly abolished in the U.S.A. the political and economic leaders continued and continue to this day, to foster political and economic instability and a double standard of treatment of Haitians versus other groups living in the Western hemisphere. In Haiti, after the legitimate elections, the support for the opposition led to a *coup* that was supported by the U.S.A. under the republican party president George H. Bush (Bush Sr.). After the *coup* the U.S.A. under president Clinton, a member of the democratic party, supported the military junta that ruled the country and even authorized the U.S.A. oil companies to deal with them. After the people suffered under the rule of the junta Clinton sent in troops and more people died. The democratically elected president, Aristide, was restored to the government but only if he agreed to include the policies of his opponent who lost the 1990 election, the opponent who was in favor of U.S.A. corporate policies. Haiti s economy failed and people suffered more violence and disruption until on February 29, 2004, the governments of France and the United States abducted and exiled president Aristide by forcing him to leave the country and stay in Africa.[41] This move was strongly protested by several governments in the Caribbean and elsewhere. This episode was only the latest display of U.S.A. policy that Noam Chomsky referred to as *"another illustration of the near passionate hatred of democracy, which is consistent and is indeed recognized."*[42]

The traditions of interventions and support of dictators and corporate exploitation in Haiti has rendered the country used to political unrest and violence which has led to a degraded culture of lawlessness and crime as well as political corruption, *coup d'états* and easy prey to political manipulation and control by the U.S.A. government and the power elite that control it, people who are still predominantly white.[43] Those policies that promoted destabilization led to generations of civil unrest,

---

[41] http://en.wikipedia.org/wiki/Aristide

[42] ibid

[43] Note: even though Barack Obama, an African American, has become president of the U.S.A. he apparently has continued the previous policies towards Haiti. See the section in this book entitled: *Barack Obama, Racism, and the Folly of Ignorance and Delusion in Politics, Economics and Social Change*

dictatorships and social degeneration that are still playing out. What would the culture and government of Haiti, the first country with a majority of African decent to achieve independence from colonial rule, look like if the U.S.A. had not committed the illegal interventions, economic subversions and political regime changes throughout history?

Nationalism V.S. Culture

Many people in the struggle for liberation and self determination have come to believe that national pride is the way to promote cultural cohesiveness and pride, in this case of black people, African Consciousness and African Pride. This would seem to be a logical statement since it would appear that the downfall of African society was due to a lack of cohesion among African peoples and or a lack of pride which led to the many cases of Africans selling out their countries and its peoples to enslavers and the later situations of tyrannical governments managed by African peoples, African dictators, exploiting African peoples, independently or under the orders of foreign powers, as well as the neocolonial systems in which Africans assisted in the continued enslavement and depletion of the resources of their own countries for personal gain and to enrich the foreign cultures.

Upon reflection the notion of nationalism, as it is practiced and espoused by many of its adherents, cannot be viewed as a righteous means to promote justice because from a high philosophical perspective there is a flaw at its core. Nationalism is actually a concept that developed late in human history that supports the view that nations are separate and distinct and consequently peoples are separate and distinct as well. It adheres to the idea that human beings belong to certain groups, which should exclude others. Many people cite statistics and the bloody history of humanity, often focusing on certain groups and their actions as a basis to say that people should naturally be separate or even that God created them separately and that they should remain so forever. The idea is that by eradicating interference or intermingling between the so called races one can somehow purify one s own group. This is of course ridiculous since, first of all, there was never any "pure" group to begin with, unless we want to consider the original group from which ALL human beings alive today originated, the African ancestors that left Africa more than 100,000 years ago and populated the rest of the world and who, due to geographical and environmental conditions changed in appearance to look like Asians, Europeans, Aborigines, Native Americans, etc. of today?

This notion, of the separation of peoples due to race, ethnicity, etc., is flawed because no matter how one may try there is no separation from humanity, the greater community. All human beings are inexorably linked in a web of life, which goes beyond borders, language and even genetics. The earth does not recognize any borders. If you were to go to the border between two countries and ask a tree growing there which country she belongs to or how does she feel about her brother tree living in the different country across the border , five feet away! If the tree could respond it would be puzzled at the question, perhaps wondering whom is this insane person asking the foolish question! Air has no trouble crossing borders; when people in the USA put out pollution it travels to Europe and around the world, and vice versa. People create borders and walls and obstacles based on their parochial or cultural values and traditions, which are based on the ignorance of culture and nationalism; they do not exist intrinsically. Further, in a global society there can be no real borders except those, which human beings set up artificially and what country can survive and prosper without the wealth of intercultural relations?

Another detrimental factor of nationalism is that it allows the development of not only the idea of international cultural selfishness, prejudice and hubris but also intra-national cultural selfishness, prejudice and hubris that manifests as negative features found in unrighteous societies such as: Nepotism, narcissism, preferential treatment, partiality, or favoritism based on class, race , gender, etc. So the society as a whole, for example the USA, operates as a racist entity internationally, in reference to other countries with majority non- white populations, and or as a superpower in relation to other countries with weaker economies and armies. However, the USA also has an internal group within itself that acts as an aristocratic oligarchy [politicians, leaders of large corporations, the super rich upper 1% of the population that owns most of the wealth of the country], seeing itself as the rightful rulers and others within the society as minions.

The unquestioned faith in religion or in secular systems of government or economics leads to religious and political/economic dogmas promoted by the elites of the society that support and elevate their own standing in the society while lowering that of others, eventually leading to great imbalances and injustices in a society and between societies. One cannot create a righteous society by adopting techniques used by unrighteous societies. You cannot act as a tyrant in order to spread democracy! Be righteous, and ally yourself with those who are righteous and bring forth righteousness in all your actions and you will overcome all evil forces within and from without and at the same time create a well ordered and just society.

Motivating People: Why Anger does not work

Nationalists usually try to set up a dichotomy by creating an exaggerated, simplistic and outdated view that all peoples of an opposing group are evil or that all actions of an opposing group have evil intents, etc. On the other hand a group may try to say that they are all good. In both ways of thinking there is ignorance and flawed philosophy due to ignorance and egoism. Often the rabid nationalist tries to engender fear, anger and even hatred in order to motivate people to action.

The demonizing of a particular group is a tried and successful way to engender some near term social action but soon after, that is accompanied by prejudice and discrimination as well as animosity mistrust and resentment that can last for generations. Its primary element is the underlying falsehood, which it seeks to prove to the world, that human beings are separate and distinct from each other as well as locked in intrinsic conflict and cannot and should not come together physically, ideologically, politically, culturally or otherwise but should struggle to defeat the other groups and keep them subjugated or at least at bay, insuring that there will always be segregation and conflict and of course that means that there will always be a need for the dogmatists, warriors and others who say they will protect the society against the outsiders , evil others, etc. For example, racists, intent on justifying the enslavement of other races, have used this platform as a rallying point to summon up the fears of the masses in order to rouse them to move against a group, usually a minority or weaker group. Is it not a form of nationalism that the Ku Klux Klan practices? On the other side, some black nationalists have attempted to rouse ire and hatred against white people to motivate black people to take action against white oppression and racism. So, this form of social motivation, through anger, hatred, segregation and conflict, has been used by groups that have been victims of racism, and or genocide to motivate their people. Even some spiritual leaders have said that the perpetrators of social injustice are the devils themselves. What reaction can we expect from those to whom the accusation is levied?   fear, resentment, anger, hatred?

It is certainly a reality that by the standards set in most spiritual traditions, which are the moral guides for humanity, the actions of those who have enslaved others, maimed them, raped and stolen from them, etc. can be considered demoniac. However, the actions of a person should not be confused or identified with the person s higher essential being even if the person is egoistic, highly disturbed or evil. Just because you commit a demoniac act, this does not mean that you are a demon.

Nor should it be said that you are under the influence of a demon (The Devil Made Me Do It). Evil actions occur when a person degrades his or her mind, due to ignorance of spiritual truth and have led a life of egoism and selfishness which has guided them to a degraded state of feeling, thinking and behaving. Evil actions are a result of living life in contradiction with the truth. Otherwise if a person is a devil by simply being a member of a particular group then since all groups are mixed what is the percentage of devils in the European community, the Chinese community, the African community, etc.? There are no pure races or ethnic groups in the world so what percentage of so called white people are devils and what percentage of so called black people are devils? Most African Americans have some European ancestry so if all white people are devils, what percentage of the genes of the so called black people are devilish? Is it possible to excise these? Since there are no ethnic groups that contain all evil people or all good people it is not possible to say that any group is all bad or all good. Again, what it comes down to is a question of universal truth or untruth. Who are the people following the path of universal truth and who are not? That is the real question! The fact that human beings of all so called races can mate and bring forth progeny, bleed the same blood, share the same desire for connectedness, fulfillment and spiritual enlightenment, means that all human beings have a common origin and equivalent potential. The proof of this is reinforced by the modern discoveries in genetics but the Sages of Sema-Yoga understood this truth several thousands of years ago.

Therefore, the philosophies of separation and divisiveness are merely illusions, smoke screens, which are distracting the human race from its higher ideal, of establishing peace and harmony on earth. Further, since modern science has revealed that all human beings on earth originated in Africa, from the same ancestors, how can it be possible to sustain the illusion of differences and separation?

In reality we should understand ALL humanity as being Africans then since they all originated in Africa in the distant past. If you want to bring the point out in a dramatic way why don t you greet people of other races with this great truth? When you see persons of European ethnicities refer to them as Africans; while in their company and when in the company of others. When you see people of Asian ethnicity refer to them as Africans. See what happens!

Race classifications and color distinctions are part of the rhetoric of racism, a bogus notion since as we know there is only one human race! As long as we support these notions by calling ourselves white or black, etc. we will never be rid of racism. Therefore, the next time a form is given to you asking your race, choose Other until they have a choice for Human Being or World Citizen! Again, if the environment to promote and support truth is not there make it!

Do not allow yourself or others to live in a world of illusion. People living lives in a state of delusion is the sure way to degrade humanity. For only when people see themselves as separate individuals in a jungle of competing groups, can they entertain ideas of segregation, conquest, enslavement, and mistreatment of others. When living in truth one cannot harm others because one will soon realize that one is harming oneself and one s own family. Have you ever seen a normal person hurt his or her own family members for political or cultural or ethnic reasons? Certainly they will harm non-family members sooner than their own kinfolk. Therefore, work towards bringing forth the truth to all peoples, that the world is not a conglomeration of competing races but a great family of humanity. The task of one who wants to *grow beyond hate* is to ally with all those who espouse truth while working to overcome those who are not following truth; not through denigrations, dogmatic labels or stereotypical racist, nationalistic or accusations based on blind faith in destructive religious[44], social[45], political[46] or economic[47] dogmas but by affirming truth and justice for ALL peoples. In this sense, growing means to accept the entire human community as a family of peoples who all originated in Africa.

While the complacency and ignorance of the group, that the activist is trying to motivate, are great ills, in the long run the promotion of anger and hatred as motivators will lead to the failure of the activist agenda, further expanding and perpetuating conflict and perhaps even the self-destruction of anyone who believes in it. This is because the greater psychology of a human being is not fully understood by the activist.

A human being is composed of spirit and mind/body. The spirit has an intrinsic tendency towards the universal, towards peace and expansion. The mind/body complex tends towards contraction, narcissism, egoism and segregation [of thoughts, feelings, between persons, politics, likes and dislikes, etc.]. From a psycho-spiritual perspective, the mind is, among other things, like a storehouse. This storehouse lodges impressions in the unconscious mind every time a person has a thought, or performs any action. These impressions sprout up later on in the form of new thoughts and desires and these impel people again to more thoughts and actions. This leads to serious implications as far as the

---

[44] [our religion is true and we are going to heaven and the religions of others are lies and their all going to hell]

[45] [our group is genetically superior]

[46] [our system of government is the best and others is wrong, and anyone who does not agree is an enemy]

[47] [capitalism is the best and only way, anyone who does not agree is an enemy]

future actions of a person being based on their previous thoughts, feelings and actions. The actions, feelings and thoughts of the past foment like thoughts, feelings and actions in the future. So, thoughts and feelings of anger, hatred, greed, etc., beget similar thoughts, feelings and actions in the future. If the impressions are in contradiction with the deeper self of a human being there will be a conflict which will manifest as mild mental complexes in the mind in the form of addictions, lack of concentration, lack of will, lack of insight, lack of patience, mental dullness, dissatisfaction, frustration, depression, etc. to the severe mental complexes: psychoses, self-destructive behavior, suicide, murder, genocide, ethnic cleansing, sadism, socio-pathology, violence, war, etc.

> Human beings are mortal gods and goddesses,
> The gods and goddesses are immortal human beings.
> Ancient Egyptian Proverb

Once again, the underlying problem of life is not the conflict between peoples, races, governments, etc. It is a conflict in the human heart; a conflict between what the deeper self tells a person and what they do in life based on egoistic notions; it is a spiritual conflict and adversity in life is caused by a spiritual deficit. This state of conflict is explained in the Sema-Yogic wisdom texts as a wretched condition, a form of hellish living. It is a state of suffering, for there is no true peace to be found anywhere in the world if a person is in the state of spiritual conflict and yet this is the state that most people considers to be normal. The state of **Spiritual Conflict** may be defined as a subconscious disconnection between a person s personality and their higher essential nature, for when a person acts in contradiction with their own higher nature they are acting against their own spirit, and the Cosmic Law of order demands that when a person deviates from the path of righteousness they will be met with pain and suffering for their transgression. This pain and suffering is not meant as a punishment but as an instruction. However, most people do not think deeply about life so they never learn the lessons that their experiences, through the situations of life, are trying to teach them. It is like a person who does drugs or smokes, commits adultery, steals, or commits other transgressions. They see others as ruining their lives in similar ways and dying but they still continue to act unrighteously. They are unable to learn or change their behavior, even if they know the behaviors are unrighteous or counterproductive because they have followed a life path of thinking, feeling and acting based on illusions and ignorance about the nature of life and the danger of desiring and hating.

The essential nature of every human being is the Higher Self. That Higher Self is the embodiment of peace, universal love and caring. Therefore, any philosophy or way of life, which limits a human being s capacity to express what is honorable, righteous, just, will cause a conflict in that person. The notion that people belong in distinct groups, separate from others, and the notion that this separation should be supported by government institutions or even military force is an even deeper expression of the depth of delusion in the heart.

If there is no unity in the world it is not because the teaching is not true but because most people are too ignorant to see it and understand it and live by it. However, there have always been those people in every period of time, in every corner of the world, who have kept this great teaching alive, they are the spiritual masters, the Sages of the world. They teach a select few in every generation who will listen to the great mystical truths but also to the means to understand and discover these within themselves. So the task of liberation from political, economic, social, gender, cultural, economic, psychological, etc. oppression cannot be accomplished with guns or brawn. It is to be won by enlightening the majority of human beings and their leaders to the higher truth, the underlying kinship that is the higher nature of all human beings. For when there is self-knowledge there can be no degradation, complacency, greed, violence, hatred, separation or injustice. We are one and the failure of leaders to see this and the failure of their followers to see this is the source of all strife, injustice and suffering in human history.

The leaders of society should work towards their own wisdom awakening and at the same time promote that of their followers. This means helping to create situations of order and justice instead of confusion, corruption, injustice, favoritism and discrimination. People should be motivated with truth instead of agitating rhetoric, which will stir up emotions and incite people s negative feelings and eventually to violence. Truth survives all challenges. It always wins in the end but it can only be advocated effectively by those leaders who are not in it solely for personal gain and do not fear the repercussions of speaking out. This requires true spiritual strength. A politician may say things to incite people by tapping into their desires, even altruistic ones or may play on their prejudices and fears of other groups or may lull them into a state of complacency, allowing them to think they will have prosperity even though the politicians are imposing capitalist economic policies at home and imperialist policies around the world [in which case the followers are complicit in the harm done to themselves and other countries and peoples], or leaders may just lie for the purpose of keeping their political position or at the behest of people who are paying them off. These injustices do not escape the mechanism of cosmic order, the universal principle of order and justice that leads people to the fate which they have destined themselves to through their own thoughts, desires, feelings and actions.

Is the present condition of modern society not a prime example of the results of an unrighteous system of economy and government? Therefore, who should support the status quo? As individuals there is a great feeling of impotence but this need not be the case. You can affect your family and your community. You can make your community a righteous place. You can create community centers where you can support the culture and values you hold dear. Other groups have done this why can t you? If you have not done so by now why not? Who are you supporting and where is your money and time going? Can you say you are righteous and stand for truth if you continue to support ignorance, degraded foods, injustice, or prejudice? Even if you do not practice these, if your government or social groups or family do and you do not take action, at least to inform others of these issues, you are complicit in it. Begin with yourself, then talk to others. Find one person that is interested in these issues or one who is questioning the problems of life, as you are, and your group of two will soon grow to three and four and so on. The effect of your group will be added to that of other groups that seem to exist in isolation but which are in reality promoting the same objectives. Study the teachings, make yourselves strong and determine to succeed regardless of the obstacles. The work of following order and truth is higher than the success of the efforts, for without effort there can be no success and even if we do not see the ultimate success, the work enlightens, purifies and affects those who engage in it and many others who do not even know of it.

Healing V.S. Revenge (and retribution)

There are many people who believe in the Eye for an Eye and Tooth for a Tooth philosophy and this philosophy, based on retribution and revenge, has caused the United States, the supposedly richest nation on earth along with other so called civilized nations to have the greatest percentage of incarcerated people and the greatest disparity between those who have and those who have not. If there is such a high degree of wealth shouldn t there be enough to go around? And, if punishment were the best way to prevent crime should the result not be less people incarcerated instead of more?

"To be satisfied with little is the greatest wisdom; and they that increase their riches, increase their cares; but a contented mind is a hidden treasure, and trouble find it not."

-Ancient Egyptian Proverb

110

What would you say about a wealthy man who refuses to share his wealth with his family? All human beings are part of a family of humanity. As equal citizens of the earth all human beings are entitled to three basic needs: Shelter, Sustenance and Opportunity to live a fulfilling life. If any of these factors are missing then there is an opportunity for resentment, anger, and violence to emerge.

"An immoderate desire of riches is a poison lodged in the mind. It contaminates and destroys everything that was good in it. It is no sooner rooted there, than all virtue, all honesty, all natural affection, fly before the face of it."
-Ancient Egyptian Proverb

The lack of equal distribution of resources in the world is not due to a shortage of resources or a lack of technology for transporting the food and other goods where they are needed. It is due to one problem: Greed. Greedy government leaders want to keep control of resources to control people s lives and become rich off of the suffering of others. Greedy business leaders control the distribution of resources to get more money, regardless of the negative effects [pain and suffering] this may have on entire populations (sometimes including their own). Again, greed exists due to ignorance of the Higher Nature of the Self. Egoistic people in wealthy countries are so intoxicated with their wealth that they are oblivious to the suffering of others, whose resources they are exploiting in order to achieve and or maintain the lifestyle of wealth and or the power and influence that wealth allows.

Many times, there are victims of suffering who are so degraded in their will and self esteem that they do not know how to escape a bad situation. In the case of a battered wife that keeps going back to her husband, for instance, one may ask why doesn t she get out? The answer is that she is psychologically incapable since she does not know a better way and she is psychologically disturbed due to the psychological and or physical trauma. She may be suffering from intimidation, fear and the feeling of impotence. She may even think that this is her own fault or that this is how life is supposed to be. Why? Because this is what she was taught or what she learned in her life and this may be complicated by innate feelings of inadequacy, immaturity or mental impressions from the past that force a tendency to be acquiescent or masochistic. When a battered wife goes to a shelter should she be told to go back to her husband to receive more beatings? Of course not, she should be encouraged to see a better way of life even if her husband does not change. She should be bolstered in her self-esteem and she should be encouraged to find her faith and the spiritual strength that lies within. In the same way, cultures which have been abused and misused, enslaved and miseducated by others should be encouraged to seek a better way, to grow in self esteem and to seek the faith which will carry them through to freedom. However, just as a counselor would not tell the battered woman to remember every single incident of abuse and develop ever-increasing anger and hatred towards the husband, in the same way, leaders of the battered culture should act towards the members of the culture as the counselors of the battered woman. They should promote cultural pride but not by bashing the culture of others, but by extolling their own culture s wisdom, altruistic achievements and contributions to humanity and encouraging the respect for the wisdom, altruistic achievements and contributions to humanity of other cultures. They should encourage the people to match and surpass the greatness of their forebear s. This should not, if possible, be done by attacking the perpetrators of injustice but by demanding that they too seek treatment for their unrighteous acts. This action is not to be taken with bitterness and resentment but with compassion and sympathy. Such a person who is capable of acting in this manner even in part, is poised to receive Divine Grace and this is the true objective of the struggle of life, to give human beings the opportunity to discover the glory of their inner divinity.

"If you meet a disputant who is not your equal or match, do not attack, they are weak. They will confound themselves. Do not answer the evil speech and give in to your animal passion for combat by venting your self against them. You will beat them through the reproof of the witnesses who will agree with you."

"If you meet a disputant who is more powerful than you, fold your arms and bend your back. Confrontation will not make them agree with you. Disregard their evil speech. Your self control will match their evil utterances and people will call them ignoramuses."

Sage Ptahotep (Ancient Egypt)

Maat Philosophy includes the teaching of nonviolence. Many people think that the philosophy of nonviolence means that they should allow themselves to be hurt. Nonviolence does not preclude self-defense. You need to protect your body and mind because these are your instrument you must use on the path to freedom, wisdom and evolution in this lifetime. The practice of nonviolence is a manifestation of the recognition of your higher spiritual attainment. You recognize that you are in a higher plane, connected to all people, even the ones who have wronged you and yet you forgive them, understanding they have acted out of ignorance. Nonviolence is also the eradication of hateful speech against your attacker, and also the eradication of evil thoughts against them.

This does not mean that you should not speak out against injustice. It means that you should speak out without bitterness, resentment and egoism. If you have a family member who is insane and that person hurt you physically would you be angry and would you hate that person? In the same way, why do you hate your attacker, they are already suffering the burden of egoism, a form of insanity, which will prevent them from attaining the glory of inner peace through higher wisdom and this will bring them much suffering in the future. This is a great punishment. Does this have to be your fate also?

You should practice self-defense and seek to neutralize your opponent but not to hurt them in a permanent way if possible. Do not forget that your unconscious mind records the truth deep down even if you outwardly manifest what would be seen by others as apparent balance, peace, evenhandedness, etc. If you act out of spite and pleasure in hurting others your unrighteousness will lead to your own suffering and downfall even if you are retaliating towards an authentic injustice.

The greatest weapons a nonviolent person has are righteousness, universal love, sharing and caring for the well being of others. All of the strife in the world occurs because of selfishness, born of spiritual ignorance. This is the source of all resentment, anger and hatred. When people feel discarded, marginalized, denigrated, abused and disconnected resentment and hatred grow because there is an instinctive but unfulfilled need to connect since the underlying reality of all people is the universal spirit. In the heart of the perpetrators of such injustices fear grows due to their inner understanding that they have done a wrong. That may lead to resentment against others, including the one s they hurt, if they are unable or unwilling to forgive, leading to hatred and violence against the same oppressed peoples. In all human beings there is a desire to affirm this great truth and the inability to do so is the source of great pain and anguish deep down in the perpetrator s heart.

Universal love is caring for all without restriction and without conditions; loving not only your family but people you don t even know, in countries far away, for they are expressions of the same higher nature, as you are. Sharing is not only to be performed through money, resources or other materials, even though this is the first necessity. You must also share of yourself, your touch, your caring, and your words of encouragement, compassion and goodwill. You must share in tangible as well as intangible ways. You must work towards a world where everyone is cared and provided for and not just those of your own culture or ethnic group, although this is a good place to start.

Wait to get paid or discover your Inner treasure

A culture, which has been wronged by another, should not seek revenge for this leads to more revenge in a bloody cycle which scarcely knows an end. The various ethnic conflicts such as the ones in Yugoslavia and Kosovo are stark examples of this point. However, the wronged culture should not cease to remember the injustice but it should not attach this to a culture but to the individual perpetrators as well as those who are supporting or benefiting from the original unrighteousness and who do not acknowledge the wrongdoing or continue to promote the unrighteousness. However, it is the unrighteousness itself that is the source of the trouble and the cause of that is ignorance of the knowledge of self that leads to egoism.

In any case, just as the battered woman should not delay in seeking treatment until the perpetrator does, in the same way a culture which has been wronged should not delay in seeking its own redemption even if the culture which committed the injustice continues to deny it or to seek to promote the unrighteousness. When the woman grows strong she will no longer allow the abuse and then the batterer will not have the option to batter that woman any more. In the same way, the culture that was battered in the past would not allow itself to be battered again. An example of this is the strengthened China which can no longer be hurt by the Japanese who once sought to conquer China and brutally occupied China and raped Chinese women and plundered China s resources.

Questions like reparations and restitutions should be pursued but it must be clearly understood that personal or societal redemption should not be delayed, waiting until reparations or restitutions are paid and no unrighteous person pays their debts until they are forced to by either a stronger military power or a stronger moral (Spiritual Power). In other words, there will be no substantial payment for any restitution as long as there is denial by the perpetrator and lack of self-esteem and moral will and resolve in the victim. Further, the greater wealth to be achieved will come from growing beyond the injustice, for real and abiding freedom can only come when there are no attachments, resentments and entanglements in the world. This form of payment is the reward for all who traverse the road of mystical awakening, the path of Sema-Yoga. So the issue of whether or not reparations come or do not come is irrelevant to the issue of spiritual enlightenment. Further, if one were to give money to a person with an alcohol or drug abuse problem or a gambling problem, etc., what would most likely happen? They would squander it on their vice and perhaps even overdose! So in this sense what is needed by a human being should come at the proper time and from a transcendental spiritual perspective, in time all injustices are redressed.

114

What is your Government: Worldly values V.S. Spiritual Values-Maat Philosophy

M any people ponder why there is strife in the world. Placing responsibility on some outer force they say: I am a good person, why do other people have to be so greedy? Others say I brought up my child in the right way, why did they commit that crime?

Many people delude themselves into believing that they can be part of an unrighteous or corrupt culture and at the same time get the so-called benefits and none of the detriments. People want lotteries, all-night entertainment, cable TV, music, modern conveniences, medicines, processed foods, etc. But they do not want the greediness promoted by gambling, the mental agitation caused by entertainments and music with no redeeming value, the degradation of sexuality, women and family through pornography and sex in advertising, the despoiling of the earth due to the mishandling of the earth s raw materials and the misuse of resources, the creation of drugs with side effects which are oftentimes worse than the disease even when disease could be avoided by living a healthy lifestyle. They also do not want the foods saturated with chemicals that are like slow acting poisons but they want to gluttonously gorge on tasty foods with little nutritional value.

While people on one hand say that they want culture, history and philosophy, studying their history and trying to bolster their cultural pride, on the other hand they are promoting and supporting the unrighteous way of life and then wonder why their is so much degradation and conflict in society. Even the basic study of ancient history trying to discover why ancient Egypt was so great and why it lasted so long (thousands of years!) will reveal that there was no deification of sports stars, there was no glamorizing of actors, rich people, secular government leaders, drug dealers or heads of organized crime. There were no processed foods (the diet was mostly vegetarian) there was an unparalleled respect for women, family and the law. There was the practice of meditation, regular purification and fasting and Sema-Yoga. Also, the basis of the government was Maat, the spiritual ethics philosophy of cosmic order and truth, which seeks to bring about a harmony between heaven and earth and not the acquisition of more dollars.

In modern times while people on one hand claim to be spiritual they on the other hand support a government which has perpetrated an continues to perpetrate injustices and in which some people with funds commit crimes without even setting one foot in jail (due to their money),

115

while others go directly to jail and are as if forgotten. One cannot go to heaven without dying. In the same way one cannot bring about justice and righteousness in the world if one does not lead a life of righteousness within oneself and if one does not promote righteousness in the community at large. You cannot say that you want to bring justice to the world and then seek a job on Wall Street or Madison Avenue, producing nothing real [junk financial instruments] or selling garbage products that are not needed; do not kid yourself. If you are serious about your convictions, work for organizations which support this view. If there are no such organizations, work to create them. Do not delude yourself and think that you are going to become rich and then help others. The notion of philanthropy and donations [charity] is bogus from the perspective of righteous culture that provides for the basic needs of all members of a society. In such a society there would be no fabulously rich people because individuals would not be allowed to amass large amounts of wealth and the masses would share in the wealth of the society and would not need donations. In modern unrighteous society philanthropy may be seen as an altruistic caring social endeavor but from the perspective of righteous society where the need for philanthropy and donations is eliminated the concept of philanthropy may be seen as a corruption of human culture. Why should there be fabulously rich people and a need for philanthropy in a balanced culture with adequate distribution of resources and opportunities for all?

For many people, who are not spiritually mature, wealth is a great curse. The money brings responsibilities and worries that often outweigh the advantages. The idea that money brings happiness is a trap-like delusion in which most people are caught up. Children are influenced by family members, government leaders, and peers who are also deluded about happiness and the purpose of life or celebrities such as Michael Jackson, O.J., Paris Hilton and fooled by the idea that appearances change one s inner worth and lead to abiding happiness, through makeup, hair relaxers, skin bleaching, plastic surgery and a whole host of Hollywood and Madison Avenue illusions of perfect looking models. They grow up believing in the same illusions, base their lives on these and then pass them on to their offspring. If you enjoy seeing illusions and untruths then you are supporting the system of unrighteousness. If you think that you live in a rich country that has not hurt other people or plundered other countries to amass it s wealth or that you are going to be a philanthropist and donate to the underdeveloped country that your country purposely underdeveloped so that you could have all the wealth and conveniences of modern society you are certainly deluded; firstly about your ideas about your own country and society and also about your own ethics as a philanthropist since the reason for the need of the philanthropy is the original unrighteousness that your country perpetrated, that you supported and continue to support! How can there be righteousness in this environment of delusion?

The study of Ancient Egypt is important for understanding how a well ordered and sane civilization can not only exist but thrive over thousands of years. There was no liquor[48] or narcotics in Ancient Egypt. Many people say they believe in the ancient tradition and yet continue to indulge in worldly behavior. If you say you believe in that culture, why do you drink liquor or do drugs? There was no gratuitous sex and violence allowed in Ancient Egypt, so why do you support a society that allows gratuitous sex and violence in the media and in popular culture? Or by lustfully ogling whenever a personality, the greater unrighteous society has deemed to be beautiful , is paraded in front of you? There was no promiscuity allowed either. Also, why is it that masculinity is judged by the number of sex partners and why are gangsters, and prostitutes supported and admired in modern society? You may not think you support this but every time you judge a person by their sex appeal or every time you wear a garment to make yourself attractive you are supporting a culture of sexuality and illusion. Then you wonder why is everything judged in terms of sex, appearances or perceived social status! People have traded truth for flash, fluff, smoke and mirrors and then wonder why there is confusion, frustration and psychosis in the culture! There was no hair relaxer in Ancient Egypt so why do people, who say they are Africans rediscovering African culture, relax their hair in modern times? Hair relaxer was not part of Ancient African culture. Perhaps it is part of black culture due to the desire to look like white people, an effect of the indoctrination with white supremacy ideology during the slavery and segregation periods of the United States of America s history. But slavery and segregation ended decades ago yet the lingering effects seem to continue in the lives of many, in the use of relaxers, feelings of inferiority, desire to remain dumb, and other negative cultural characteristics of black culture. Further, the last time a survey of countries on earth was performed there was no Black country to be found. Since there is no country called black there are no black people either, just as there is no white country and there are therefore no white people. That is, unless we recognize Ancient Egypt and Nubia because the original names for those countries and lands, Kamit and Kush, mean black land . But if that is the source of the term then it would mean that those who want to consider themselves under that designation black people should be seeking to follow the traditions and customs of their ancestors, including religion. While there is a minority of people of African descent who do accept that designation and try to act in accordance with its legacy the vast majority do not accept it and would seem to be perfectly comfortable acting, thinking, looking and feeling as part of the non-African culture they are associated with; in this context they may be considered genetically of African

---

[48] (liq·uor (l k   r) n. Abbr. liq. 1. An alcoholic beverage made by distillation rather than by fermentation.)

descent but ethnically they are Americans, Caribbeans, South Americans, etc.

One cannot just sit back and do nothing but say that one is part of some greater culture and that things should change somehow. If there is no positive environment you need to make it.   If you are really serious about change you can bring about the most profound change of all even with minimal funds, transforming yourself into a wise personality, capable of great, society changing works. Can you imagine what would happen if a sufficient number of people with this strength of determination, will and spiritual resolve came together? If you say that there are no such people around it is because you are not ready to see them and recognize them. Purify yourself first and then you will discover your path in life and you will also discover those who are on the same path. Do not say I will marry, have children work on my job or career and be a good person and maybe my children will make the world better.   This is not enough because the ordinary good person [that follows popular culture] is part of the problem, as we saw earlier. You must show the way by your abstinence from the indulgences of modern society and your balanced manner in adversity as well as prosperity. This will act as an example for them and will lead you to the glory of spiritual enlightenment and true power to be a transformative force in the world.

Self-Hatred and the its outer Manifestations

An important effect of ignorance of the knowledge of Self is the process by which complexes develop in the mind due to previous actions in life; specifically, actions that are embarrassing, regretful, that are indeed heinous or reprehensible or which do not conform with the values of other people and which one has been forced to accept either through upbringing or socialization are capable of causing the formation of psychotic elements in an otherwise apparently normal personality. However, those elements can form powerful forces that compel a person to uphold certain ideals or values even if they are not personally held. These elements can lead to self-hatred, due to a person s inability to cope with the feelings and contradictory thoughts or work out a way to understand the conflict and mature out of it. An example of this is politicians who condemn others for being homosexual, or not upholding family values. Later we may find out that they are the ones who were hiding their own homosexuality or had or have a close family member who is and they are trying to distance themselves or hide it or not admit their own homosexual feelings. They were lashing out at others because of their own inner conflict due to shame or self-loathing they developed about themselves or learned they should have about themselves and others based on the values of others. Other prominent examples are preachers who violently oppose homosexuality or violently promote family values and later we find out that they are homosexuals or adulterers or pedophiles, etc. This can work with other feelings of inadequacy or due to one s regrets due to feeling like a failure, and many other reasons. The racist projects his own inhumanity upon the slave, calling him less than human when it requires being less than human to mistreat and abuse other human beings, etc. The bottom line is that the personality can develop inner self-directed anger and hatred that is projected outwardly at those who are perceived as having the flaw one sees in oneself or those who are perceived as potential revealers of ones perceived flaws, inadequacies or negative qualities. In this way, a personality projects anger and hatred upon others that it is experiencing internally. This of course leads to varied levels of irrationality, supporting values and ideals not out of reason but out of fear of being exposed for what one truly is or appearing weak, etc. In order to overcome this form of mental complex it is necessary to make peace with what thoughts and feelings one has and then to realize these are a product of past actions, upbringings and or socializations and whatever the detriments there may be in the personality, they are not abiding because they are left behind at the time of death. Sex is a thing of bodies, not of souls. In any case, all people are flawed and therefore, should be forgiven for their mistakes; so what is real in life? What should be truly revered in life? The answer is forgiveness, understanding, and working towards self-improvement, peace and harmony. There are no absolute truths in the world of time and space except that eventually all people die and what value are the actions during life, after death? The value is in the negative or positive feeling and wisdom that is carried forth after death. Good feeling and wisdom of self come from ethical behavior and sane thinking about the world s problems. If this is done, the problems of the personality can be handled in a balanced and normal way.

Barack Obama, Racism, and the Folly of Ignorance and Delusion in Politics, Economics and Social Change

In November 2007 a milestone occurred when Barack Obama an African American man was elected as president of the United States of America. Many people never thought that the milestone would not have occurred in our lifetimes given the history of racial bias, oppression, animosity and violence that began in the United States with the institution of slavery. Accordingly, many people think that the election of Barack Obama means among other things that the United States has reached some kind of reckoning with the issue of racism. Many may also believe that the election also means that to some degree or another white people have redeemed themselves in reference to the issue of slavery.

It is interesting to note that Barack Obama was not winning the election in the polls during the period between the primary and the election. At that time he and his opponent John McCain, were about even in the polls and perhaps Mr. McCain was slightly ahead. Then, in September 2008 when the great financial collapse began in the United States it seemed that people intrinsically new that there was something extremely wrong with the economic system of the United States. When the banking institutions of Wall Street, which are inexorably tied in with the corruptions of the government [otherwise termed: *fascism*] began to fail, credit markets locked up, businesses ceased operations and stocks began to plunge, words like Great Depression began to be heard in the media and there developed a time of tension and fear about the economy that has not been seen since the crash of 1987, the economic crisis of the late 1970 s and early 1980 s and a level of anxiety and desperation which has not been seen since the 1930 s.

With the financial crisis, triggered by massive bank failures due to malfeasance, threatening to become an economic crisis as a backdrop, the speeches by Barack Obama began to resonate with a larger segment of the population. The ideal of his core followers was a general change of not just government leadership but also the ideal of beneficial economics, that the economy should not benefit just the elite of society but everyone. This message began to resonate with a larger segment of the population well beyond his core followers. His oratory spoke to this issue as well as the ending of the Iraq war.

In September 2008, when the economic collapse began, John McCain apparently began to act erratically and performed several political blunders. As viewed in the general news media, it appeared that John McCain did not have the temperament for handling a crisis and that he either did not understand there was a crisis or offered the same usual Republican Party ideas about *Lazes Faire* economics and government deregulation as well as less taxes for the rich that many seemed to be understanding as the cause of the economic debacle. In contrast, Mr. Obama presented a calm demeanor.

However, just because Mr. Obama appeared to be calmer under pressure did not necessarily mean that he was the better person to handle a given particular crisis, especially an economic crisis that may possibly surpass the challenges of the Great Depression of the 1930s. Would not a better choice have been someone who had experience running large government organizations and experience in economics, finance and budgeting, along with political savvy? In other words, being a gifted politician does not make one necessarily a good economist just as being a good administrator does not necessarily make one a good engineer. Furthermore, Mr. Obama would not necessarily be the best person to make the kind of fundamental change that people are really looking for in view of the fact that his history denotes a compromiser and not a revolutionary or at least a kind of politician that ushers in new eras.

Some of Mr. Obama s core followers were considered as part of the left wing of the Democratic Party. Most people who are labeled as left wing or part of the left wing of the Democratic Party are looking for fundamental changes in the way that the political and economic system of the United States should be conducted; specifically, that there should be a more progressive form of economics [more equitable in the division of resources and taxation] and that the society should be more based on sustainable ideals instead of the ideals of capitalism, corporatism and consumerism. Still, these aspirations would seem to be more delusions. Why? Those kinds of fundamental changes would mean a radical restructuring of the government and economic systems in such a way that the values upon which they are based would be completely shifted; something that would require a momentous political agreement to amend the constitution if not a constitutional convention to rewrite it. It would need to mean going from an economic system based on capitalism and consumerism to an economic system based on sustainability and fair distribution of resources.

Now, this kind of fundamental change in government and economics would be objectionable to a sizable portion of the population which would include the same group that is presently in control of the government and the economy [the rich and powerful and those who are deluded by their rhetoric (conservatives, libertarians, etc.)]. In terms of government, this would mean a shift from a system of representative government, in the form of a republic, to one that is more directly democratic and responsive to the needs and desires of the people; in other words, instead of representative government where people vote for representatives who have to be trusted to do what the people want, a more democratic system whereby elected leaders would have to follow more closely the dictates of the population and would be required to follow more ethical policies instead of being able to lie during campaigns to get elected and then do whatever they want to do after that, or get into office and be reelected through vote fraud, and or political machines or legalized bribery [political contributions].

However, though Barack Obama spoke eloquently, from an ideological perspective, on these issues he did not speak much about detailed actions he would take to bring about any of the kinds of fundamental changes discussed above. Of the changes he did specifically speak about, many were modified or completely altered later on; such as being against immunity for government officials who instituted warrantless wiretapping. During his campaign for President Obama said he would not have lobbyists in his administration; he then appointed several previous lobbyists and high level executives from the financial industry that brought on the financial crisis of 2008 and the growing economic collapse of 2009.[49] Regarding fundamental policies he did not speak about, he did not talk about ending the imperialist policies of the United States of America in the form of closing military bases around the world or ending the hegemony of the U.S. Dollar as the world currency. He

---

[49] *Bill Moyers Journal,* February 13, 2009

also pulled away from prosecutions for war crimes and violations of the Geneva Conventions by Bush Administration officials and C.I.A. operatives. On the week of February 1st Obama had his secretary of state, Hillary Clinton, reiterate the USA s continuing unquestioned support for the Israeli policies against the Palestinian people, which include the violations of international law, illegal blockades and refused to denounce the internationally recognized Israeli war crimes recently inflicted on the Arab peoples of Gaza, which included massacring women and children. Obama also signed an executive order to end torture and extraordinary rendition and shut down the military jail in Guant namo, Cuba. However, the *Los Angeles Times* also reported that the Obama administration has decided not to end the controversial policy of rendition, which gives the CIA authority to abduct anyone throughout the world and secretly transfer them to another country.[50] Obama also followed the Bush Administration policy, widely held to be deceptive and against his pledge of transparency and following the law, in arguing before the courts that allowing a lawsuit against an airline that was used by the CIA to transport prisoners to countries where they would be tortured would reveal national security secrets. Other recent activities by the Obama administration, actions that followed the Bush administration and the policies supported by previous administrations signaling not a break from the past but a continuation of it included:

Court Rejects Obama Bid to Stop Wiretapping Suit[51]

A Federal Appeals Court in San Francisco has rejected an argument by the Obama administration that the court should stop a lawsuit challenging the government s warrantless wiretapping program because a trial would potentially threaten national security. The ruling came in a case involving a defunct Islamic charity. Government lawyers signaled they would continue fighting to keep the information secret, setting up a new showdown between the courts and the White House over national security.

---

[50] *Democracynow.org,* February 05, 2009
[51] *Democracynow.org,* Headlines for March 02, 2009

Obama Mirrors Bush in Opposing Release of White House Emails[52]

The Obama administration has again sided with former President George W. Bush on a case involving government secrecy. The White House has already continued Bush stance s on seeking dismissal of a lawsuit by former CIA detainees and to prevent a federal court from reviewing the Bush administration s warrantless spying program. Now it s refusing to reverse the government position on opposing a suit seeking access to millions of missing White House emails over Bush s two terms in office. The groups Citizens for Responsibility and Ethics in Washington and the National Security Archive want the emails publicly released.

Obama Backs Bush Policy on Bagram Detainees[53]

The Obama administration has embraced another key argument of former President Bush s counterterrorism policy. In a court filing on Friday, the Justice Department told a federal judge that prisoners held at the US Air Force base at Bagram in Afghanistan have no legal rights to challenge their imprisonment. Human rights groups say they are becoming increasingly concerned that the use of extra-judicial methods in Afghanistan could be extended under the new US administration. Bagram Air Base is about to undergo a $60 million expansion to provide enough space to house five times as many prisoners as remain at Guantanamo.

Obama Administration to Boycott UN 'racism' Conference[54]

The Obama administration has announced that the United States will boycott the World Conference Against racism in Geneva next month, unless its final document drops all references to Israel and reparations for slavery. Israel and Canada have already announced plans to boycott the UN conference. In 2001, Bush administration diplomats walked out of the conference in Durban, South Africa after delegates proposed a resolution likening Zionism to racism. AIPAC, the American Israel Public Affairs Committee, praised President Obama s decision. The group said, The event, which has again proven to be a celebration of racism and vile anti-Semitic activity, is further evidence of the U.N. s inability to demonstrate any semblance of fairness or objectivity on these issues when it comes to the Jewish State.

Obama: US Can Detain Prisoners Indefinitely Without Charge[55]

---

[52] *Democracynow.org*, Headlines for February 24, 2009
[53] *Democracynow.org*, Headlines for February 23, 2009
[54] *Democracynow.org*, Headlines for March 02, 2009
[55] *Democracynow.org*, Headlines for March 17, 2009

Dick Cheney s comments came days after the Obama administration said it will no longer consider prisoners at Guantanamo Bay to be enemy combatants. Despite abandoning the label, the administration claims it still has the right to hold prisoners indefinitely without charge even if the individual is captured far from any battlefield and has not directly participated in hostilities.

Obama Admin Backs Ban on Foreign Scholar[56]

The Obama administration has apparently decided to continue the former President George W. Bush s policy of banning foreign scholars under anti-terror laws. In a federal appeals court hearing Tuesday, a government lawyer argued in favor of maintaining a ban on a prominent Muslim intellectual barred from a teaching job in the United States. The scholar, Tariq Ramadan, was offered a position at the University of Notre Dame in Ohio in 2004. The Bush administration initially barred his entry without explanation and then said it was because he once gave money to a Palestinian charity. The American Civil Liberties Union is challenging the ban on Ramadan s behalf.

In assessing president Obama s policy on Afghanistan, the scholar Noam Chomsky pointed out that the foreign policy is not different from that of president George W. Bush or the typical United States of America way of imposing it s policies on other peoples against their will and not supporting the democratic decisions of other countries so as to promote the agenda of the USA.

DEMOCRACYNOW.org 4/3/09

NOAM CHOMSKY: ...And President Karzai, formerly our man, no longer, because he s getting out of control

AMY GOODMAN: How? How is he getting out of control?

NOAM CHOMSKY: Well, interesting ways. When President Obama was elected, Afghan President Karzai sent him a message, which, as far as I know, was unanswered, in which he pleaded with President Obama to stop killing Afghans. He also addressed a UN delegation and told them he wanted a timetable for the removal of foreign forces. Well, his popularity quickly plummeted. He used to be very much praised for his nice clothes and great demeanor and very much

---

[56] *Democracynow.org,* Headlines for March 25, 2009

admired by the media and commentators. Now he s sunk very low. He s suddenly corrupt and so on.

In a discussion about the current financial debacle, Bill Moyers questioned William Black about the policies that Obama is pursuing. Black pointed out that in pursuing the present course the Obama administration is not only pursuing unsound economic policies but is breaking the law.

> **BILL MOYERS:** Welcome to the Journal.
> For months now, revelations of the wholesale greed and blatant transgressions of Wall Street have reminded us that "The Best Way to Rob a Bank Is to Own One." In fact, the man you're about to meet wrote a book with just that title. It was based upon his experience as a tough regulator during one of the darkest chapters in our financial history: the savings and loan scandal in the late 1980s
> **BILL MOYERS:**   you supported Barack Obama, during the campaign. But you're seeming disillusioned now.
> **WILLIAM K. BLACK:** Well, certainly in the financial sphere, I am. I think, first, the policies are substantively bad. Second, I think they completely lack integrity. Third, they violate the rule of law. This is being done just like Secretary Paulson did it. In violation of the law. We adopted a law after the Savings and Loan crisis, called the Prompt Corrective Action Law. And it requires them to close these institutions. And they're (Obama Administration) refusing to obey the law.
> **BILL MOYERS:** In other words, they could have closed these banks without nationalizing them?
> **WILLIAM K. BLACK:** Well, you do a receivership. No one -- Ronald Reagan did receiverships. Nobody called it nationalization.
> **BILL MOYERS:** And that's a law?
> **WILLIAM K. BLACK:** That's the law.
> **BILL MOYERS:** So, Paulson could have done this? Geithner could do this?
> **WILLIAM K. BLACK:** Not could. Was mandated--
> **BILL MOYERS:** By the law.
> **WILLIAM K. BLACK:** By the law.
> **BILL MOYERS:** This law, you're talking about.
> **WILLIAM K. BLACK:** Yes.
> **BILL MOYERS:** What the reason they give for not doing it?
> **WILLIAM K. BLACK:** They ignore it. And nobody calls them on it.

In relation to the continuation of the war in Iraq and Afghanistan and the manner in which Obama criticized George W. Bush about these issues there was a report on an important policy decision of President Obama that went contrary to his campaign promises.

Obama to Request $84.3B for War[57]

President Obama is asking Congress for $83.4 billion in funding for the occupation of Iraq and Afghanistan. The request marks a complete reversal for Obama from two years ago, when he voted against war funding as a senator under former President George W. Bush. The request would bring the budgetary cost of the two occupations to nearly $1 trillion so far. Obama is also asking for $350 million for operations along the US-Mexico border and $400 million in counterinsurgency aid to Pakistan. Although the Democratic-led Congress is expected to approve the funding, some antiwar lawmakers are voicing opposition. Congress member Lynn Woolsey of California said, Instead of attempting to find military solutions President Obama must fundamentally change the mission in both countries to focus on promoting reconciliation, economic development, humanitarian aid, and regional diplomatic efforts.

All of these moves that apparently continue the Bush Administration policies or the policies of other presidents (and general imperialist policies of the USA) place Obama not only in the company of Bush and the same politics as usual but also involve him as an accomplice in the possible war crimes and violations of the USA constitution [the supposed highest law] but it makes Obama personally complicit in the continuation of such law breaking and USA imperialism. Such actions, taken so far by Mr. Obama, would seem to vindicate the presidency of George W. Bush, which many held to have been the worst in terms of human rights violations, violations of the constitution, fiscal mismanagement and unethical behavior, in the history of the United States of America. Some may consider these as proofs revealing his deeper ethical duplicity based on his contrary statements during the campaign and or his present moral degradation from his previous status before taking on the presidency. Considering the promises he made during the campaign, these actions would seem to confirm the typical political bait and switch political

---

[57] *Democracynow.org*, Headlines for April 10, 2009

practice. Obama s supporters might be considered by some to be mesmerized by the desperation of hope due to the dire conditions brought on by corrupt politics and economics, so much so as to overlook or ignore the contradictions of his actions thus far, in a manner not unlike cult or faith-based religion wherein the leaders ideology or rhetoric is not questioned even when the actions of the leader do not conform to the dictates of the rhetoric. In much the same way as the majority of the population ignored other points of view and agreed with the actions of George W. Bush especially in his first term, making war on Afghanistan and Iraq, warrantless wiretapping, torture, etc., many of the followers of Obama seem to also ignore, overlook, discount or outright deny that his actions, thus far, fail to meet their hopes and expectations.

These contradictions were presented here to demonstrate that, just as many had written or had spoken publicly about, Mr. Obama would not or could not be the kind of change agent that many people either thought he would be or wanted him to be. In other words, the delusion about assigning one man or woman, and in fact, any man or woman the responsibility to change a country is really quite ridiculous in terms of a premise for serious political and social change. Yet, this is the kind of hope that presidents have been invested with especially since the 20th century; and in every case, the desired change has never come about. Rather, the system of government and economics has remained the same and the same people belonging to the same segment of the population [corporations, the wealthy and powerful] or their assigns, remain in control of them.

Figure 17: President George W. Bush and President-elect Barack Obama meet in the Oval Office of the White House Monday, Nov. 10, 2008.

This delusion also ignores the fact that the presidency is only one part of the government. There are hundreds of people in Congress and of course, the nine Supreme Court Justices who also affect the direction of government. So it is irrational to invest a president with the power to take the actions many people would like that person to take [either power to be conservative or liberal]; and of course, there are the moneyed interests who pull their strings. The point here is that, setting aside the issue of Obama s ethics, the system is corrupt and even the most ethical or well meaning person in the presidency would fail as long as the same protracted values and institutions that promote the views and agendas of the power elite remain in place. This is the higher delusion, not only about whether Mr. Obama is a good man or not, but that the system as it is can be changed for good, to work for all and promote peace, prosperity and the rule of law, etc. Even if we were to see a wonderful person act as president and the country turning towards the rule of law and righteous government, how long would it be before a new servant of the plutocracy would come into power, reverse all the progressive gains and lead the country once again down the road to deregulation, capitalism, imperialism and globalization? In other words, how long would it take for one George W. Bush to come along and reverse the policies of all the previous presidents through inciting fear, touting the fallacy of free market capitalism, arguing for tax breaks to the rich and bias towards corporations instead of the public good? This issue points to a systemic problem in the politics and economics of the United States of America and not just a legal problem; so changing laws is not enough, the culture itself needs to change, that is, the values of the culture need to change such that unfairness, crime, corruption and ignorance are not acceptable but are repudiated. Until such time there may be a tendency towards the positive or the negative from time to time but a sustained positive culture will not be achieved.

In reference to the treatment of the people of Haiti, in an interview on *Democracynow.org,* the civil rights activist and Haitian historian and advocate, Randal Robinson, pointed out the failure of the Obama administration, now more than four months old, to reverse the disparate treatment of Haitians and policies towards Haiti.

Protest Planned Outside NY Immigration Office to Stop Deportations of 30,000 Haitians[58]

JUAN GONZALEZ: And, Randall Robinson, is there any indication from your contacts that the Obama administration will be more responsive on this issue than the Bush administration has been?

RANDALL ROBINSON: Well, I m troubled that my understanding is that the Justice Department will leave this to the Department of Homeland Security and will not intervene. I am deeply troubled by that. This is a profound unfairness and continues this egregious discrimination against Haitians. When compared with our treatment of other people who enjoy the same status in the United States, it makes absolutely no sense.

---

[58] March 20, 2009

The *New York Times* editorial page has criticized this
continuation of the Bush policy. And we would invite the
administration to change course and to instruct the Department
of Homeland Security to grant TPS to these Haitians who are in
the United States, and we would invite Americans to call the
White House to do this. This will wreak havoc not only in the
lives of these people, but it will wreak havoc for Haiti trying to
recover from last season s devastating hurricanes.

In order to move towards what is righteous or at least redressing wrongs
of the past, many would like to see reparations for Native Americans,
and Africans. Yet, like his white predecessor, Obama continued the
policy of denial of the issue of worldwide racism and refusal to make
amends for the past racial injustices of the United State of America.

Reparations, Israel Dropped from UN 'racism' Text[59]

Negotiators drafting the declaration for next month s UN
Conference Against racism have acceded to US and
European Union demands and dropped references to Israel and
reparations for slavery. The Obama administration has vowed
to boycott the conference unless the two issues are dropped
from conference text.

Others would like to see the withdrawal of the US military forces from
the over 156 countries where they are now.[60] Still others would like to
see the equitable distribution of wealth to all members of the society
instead of most of the wealth going to the highest 1% of the population,
and also would like to see full economic equality of the genders, and
healthcare for all. If these things are not done does it not mean the same

---

[59] *DemocracyNow.org, Headlines for March 19, 2009*
[60] More than 1000 US Bases and/or Military Installations
The main sources of information on these military installations (e.g. C. Johnson, the NATO Watch
Committee, the International Network for the Abolition of Foreign Military Bases) reveal that the
US operates and/or controls between 700 and 800 military bases Worldwide. In this regard, Hugh
d Andrade and Bob Wing's 2002 Map 1 entitled "U.S. Military Troops and Bases around the World,
The Cost of 'Permanent War'", confirms the presence of US military personnel in 156 countries. The
US Military has bases in 63 countries. Brand new military bases have been built since September 11,
2001 in seven countries. In total, there are 255,065 US military personnel deployed Worldwide.
These facilities include a total of 845,441 different buildings and equipments. The underlying land
surface is of the order of 30 million acres. According to Gelman, who examined 2005 official
Pentagon data, the US is thought to own a total of 737 bases in foreign lands. Adding to the bases
inside U.S. territory, the total land area occupied by US military bases domestically within the US
and internationally is of the order of 2,202,735 hectares, which makes the Pentagon one of the
largest landowners worldwide (Gelman, J., 2007).
http://www.globalresearch.ca/index.php?context=va&aid=5564

class, racial and economic divisions for profit, control and domination are being maintained and no other outcomes should be expected beyond what we currently see: a caste system based on social status tied to wealth and connection with a power elite, racism and a permanent underclass? Keeping in mind the aforesaid, if we have a permanent underclass this would mean there is a permanent overclass and both groups exist by design. In other words, unless we see fundamental changes to the constitution and values of the society, and not just changing the personnel that manages the government, what we had, have and will have is the same.

Clearly, the radical and fundamental changes would be impossible given the large segment of the population that believes in libertarian ideals and *laissez-faire capitalism*, market economics, as well as racism and gender bias even though those systems of economic and social order have been found to be faulty, as the current social, political, financial and economic debacle have starkly demonstrated. Regardless, that segment holds on to those views because they work to keep them [the overclass, power elite, plutocracy, etc.] in power.

Mr. Obama s actions, as of the first month of his presidency, as did his actions during his campaign and prior to being elected to the Senate, would tend to suggest he would act as a supporter of the system, that he is not beholden to or a supporter of the ideals of the left segment of the Democratic Party, to progressive principles, and that in fact he is more of a supporter of the system and is indeed trying to repair and restore the current government and economy essentially with the same kind of policies and economic theories as his predecessors even to the extent of continuing wars and war tactics that have brought shame on the presidency and the US Government, such as attacking villages in Pakistan, supposedly trying to kill enemy *Taliban* and or Al *Qaeda* soldiers, with unmanned drones that led to the deaths of civilian women and children in his first week in office.

We may consider that he would not have had another choice since if he had refused to order the attacks he would have been excoriated by his political opponents. Also, he himself stated during the campaign that he would indeed escalate the war in Afghanistan [one of the early compromises of his core constituents was to accept this idea of the necessity to escalate the war in Afghanistan as opposed to a complete end to the Iraq and Afghanistan wars]. In any case, the country would

132

appear to be left with a person who is carrying on with the same policies he was, according to his followers and supporters, not supposed to continue as part of his promise of new ways of governing that rejected the policies that his supporters repudiated about his predecessors and especially his immediate predecessor. This would mean that, due to blind faith or willful ignorance or hope in a defunct, though destructive, political system, his supporters fell under the illusion that the same two party system which espouses the ideals of liberty and justice for all but which delivers neither nor allows dissenting opinions to be heard or introduced to government policymaking could be reformed in a new era of governance that espouses the ideals supposedly contained in it s founding documents [ideals, such as freedom, opportunity or democracy] which never have been extended to all members of the society]. Thus, we would need to conclude that acquiescence to the current system and self-delusion, on the part of most of the population that voted, are more responsible for Obama s victory than right thinking and sound reasoning about the serious deficiencies of the government, economic and social order of the society and what is real meritorious experience that should qualify a person to be elected to be president as well as a member of congress and delusion about the real purpose[61] of and power behind the government [elite segment of the population {top 1%}] and what is needed to change those realities.

It is important to keep in mind that the masses of white people are also economically and socially subjugated by a higher class through social hierarchy that is part of the oligarchy. The United States of America appears from the outside as a **particracy** or government by political parties but within those parties there is a comon group that controls both. The two political parties are controlled by aristocracy, or government by a ruling class. That aristocracy is composed of *plutocrats* the wealthy; that plutocracy is composed of *oligarchs* the Kennedy family and the Bush family are examples of the families or small groups that control the politics and economics to the country. [62]

Racism and white supremacy, from an institutional perspective, are not the essence but are aspects and instruments of the republican form of government and capitalist market economic system [fascism] of the USA and other countries, used to manipulate and pit groups against each other to promote distraction and confusion about the real problems and causes

---

[61] [maintain the power and wealth of corporations and elite segment of the population and maintain others in economic distress or poverty]

[62] government by a few, especially by a small faction of persons or families

of the problems of the society, in order to control and exploit the population. Nevertheless, it was Obama s choice to seek and accept the position of presiding over a country that has manifested perhaps the greatest military and economic imperialist agenda and worldwide military and economic crimes in human history.

So, keeping the aforesaid in view, it would seem that we are left with the notion that Mr. Obama was elected not due to his experience, as a person qualified to run government[63] and economic systems[64] or an outstanding agenda for real and fundamental changes to the government and economic systems but due to special circumstances; namely the economic crisis that caused an already distressed and weary public to, out of fear and desperation, grasp at a person that was made available to them that was more attractive and would at least be able to speak to what appeared to be their deep-rooted fears and desires for righteousness and hope but what may have been in reality seductive beguiling sophistry and chicanery that ensnares even its greatest practitioners along with the tired, weak-willed and deluded pleasure-seeking and entertainment intoxicated masses, like the rats that followed the fabled pied piper.

It was amply demonstrated through the primary season that Mr. Obama was not the most qualified person in the field of candidates. However, it was demonstrated that Mr. Obama had advanced intellectual capacity, unlike his predecessor, George W. Bush, and a Obama also displayed a masterful capacity to communicate with the public and deliver rousing speeches, matching if not surpassing the political and oratory skills of Ronald Reagan and Bill Clinton, who are widely recognized as top communicator presidents of the late 20th century if not of the entire 20th century. Therefore, we are left with the idea that Mr. Obama was elected not because he was the better of all possible choices; rather, he was chosen out of fear of a collapsing economy and a deluded notion that a multicultural person who appears to practice compromise[65] politics could break through the morass of United States of America politics and economics and social degradation. This desire was in the hope that a corrupt government constitution and bankrupt economic system could and should be fixed or saved instead of reworking, if not, overhauling it entirely or even throwing it out and starting it over from scratch.

This is not to say that other candidates from either party were good or better choices and we should remember that the system only allows candidates from the two parties and no outsiders. And, the candidates are

---

[63] trained (university degree) and experienced in **Public Policy & Public Administration**

[64] trained (university degree) in economist

[65] instead of winner take all and lock step government that does not care for anything but its own agenda, which is what the republican party displayed in the last 15 years

put up by the parties and are not selected by the masses. Yet, Mr. Obama had an important characteristic that the other candidates did not have, charisma. Even though charisma is not necessarily a qualification for managerial or professional positions it is a qualification for successfully navigating the media aspects of a political campaign as it has developed in the U.S.A. because the culture is so dominated by entertainments [especially in the forms of political and celebrity scandal, sports, movies and music]. The weak willed and weak minded personality is prone to select visually and audibly appealing candidates instead of substantive ones regardless of the level of capacity or expertise of the substantive candidate; this is because of the atrophied intellect of the weak minded personality and the reliance on emotions and surface appearances instead of relying on evaluations based on reasoning and factual evidence. In other words, just as the religion of most people is faith-based, relying on preachers who look and sound convincing as they espouse the virtue of faith instead of wisdom and become rich while their followers remain in a lower state, so too is their political practice. Of course, being based on delusion instead of reality sustained by facts, both the politics and religion of most countries, including the United States of America, leads to political failure and economic destitution for the masses and more wealth for the rich and powerful. Under these circumstances it is understandable how charisma forms such an important part of politics; charisma serves as a benchmark for public selections and it more easily manipulates people s minds when the public is weak-willed, ignorant and especially when in the grips of fear or despair. In other words, the faults here are twofold, in the flawed systems of government and economics and the ignorance and weaknesses of their followers and administrators.

These and other factors have given rise to speculation in some quarters that the financial crash of September and October 2008 was orchestrated to embarrass the Republican candidate, John McCain, in the eyes of the public so that Obama would win. The purpose was two-fold, first to panic the society into allowing a massive bailout of the financial sector and secondly, to put Obama in place as a strategic move to quell, through the power of his oratory, charisma and ability to connect with and apparent ability to speak to the desperation of the populace, the anger of the population which was essentially fed up with the republican party rule of the last 8-15 years which is seen as the cause that brought on the current crisis [in reality it is the system of politics and economics that is part of the cause and not just the people that manipulated and operated the system]. The idea is that Obama s charisma and power of oratory along with the goodwill he developed through the campaign and the delusion that most people have about him, that he is a real agent of change, would allow them to control the mainstream and left leaning segment of the population long enough for an extension of the current systems of government and economy and more bailouts, which means more transference of wealth from the population to the wealthy, and more time to put into place plans for population control. There is also one more idea that is part of this theory, that a further extension of time would produce more of an emergency that would eventually justify the need for extreme measures, like martial law, and the devaluation of the current US Dollar, thereby invalidating the present currency and consequently devaluing the wealth of anyone who holds US dollars, ushering in the introduction of a new form of currency, which would be more acceptable coming from Obama than from the Republican party. If Obama is in collusion with this plan it would mean that he is obviously part of a conspiracy to deceive and steal the wealth of the USA and prepare the ground for a so-called new world order governed even more tightly by a worldwide power elite.[66] If he is ignorant of such a scheme, this premise, therefore assigns Obama the role of a patsy or stooge of the power elite that control the economy, which means they also control his politics either by manipulating him by means of opposing actions through other government elected and non-elected persons, to block his policies or by manipulating events in such a way that he has no viable options except the one(s) they desire. An example of such manipulative subterfuge has already been documented:

Lawyer: Torture Evidence "Hidden from Obama"[67]

Meanwhile, *The Guardian* newspaper reports US defense officials may be preventing Barack Obama from seeing evidence that Binyam Mohamed, a former British resident held in Guant namo Bay, has been tortured. The prisoner s lawyer, Clive Stafford Smith, says he sent Obama evidence of what he called truly mediaeval abuse, but substantial parts were blanked out before the President could read it. Smith says Obama should be aware of the bizarre reality of the situation. Smith said, You, as commander in chief, are being denied access to material that would help prove that crimes have been committed by U.S. personnel. This decision is being made by the very people who you command. *The Guardian* reports US defense officials might have censored

---

[66] see the book *Collapse of Civilization/Death of American Empire* by Muata Ashby
[67] *Democracynow.org, Headlines for February 13, 2009*

the evidence to protect the President from criminal liability or political embarrassment.

Furthermore, once Obama would fail to control the economy and fails to keep his main promises like introducing new politics, transparency and honesty in government, ending the wars in Iraq and Afghanistan, etc. but especially, if he fails to turn around the economy, or if he would institute or continue radical security measures such as those introduced by republicans [Patriot Act, wireless wiretapping, martial law, etc.] to keep the country functioning or in another scenario, even if he were to not institute those policies of the right wing, his failure would be seen as a failure of the Democratic party and he himself would also be seen as being no different from all other corrupt politicians and would lose the presidency after only one term, to another Republican who would finish the job of devastating the economy in favor of the wealthy and usher in a new era wherein the USA and in fact all countries are economically debilitated, in debt and fully under the control of and whose wealth goes directly to the moneyed interests.

While this is not a political treatise,[68] it is an essay attempting to show how the predicament of ignorance leads to not only delusions and egoism in the life of an individual but also the life of a society and how it promotes negative outcomes in politics as well as the socio-economic order of a society, which can affect other societies. The political motivations of those who do not necessarily care about racial issues but who care about power and wealth, are integral to understanding that racism is no longer the overriding factor of USA society in terms of those who fill the positions in it s management staff [president, congress, supreme court]. Since the 1960 s there came into office perhaps thousands of officials in various levels of government including mayors and governors, that were either black or latino . That development has not elevated the political and economic ethics of the culture or prevented the same ruling class from controlling the politics or economics of the society. At one time, prior to the 1970 s, overt racism was used as a means to pit groups against each other and occupy their energies; blacks were busy surviving and working for meager wages while the masses of whites were busy holding them down so that they could consider themselves in good social standing [relative to blacks but of course, not in relation to the class of whites that occupy the social level

---

[68] For a detailed study of USA politics in light of High Wisdom Philosophy see the book *The Collapse of Civilization* by Muata Ashby

we may term as *aristocracy/oligarchy/plutocracy,* highest 5% of the white majority]. Now, racism is till used as a wedge between the so called races and social classes [middle class and lower class whites and middle class and lower class blacks , latinos , asians and native Americans] but the strategy is not to maintain distraction through overt racism but rather to maintain the class structure [the very wealthy and everyone else] through fear of terrorism, worker insecurity and institutionalized racism while at the same time appearing to promote economic, racial and gender justice and highlighting the virtue of fighting against racism in order to keep the masses [everyone besides the moneyed interests] busy believing that it is worthwhile upholding a failed political and economic system, and that it can be repaired or made to work well for everyone. In reality it is a system that produces the illusion of democracy and which is in reality designed to sustain the wealth and power of the oligarchy / plutocracy and an economic system; it is also in reality designed to produce consumerism, and the destruction of the environment. As of early 2009, most people in jail were still blacks and latinos , women were still being underpaid for the same work that men do and get more pay, the working class was more economically stressed than ever and the rich were wealthier and the poor were poorer than at any time in history. In terms of political and economic systems, the delusion of the masses and the collusion of the masses with the politicians and moneyed interests allows clearly predatory and tyrannical systems of government to be accepted.

Many people view the rise and influence of corporations on the legislative branch of government to be troubling. However, though *Corpocracy* may be thought of as government rule by corporations but in the case of the United States of America, the corporations are merely social instruments of the aristoligarplutocracy [a simpler term we may use is *"The Power Elite"*] which they use as instruments of commerce to enable wealth accumulation and extraction of resources from the economies of the world that operate within a larger context called *fascism* [rule by corporations in collusion with government]. So the vaunted ideals of the US Constitution which set up three branches of government [legislative, executive and judicial] operate as one of two instruments [the other being corporations] for controlling politics and economics. This means that in reality there is no democracy , only aristoligarplutocracy or rule by a wealthy elite through government institutions and corporations.

Finally, it is important to understand that even those persons that are part of this aristoligarplutocracy may be considered as evil in the sense of devilish if they have malice of forethought in creating, and sustaining the current system of politics, economics, social order. However, rather, they may also accurately be described as degraded human beings due to their ignorance of the knowledge of self as being connected with others and with nature, for only when people are disconnected and degraded due to egoism and ignorance is it possible for man s inhumanity towards man to flourish into the violence, injustices, degradations and atrocities of the society. We know this because studies have demonstrated that the reverse condition produces the reverse outcome: when people are more altruistic and when there is more justice and more equitable distribution of resources in a society there is less inhumanity, violence and unhappiness. In this sense the plutocrats, and the people who support them, have *traded* the happiness and well-being of the society, as a whole, in an attempt to insure their own happiness, well-being and power.

Society as a whole, places a value on human life. However, the leadership of society has more responsibility as they have more knowledge of the issues, and impacts of their policies. By promoting policies that foment economic systems that promote injustice and inequity in the distribution of resources such as free market *laissez-faire* capitalism there will be no balance or sustainability in the economy; rather there will be boom and bust periods and also these systems promote disparities between the rich and poor as well as varied forms of crime. Consider that if this is true then it means that those who promote these forms of economies instead of forms that promote full employment, are knowingly also promoting levels of crime that would otherwise not exist and are therefore morally guilty accomplices to those crimes even though they may prefer to place the blame on the perpetrators of crime. From a moral standpoint, if a person, through omission of action, fails to provide some situation that it is in their power to provide which they know will create a fertile ground for crime are caught in a moral hazard of criminality.

> The results suggest that both the variables chosen as regressor are significant in determining the level of criminal activities. The results are consistent and concurrent with the finding of Agell and Nilsson (2003), and Papps and Winkelmann (1999) whose studies all

139

found strong positive and significant relationship between unemployment and crime. As for the negative relationship between unemployment and violent crime, it is also consistent, whereby as explained by Poutvaara and Priks (2007), it is due to substitution effect in their studies which examined a model of criminal gangs. They further explained that unemployment increases the relative attractiveness of large and less violent gangs engaging more in property crime. The results of this paper suggests an explanation to the empirical regularity whereby unemployment tends to increase property crime, but not violent crime same sentiments are also shared Becker (1968) who emphasizes on the cost and benefit of crime, and Ehrlich (1973) who extends Becker s crime model by including the role of opportunity cost between illegal and legal work. It also does explain the negative relationship between income and domestic burglary.[69]

Furthermore, the spikes of unemployment are especially injurious to some members of society. So, systems of economy that promote unemployment are inherently immoral and destructive. At those times many people suffer not only due to crime increases but due to other social ills such as disease and stress. Knowing this and still promoting a form of economics that allows such conditions to ensue is, again, a choice, but a morally hazardous one in which the leaders of society and those who follow them, have placed a value on the lives and well being of the members of society, the price of which is the cost of partial employment. They refuse to pay for full employment [taking less profit and allowing more people to be employed], so that they may maintain an advantage, as well as become more wealthy and powerful and maintain others in a state of subsistence living, ignorant and powerless to change their conditions. Nevertheless, we should also not forget that the followers, the masses, have the responsibility to stop the negative situations and if they do not, then they are also blameworthy for the conditions of their society and their lives.

---

[69] Is crime cointegrated with income and unemployment?: A panel data analysis on selected European countries Baharom, A.H. and Habibullah, M.S. Universiti Putra Malaysia
http://mpra.ub.uni-muenchen.de/11927/1/MPRA_paper_11927.pdf

This Economy is a Real Killer[70] by Peter Dreier

After crunching the numbers, Brenner calculated that for every
one percent increase in the unemployment rate (an additional
1.5 million people out of work), we can expect an additional
47,000 deaths, including 26,000 deaths from heart attacks,
about 1,200 from suicide, 831 murders, and 635 deaths related
to alcohol consumption. If, for example, the unemployment
rate jumps from 8.1% to 9.1%, we can expect roughly an extra
1,200 people to commit suicide and another 831 people to
commit murder.
For most people, losing their job, their life savings or
pensions, or their home is traumatic, even when its through no
fault of their own. Our individualistic culture leads people to
blame themselves and to think of themselves as failures.
When the economy goes south, the hardships in people's lives
get translated into increased stress, anxiety, and frustration.

Obama, was seen by many as a perfect choice because of his supposed
multicultural background which offered something apparently new or
novel, if not even exotic yet familiar and steady to offer to the political
stage, as opposed to the traditional rich white men that have occupied
the presidency and have practiced the traditional politics of saying
anything to get elected and then doing whatever they wanted, but
nevertheless supporting the system and the interests of the wealthy and
white majority. He is new and different in terms of his appearance,
brown skin, as opposed to the white skin of all other Presidents.
However, he is familiar in terms of his politics, having brought in the
same people who were in government before,[71] that have so far
demonstrated they hold the same beliefs and have the same corruptions[72]
as previous presidential staffs instead of selecting new and capable
people, to fill the positions of government, from a population of 300
million people.

During his campaign Obama was hounded by the question of his
blackness , specifically its adequacy or inadequacy. In accordance with
the racial politics of the country from the inception of slavery as an
accepted institution, the definition of a black person is anyone that has
a black ancestor. So it is interesting that his blackness would be in

---

[70] *Huffingtonpost.com*, March 21, 2009, http://www.huffingtonpost.com/peter-dreier/this-economy-is-a-real-ki_b_173515.html
[71] Mostly people who served under president Bill Clinton, or the Bush, Reagan or Carter administrations.
[72] Several Obama appointees were found to be breaking the law by not paying their taxes.

question since he obviously appears to have had a black ancestor. This raises the question of if his blackness is in question, are those who question it referring to his skin color or his culture, which implies his belief and values, and does that relate to his having a recent white ancestor, his mother, or does it relate to his not having grown up in the circumstances that most black people experienced? If this refers to the latter it is a question of culture and not of so called race ; so it is interesting that such a distinction would be made since the mere appearance of blackness would lead any black man to be treated equally throughout the country; in other words, he would be discriminated against. If this issue relates to a cultural difference then it is not a racial issue unless we consider all people who believe in the ideals of racism to be white racists.

Figure 18: Right-to-left: Barack Obama and half-sister Maya Soetoro, with their mother Ann Dunham and grandfather Stanley Dunham, in Hawaii (early 1970s)

While many accepted him, as a real black man because he selected a black wife, instead of a white wife, as any Harvard educated black man could have acquired, his campaign made specific efforts to highlight the whiteness of his mother and her family.

Having such relatives so recently in his history allowed that to be possible, for him to be referred to as a half black half white person, a multicultural person, or a biracial person, someone that whites and blacks could equally embrace. This idea would mean that the subsequent generations, the descendants of black and white people who mated and produced offspring, who today are appearing as everything from light to dark complexion, cannot make this same claim [half black , half white ,   multicultural , biracial] even though it is obvious that most people who are today referred to as blacks or latinos have black ancestry; some are referred to as latinos and others as Caribbeans, etc. But those designations relate to culture and not the dubious but still recognized idea of human races.

Let us not forget that white people are not really white, but rather Africans, like everyone else, since all human beings alive today originated from the same African ancestors! Perhaps if we were to use this higher and general designation the delusion over races that gives rise to racism could be reduced or even eradicated. This idea has more pertinent implications than just the common origin of all human beings, though that is momentous in itself; if we were to go back just a few generations it is remarkable that many people are recently related to each other even across so called racial lines. It is interesting, as a side note, that it was revealed, during the campaign, that Mr. Obama is related to the previous Vice President, Dick Chaney, a white man, who was euphemistically referred to as Darth Vader , the evil villain of the Star Wars movie saga. It has been discovered that many of the past Presidents and Vice Presidents have family relations and some going back to the royalty of England. Some may also wonder if Obama would proceed with criminal charges against his own cousin. This is of course another delusion since all human beings are related and if we were not to impose the law on our kin we would never build any court or jail.

The term multicultural is misapplied here because it is being conflated with the idea of race which is itself a misconception. People from different races may exhibit the same cultural characteristics. Culture is not the same as race and could not be since race is a bogus concept. If we consider ethnicity this too is not synonymous with culture since it is the idea of association with a culture. Again, is the sum total of the distinctive actions and manifestations of a society through human activities such as language, art, religion, music, clothing, etc. If we are to apply the term culture in the context of seeing black people s way of life as being different from that of the majority white people then the term might possibly apply but does that mean that

143

blacks have a different culture from the whites ? If that is the case then are the proponents of this idea saying that the white people that supported and voted for Obama see him as representing a different culture and that other culture was acceptable to them? Likely not, for can we envision a white person from the USA voting for a person that speaks Hindi and lives in accordance with Indian values? The answer would likely be no. In the same way we would not expect to see wide scale support for Jesse Jackson or Al Sharpton either. That is because Jesse Jackson and Al Sharpton are indeed perceived as representing a subculture which we may refer to as black . Neither Jesse Jackson nor Al Sharpton was able to achieve any sizable support from the majority white population; also, some may note that the speech patterns, lifestyles, associations, politics and social circles traveled by Jesse Jackson and Al Sharpton could be perceived as being more akin to those of inner city blacks , in other words, black culture, as opposed to Obama s which are more akin to that of the white majority, in other words, white culture. Furthermore, during the campaign, Obama spoke about inner city, race and social issues in a different way than Jesse Jackson or Al Sharpton did. Obama purposely sought to downplay any racial distinctions or issues during the campaign. Obama grew up with his white family and in a foreign country, all of which in the eyes of many can cause him to be seen as not fully belonging either American culture [majority culture of the United States of America] or black culture. To others he may not be perceived as something other than a part of the black culture that is associated with inner city life, Hip Hop music and the history of slavery, segregation and the anger of some blacks who experienced that history along with the concomitant guilt, fear and resentment held by many whites who feel sorry about slavery or other who may feel umbrage about being associated with what they perceive as a problem of past generations that they had nothing to do with and which they do not understand how they are still benefiting from. In that sense also, Obama s multicultural-ness allows some people to feel that they have redeemed themselves for any past wrongdoing since his culture is not a stark reminder of that past and it s ever-present consequences, as opposed to that of Jesse Jackson or Al Sharpton which might.

So this would mean then that the white people that supported and voted for Obama maintained an illusion of Obama s supposed multicultural-ness when in reality they were supporting their own culture behind his skin color, since his politics, and way of life may be able to reflect the ghetto and the struggle of black people against racism, discrimination and slavery, but is not intrinsically of or from it in the manner in which Jesse Jackson or Al Sharpton may be perceived as representing their origins, feelings and connections to the struggle of black people. It would seem that what the white people who supported Obama really mean, therefore, is that he is somehow part of the black culture of the USA but representing the majority culture which also happens to be white . Under these conditions some may perceive him as the most prominent in a long list of people of color [Blacks , Asians, Latinos, etc.] that have been elevated to managerial positions to run companies for the owners, who have been white. Again, let us remember that the term race is the description of a form of life, i.e. the human race . The use of the racial terms is for the purpose of discussion and is not an acceptance of their validity. There is no such thing as a white race or a black race .

If this idea of multicultural ism is being applied in terms of the idea that he represents whatever we might call the culture of white people and or the culture of black people then does that mean that he represents the culture of Jesse Jackson and or Al Sharpton? If he does, why is it that Obama was elected by the majority of the population, which is white , and they were not? Is it because they manifested the black culture and not the white culture? Then it would mean that the white people would not elect anyone that does not represent and manifest white culture. If the white culture appreciated and desired to elect someone who represented the culture of black people why were Jesse Jackson and or Al Sharpton not elected or at least given serious support in the white community? If this means that white people wanted someone who represented both cultures that would mean that they did not fully embrace the culture of black people and wanted some security in their own culture.

If we are to say that Obama s blackness is due to his skin color could we not say that about the rest of the 14% of the population which is recognized as black ? And if we are to say that he is also half white is that because he had a mother who was white ? If that is so what about the people who have say a grandfather or great grandmother who was white; they are not biracial too? If we were to include the numbers of people that pass for white but that have some black ancestor we would be looking at a sizable number of the population. The idea here is to point out the illusoriness and the nonsense of the considerations that

145

most people live by and which lead them to a myriad of problems in society and in their own lives, through prejudices, misconceptions, unfounded fears and other delusions.

Pan-Africanist Scholar Ali Mazrui on the Election of Barack Obama as the First Black President in the Western World[73]

AMY GOODMAN: How do you respond to someone like critics like Glen Ford   he writes for the *Black Agenda Report*   who says, **Obama** will provide US empire with a black face, and that could be very destructive.

ALI MAZRUI: It is a risk, really, because sometimes people are swallowed up by the position they occupy. I would hope he would help reshape the position he occupies, the presidency of the United States. And I ve spoken, including in India   the one thing I hope he will avoid is initiate another military conflict for the United States, because since the 1930s, every single American president has initiated a conflict, either large-scale war or some kind of confrontation with another country involving weapons   everybody since Franklin D. Roosevelt. So, my hope is he will break that tendency for the American presidents to feel the way to be really presidential and commander-in-chief is to be ordering an army into action on another society.

AMY GOODMAN: And what sense do you have that he will go that way? I mean, since he has come into office, we see one after another of these unmanned drone attacks in Pakistan. Of course, while he says he s going to draw down in Iraq, he s talking about a surge that will double the force in Afghanistan.

ALI MAZRUI: Absolutely. So, at the moment, I m not optimistic that he ll necessarily be just a peacemaking president with the conflicts that are on. So my dream was he will be the first president not to start a conflict, not that he would be the first president not to preside over a war, because he s inheriting two wars, anyhow. And then, with one of them, the Afghanistan, he s not planning to end it, really. He s planning to escalate it for a while, so that is disappointing

---

[73]*Democracynow.org,* Monday, February 16, 2009

In examining the Obama Phenomenon we should perhaps draw a distinction between what he may represent from a sociological versus political/economic perspective. From a sociological perspective, while Obama s election may lead to some social change, change in relation between blacks and whites in the future, by all members of the population experiencing a black / multicultural / biracial , etc. person in the office of President of the United States, and through that experience witnessing that the unfounded fears of many whites do not come true, namely: the country does not cease to exist, that black people will not take over the world, that black people will not kill all the white men and rape all the white women, etc. This experience may allow the idea of a black person as leader to become acceptable and mainstream, if not desirable.

This would certainly affect race relations if his persona is seen as a representative of the black population as a whole; but if Obama is seen as something other than an ordinary black man of the United States, that imagery could relate to him and those who can project his type of image of a black man, and that would be the standard which is acceptable to the majority white population, something other than the general idea of a black person in the United States of America. If Obama were only to be seen as representation of an ideal of blackness that is comfortable and familiar to white culture and not represent the general black culture, Obama could be seen as an exception, an aberration, a special case; and the social change would not develop into political and economic change wherein black people, as a whole, would be seen as equals and as partners in setting political and economic policy for the country. Only those blacks that represent the system, that operate within the cultural comfort zone of most whites who vote, would be allowed to partake in cultural and economic policy making and that would not mean change but just more people supporting the same ideas, agendas and policies. In other words, this would be only a superficial change in the society where even though Obama was the president he would be seen as different from the rest of the black population and thus the relations between the black population and the white population would remain little changed even though the white population might even have developed respect and admiration for a black person acting as president. On the other hand, black people might, through Obama s success indeed see that they can have more than the black culture that has been developed but they may also see the contradictions of Obama s persona and his relationship with white people, which may still exclude them. In this scenario Obama would be seen as a token black person instead of a representative of real opportunities for all members of the population.

Therefore, it is not necessarily correct to assume that because he was elected that that means there was a fundamental change in the dynamic of relations between blacks and whites . If he had lost would that have invalidated those who voted for him? In the same way it does not invalidate those who did not vote for him, many of whom did not specifically vote for him due to racial reasons.

From an economic and political standpoint, it is perhaps likely that there will be no net positive effect since regardless of who was in the office of president, the situation is so dire that no one could substantially change it right now. More importantly though, even if it were changed for the better, the problem is not who occupies the office of president but what system of government and economics does the president preside over, support and sustain? This is the real issue; from a philosophy of politics point of view, all else is a distraction and no amount of protests, hope or good people filling government posts will change the outcome as long as the government and economic systems remain corrupted by social values of greed and the lust for power, again, all of which are born of ignorance of one s higher nature.

> *There is no political solution*
> *To our troubled evolution*
> *Have no faith in constitution*
> *There is no bloody revolution*
>
> *We are spirits in the material world...*
>
> *Our so-called leaders speak*
> *With words they try to jail you*
> *The subjugate the meek*
> *But its the rhetoric of failure*
> *We are spirits in the material world...*
>
> -Sting & Police, 1986

The contradictions above highlight the delusions most people have about culture and race as well as politics and economics. It is meant to provoke thoughtfulness about how the erroneous notions lead a person and in fact entire populations and societies to live in ways that are against their own higher ideals and lead to financial, economic, social, political and environmental disasters. For the purpose of our discussion, the understanding of the meaning of the contradictions requires the reader to realize the difference between substantive and superficial change. If Mr. Obama closes a prison (superficial change) at Guant namo in Cuba it is not the same as restoring diplomatic relations with Cuba (substantive change); If Mr. Obama reverses (superficial change) the signing statements of President Bush but does not seek to have a constitutional amendment outlawing (substantive change) them the situation will continue if not with Mr. Obama, with other presidents in the future. If this metric is applied to the understanding of politics, sociology and economics it will be easier to understand the predicament of humanity and why problems do not get resolved permanently as well as why the apparent changes of the present are insubstantial and ultimately inconsequential distractions that lead to an illusory notion about change and eventually lead to more strife, suffering, frustrations, unrest, hatred, and violence in society. We may conclude here with a passage from the book of a person who gave a significant portion of his life to the elevation of African American peoples and the introduction of ethics and good governance to USA politics.

> America is a huge fraud, clad in narcissistic conceit and satisfied with itself, feeling itself unneedful of any self-examination nor responsibility to right past wrongs, of which it notices none. It s the kind of fraud that simply wears you out.
>
> -Randall Robinson, *Quitting America*

It is unlikely that a deluded society can change from corrupt to ethical as it wallows in entertainments or self-congratulatory illusions about it s own power and greatness; those who holds such notions like my country love it or leave it, or my country is the best and we may have our problems but all other countries are worst or we have freedoms that no other country has and that makes us the greatest country etc. might be confronted with the fallacy of their own convictions IF they were willing to face their ignorance. There are other countries that have the same freedoms and more ethical social orders, better health care, less crime, etc. So what makes the USA great? Is it the power of the military or the capacity of some people to become wealthy or the ability to make blockbuster movies or the ability to have the biggest economy and hoard most of the wealth of the world? Certainly one should not have to leave one s country if it needs to be criticized or have to love it no matter what injustices or atrocities occur there. Should a child be forced to love her father who raped and mutilated her? Does the father deserve no criticism, no reproach? Should a country that devastated the African population through the transatlantic slave trade, raped the slaves and discriminated against them for over 100 years, killed, humiliated, and usurped the land of native Americans be loved unconditionally simply because it is possible to become fabulously rich there? Is this a virtue worthy of unconditional love ? Should the United States of America be loved unconditionally because it became the greatest empire, and military power seen in history?   With no acknowledgement of wrongdoing, no compensation to victims or their descendants, no admission of guilt and continued disparities and injustices how can the illusion of greatness be sustained except in the rhetoric of political leaders and the mindless, thoughtless march of the ignorant masses waving patriotic flags as they rush into the abyss of endless wars, perpetual fear and continued propping up of the social ego of American society through a complicit entertainment and media infrastructure. This is why in many quarters it has been advanced that the society will not be able to improve due to the self-perpetuating machine, which Noam Chomsky once referred to as Manufacturing Consent in which the society goes along with it s media that constantly feeds it illusions about it s condition and standing at home and abroad and never provides it with anything contradictory. Not to place the entire blame on the media, if negative or contradictory information were to be presented it is more likely that people would turn it off and find entertainment channels, sports channels or other news media that would support their concepts of self, culture, nation and religion. The media outlets have a vested interest in presenting what people want instead of what they need even though those people are like children who want candy and no vegetables, that steady diet of narcissistic misinformation will lead to corruption and the social, economic and political degradation of the society.

Those who hold the view, of the incapacity of such a society to change in a substantial and not just a superficial way, to the positive, might see a need for total collapse of the society in order for there to be even a chance for real and substantial change; a chance because, even after a complete collapse, those currently in power would seek to reconstruct a new society but with the same failed ideals that would eventually lead to the same corruptions. In other words, while there are other ideals those would not come into the political arena due to the self-deluded system of media and entertainment consumption and general ignorance about the nature of being and the lack of ethical conscience, all fomented and promoted by the leadership and accepted by the population at large.

PART II: PATHWAYS TO FREEDOM FROM HATE

DETACHMENT IS THE PATH TO LOVE, HAPPINESS AND ENLIGHTENMENT

The discipline of detachment is an important key to discovering freedom from hate and must be properly understood to be properly practiced. Most people shun the thought of spiritual detachment, feeling that anyone who promotes its practice is selfish and cold-hearted. This is due to the erroneous understanding of what detachment means. The practice of detachment is not a physical turning away from the world, but a psychological letting go of the world as the source of happiness and peace you are seeking. Instead, you mentally turn and go to drink the nectar of truth and peace (*hetep*) from the fountain of true happiness and peace, the Higher Self which is your innermost essence. You develop the understanding that the experience of happiness and peace is not a worldly attainment, but an inner attainment. Therefore instead of directing your attention to chasing after situations in life or objects of the world, including people, to feel happy, you now concentrate on practicing the spiritual disciplines which will allow you to cultivate this inner experience of abiding happiness; thus, having discovered the inner fount of happiness, one renders the need for external sources of fulfillment and the associated frustrations and hatreds that develop from those desires, nil.

Many people think they are to remove themselves from the world in order to attain the goal of this philosophy. In the practice of Sema-Yoga you are to go back into the world, but not to try to find happiness there and become frustrated and angry when it does not materialize, like you did before. There are several spiritual benefits to be derived from interacting with the world when one has some spiritual insight into the source of happiness and the purpose of life. It must be clearly understood that when spiritual teachings speak about attaining enlightenment, it is not talking about something that is to be achieved at the end of some long journey. Essentially enlightenment is the journey itself. Enlightenment means becoming a being who embodies compassion, patience, universal love for all, understanding, peace and who understands that he/she is essentially one with everything in creation, all existence. Like any other attainment in life, how can you achieve it if you don t practice it? You can read everything about being a doctor or a basket ball player or a gymnast, but if you do not practice these disciplines, you will never attain them. So, to develop compassion, you must practice being compassionate with others. To develop selflessness, you must go beyond selfishness and practice helping others selflessly. To develop patience, you must practice being patient. To develop the ability to love all, you must practice loving all. To become the embodiment of peace and bliss, you must practice being peaceful and blissful. To become free from the attachments of the world you must practice detachment. To become one with everything in creation, you must correctly understand what it means to be one with everything in creation and act like you are essentially one with everything in creation. What better place to practice these qualities but in the world with its varied situations and people with different levels of spiritual evolution. Each day you encounter people and situations which challenge you to be patient, loving, understanding, giving and to. through constantly experiencing disappointments, force you to remember that happiness and peace are not to be found in the world.

Situations challenge and test your level of spiritual attainment so as to promote the integration of your whole personality. And the greatest challenge is really an internal challenge, in dealing with yourself when you act in ways which promote the lower nature (anger, hatred, greed, impatience, lust, envy, jealousy, fear, etc.). If you cannot be compassionate, understanding, loving and patient with your very self, you are going to have difficulty being compassionate, understanding, loving and patient with others. So the world is really reflecting (exteriorizing) and amplifying your inner struggle. So the world does not give you inner (emotional) experience; it fulfills the inner experience you are already having. This is what is meant by the illusoriness of the world. You experience the outer world according to your inner experience. Haven t you noticed when you are internally upset and angry that you feel whatever occurs in your life during that time seems to be specifically there to frustrate you, personally, more. And likewise, when you feel great, nothing that occurs in the world frustrates you until the great feeling disappears. When people do not have this insight into the world they truly believe that the world is out to get them and feel like they are helpless victims. However, with deeper insight you can realize that the world is essentially always the same. There are always people who are going to praise you and people who are going to criticize you. There are always situations which will meet your expectations and situations which will drown your expectations. That is just the nature of the world. Some people like to reminisce and believe things were better back in the olden days, however, things were always just like this, though the specific circumstances may have been different. Even back then they encountered frustrations when they looked to the world for lasting happiness; otherwise they would be enlightened now. So, you cannot allow the outer world to control your inner experience, otherwise you will forever be on a roller coaster ride, one moment happy when things go your way, and the next moment unhappy when things do not go your way. Instead you need to work on cultivating your inner spiritual experience, in which may be found that for which you have been striving to attain through all your past worldly actions, true happiness and peace.

As your personality integrates and you more and more embody these spiritual qualities, you become a source of inspiration for others. In the beginning you may not be able to practice these virtuous qualities to a great extent, however, you must persist to the best of your capacity. When a seed is planted in the ground it does not become a big tree overnight and start to bear fruit. No, it starts off small as a tiny seedling which must be nurtured. The weeds must be plucked away from it to allow it space to grow. It takes a while to grow, but eventually it will attain its full maturity and bears fruit. Likewise if an aspirant practices these qualities faithfully and with perseverance, it is inevitable that he/she will attain them.

To some extent there is a physical turning away from the world which occurs with the practice of detachment, but it is positive and occurs because you no longer pursue those egoistic endeavors which you were pursuing because you thought they would make you happy. So you find that you have much more time to dedicate to your spiritual studies and practices. You no longer desire, for example, to go to bars and engage in other negative associations to find happiness or temporary escapes from the disappointments of the world. Instead you will find greater fulfillment in meaningful relationships, self-discovery pursuits and or spending your time helping others as individuals or humanity, in general ways, like, for example, making an invention that makes people s lives better or helping those who are less fortunate than you, by taking care of their basic needs by volunteering, or teaching them this kind of philosophy, which relieves stress and leads to true happiness and saves them from the karmic bond. You may decide to spend your time assisting in programs which help the homeless, AIDS patients, abused children, etc. To those people who had gotten used to you hanging out with them, engaging in negative (egoistic) acts, you may seem to be turning away from their world and they may even label you selfish for not wanting to spend time with them. However, turning away from projects that only indulge the ego and can never lead to true happiness and turning towards projects which open up your consciousness, promote the spiritual experience of happiness and peace and uplift humanity at the

154

same time are discovered as a higher path and thus can never be selfish as they are a great service to humanity. Therefore to properly practice spirituality and detachment you do not have to stop working and negate your practical duties in the world, but instead you perform all of those duties with greater sensitivity and wisdom, thus not only fulfilling your practical duties in the world as and employer or employee, father or mother, daughter or son, brother or sister, friend or acquaintance, but at the same time fulfilling your spiritual duty and purpose as well.

The sun is the embodiment of the quality of detachment. The sun knows nothing of differences. It knows nothing of good and evil people it shines on all alike. It is the embodiment of duty and righteousness. It performs its task of rising (duty) and shines on all (righteousness) giving them an opportunity to live and see their way. Some use that light to see what they want to see while others use it to see what there is to see. Some live in ignorance and delusion about the world even though they have the sunlight to see what occurs in the world while others, using the same light, pursue wisdom and reality behind the fleeting and frustrating objects and situations of life. Yet, the sun does not ask for anything in return for the service. An aspirant must do the same. One who aspires to attain this wisdom should strive to do their duty (service to humanity) in a selfless manner, not looking for rewards, not looking for attachments and not making distinctions between people and objects based on egoistic notions. If you were to practice this wisdom, it would eventually lead to enlightenment. You must make a choice, either to act out of egoism or to act in accordance with what is true. In this manner an aspirant cleanses the heart through action. This is known as the Sema-Yoga of Action, Maat Philosophy. The reduction of egoistic desires, attachments and hatreds will render the mind peaceful, serene and calm. This calmness will allow the vision of the Self Enlightenment, to emerge. A true teacher of high wisdom philosophy, such as that of ancient Egypt, is like the sun shining the light of wisdom on all alike for the sake of uplifting all humanity. The trouble of ignorance is a universal problem for humanity. Therefore, one objective of wisdom education is to uplift all humanity. This is the real desire of the inner most Self which is manifesting as the actions of the teacher and the desire of the aspirant.

This teaching is not to be understood as a morose outlook or a lack of dealing with the world. When you become more established in the Self and no longer depend on the world you can most effectively deal with the world, while experiencing abiding peace at all times. In fact, in order to achieve any greatness in life it is necessary to grow up, to transcend the world and then by example to lead others to a higher vision. A person who is impervious to censorship or praise cannot be perturbed or deterred from their goal. But a person who is dependent on praise and who is hurt by curses from others will never succeed because they will always be agitated, insecure and consequently compromised. For that kind of person there will always be a need to seek approval from the world. How powerful people could be if they did not allow their mental energy to be drained by attachments and desires for perishable and illusory things. Ironically, when a person truly succeeds in detaching from the world from an egoistic point of view, it is then that it becomes possible for them to truly love and serve others as well as profoundly enjoy life. This seems like a paradox but when there is a personal stake in something that one is attached to, this attachment clouds the intellect, and this cloud of delusion renders the mind dull and incapable of making the right [non-egoistic] decisions and choices in life or understanding the underlying nature of one s own existence. This mind will stoop to deception and outright scheming to get what is desired even if it hurts itself or others   all in the pursuit of happiness because it has little or no conception of the innermost reality or the existence of God within.

> "When opulence and extravagance are a necessity
> instead of righteousness and truth, society will be
> governed by greed and injustice."
> Ancient Egyptian Proverb

When there is ignorance and delusion in society, running after illusory pleasures and empty values, any and all forms of degradation can occur. Therefore, in order to eradicate the cause of degradation the negative values and actions must be eradicated. This leads to purity of heart. Animosity and conflict among people is a practical factor of life but this does not mean that an aspirant should allow him/her self to be affected by it internally. A person should do what is necessary to promote the well being and safety of their body and that of their family but always with the understanding of detachment derived from the teachings. The understanding must always be there that a higher power, manifesting through a person s *ariu* (karma), is in control and that the higher power (of the Higher Self) is allowing the world to proceed in its course for a purpose, to lead souls to attain enlightenment and realize their oneness with existence. Though, from an egoistic perspective, the world is seemingly filled with contradictions, from a spiritual point of view there are no contradictions, only the plan of *ariu* unfolding in accordance with the level of a person s ignorance or wisdom. An aspirant, one who aspires to learn, practice and succeed in this discipline, should work diligently to purify their heart (get rid of anger, hatred, jealousy, hypocrisy, vanity, pride, etc.) and in this way show the world how to live in peace and freedom from hatred.

CULTURAL EGO

Generally speaking, there are many groups in society that exemplify a highly developed cultural ego. From an ordinary perspective, the cultural ego, the identity within the larger body of humanity, serves the purpose of protecting the group and individuals from the negative elements of the outside world.

Let us look at the difference between a powerful culture and a weak culture of the world today. It would be hard to imagine Hollywood putting out movies which depict Jehovah or Allah to be an ancient evil alien who makes slaves out of human beings. This is an effect of the Jewish and Islamic ego that would protest such depictions and produce major social disruptions in the society. In other words, the respect for the power of the Jewish culture prevents such depictions. Yet, this theme was used in a movie called Stargate, where the Egyptian (African) God *Ra* was portrayed as described above. The movie was shown without significant protest by the Africans or the African American community who have the most to lose by the denigration of one of the most important symbols of African myth and mystical philosophy. Their ignorance as to the true origins of Ra and the importance of his teachings has allowed this ridiculous movie to be created and disseminated and even further developed into a long running television show. Another recent movie was The Mummy, in which the most revered saint of Ancient Egypt was portrayed as an evil murdering monster.

What happened to the cultural ego of people of African descent? Why do groups of African people, not cry out for justice at all times until the message is heard loud and clear in their own communities and the world at large and then take whatever action is necessary, as other groups would, to redress the wrong that was done? Many people feel that slavery happened long ago and that people should move on. This is like saying that a person was raped when he or she was a child but now that they are grown up the whole situation should be forgotten and the person should move on as if nothing happened. While from a deeper spiritual perspective this is what must happen eventually, once the lessons from the issues created by the negative experiences are resolved, on a societal level the entire situation must be dealt with and healed before there can be real progress, otherwise, there will always be some simmering animosity, ignorance and anger in people. In the Jewish culture there is cohesion and vigilance as to what can happen when voices in the community project denigrative ideas about Jewish culture; that lesson was finally learned when the aristocracies and oligarchies of Europe, and finally the Nazis, started the verbal attacks against Jews leading to hatred and violence against them. Now, the vigilance is followed by active lobbies working in politics, the courts, economics and the media to denounce any denigrative or disparaging statements or images against the Jewish culture. Is this because the Jews, as a culture, remember their holocaust and are determined not to allow it to happen again? Indeed, and to this extent we may consider the Jewish cultural ego to be healthy, but what of the African American cultural ego? Where is the cultural cohesion, the economic and political clout and the media savvy to present a powerful outcry, and counteract the negative, denigrative or disparaging statements or images against the African or African American culture? Where is the collective outrage and remembrance of the African holocaust that was, by any measure, more devastating than any other in the last 500 years and where is the determination to stop it and not allow it again, through the use of powerful social institutions? One who is truly righteous will not only cry out for justice when members of their own culture or ethnic group are treated unjustly, but whenever any human being is treated unfairly. Whenever anyone is discriminated against, every righteous person should protest and then take action to stop the injustice. This is the essence of Maat philosophy, the practice and upholding of truth, righteousness and justice for all.

The crying out for justice should not be taken to mean an egoistic you did this to me and now you must suffer and pay, etc. If a Sage advocates crying out for justice it is to uphold righteousness, truth and justice in a spirit of forgiveness and asserting strength in the community to prevent anyone from entering into the delusion which allows injustice to occur. The duty of spiritually advancing personalities is to continually reassert the truth and show others how to live it, and what to do about it, as done by luminaries such as Mahatma Gandhi, Dr. Martin Luther King, Malcolm X, Nelson Mandela and others.

Communities can be useful to the extent that they provide a place for people to grow, be nurtured by society and then be given an opportunity to explore their spiritual essence. This is the true purpose of society. However, if society is seen as a tool to maintain a racial identity, a religious identity or as a means for some groups to come together to further their own egoistic schemes, the higher purpose is being degraded. So while several groups have improved in one area, to protect themselves from injustices, they have degraded themselves by promoting their own segregation and advocating violence as a means to political objectives instead of righteousness, justice, forgiveness and sharing as a means to promote understanding and peace. They become egoistic communities which have instituted mechanisms to support racial and/or religious identities that keep them segregated from the larger body of humanity.

Since the soul of every human being is innately divine, it shares in the power of the Higher Self which is the greatest force on earth. To the extent that a person taps into that power and wisdom they are able to succeed in the challenges of life. To the extent that they move away from their higher nature they enter into egoism, and the negativity of the mind and body (anger, hatred, greed, selfishness, hoarding, jealousy, violence, etc.).

When people talk of becoming part of a society that promotes materialism they are in effect trying to become part of the mechanism which sees distinctions and promotes injustice, egoism, desire, hatred and greed in the world in the name of pursuit of happiness because the eventual outcome of materialism is segregation of concepts, customs, peoples, religions, philosophies, economies and cultures. So what should people want? It is all right to strive to have communities, but not closed communities. They should be open to the understanding of the underlying oneness of all human beings and this will allow them to treat themselves and others with respect, dignity and peace. How can people learn about each other and interact properly if they remain closed to each other out of fear and resentment and hoard resources needed by everyone? In ethical culture, hoarding wealth and other resources is considered to be the same as stealing, because you have essentially taken resources away from others who could be using it to subsist and maintain their well being. The selfishness of one group causes another to experience wants, disease, malnutrition and hunger, which causes more deaths than military terrorism. For example, if humanity changed from a capitalist system to globalism, the disparity between rich nations and poor nations would cease to exist. If humanity turned towards a vegetarian diet there would be no famine and no global climate change. But the selfishness, and avarice blinded hearts of those who [leaders and their supporters/followers] wish to keep the status quo, perpetuate and thus are complicit in the negative condition of humanity.

Hunger mortality statistics

- 1 person dies every second as a result of hunger - 4000 every hour - 100 000 each day - 36 million each year - 58 % of all deaths (2001-2004 estimates).[74]

---

[74] • ^ Jean Ziegler. The Right to Food: Report by the Special Rapporteur on the Right to Food, Mr. Jean Ziegler, Submitted in Accordance with Commission on Human Rights Resolution 2000/10 . United Nations, February 7, 2001, p. 5. On average, 62 million people die each year, of whom probably 36 million (58 per cent) directly or indirectly as a result of nutritional deficiencies, infections, epidemics or diseases which attack the body when its resistance and immunity have been weakened by undernourishment and hunger. .

• ^ Commission on Human Rights. The right to food : Commission on Human Rights resolution 2002/25 . Office Of The High Commissioner For Human Rights, United Nations, April 22, 2002, p. 2. every year 36 million people die, directly or indirectly, as a result of hunger and nutritional deficiencies, most of them women and children, particularly in developing countries, in a world that already produces enough food to feed the whole global population .

• United Nations Information Service. Independent Expert On Effects Of Structural Adjustment, Special Rapporteur On Right To Food Present Reports: Commission Continues General Debate On

- 1 child dies every 5 seconds as a result of hunger - 700 every hour - 16 000 each day - 6 million each year - 60% of all child deaths (2002-2008 estimates).[75]

How can people coexist equitably, respectfully, peacefully with or learn anything from others if they feel they are superior to others or have superior knowledge, technology or ability? Vanity and pride in all its forms is an extreme example of spiritual ignorance and weakness in character. As a human being you are part of the world, and if you hold back from sharing with the world you will deprive yourself and the world from experiencing spiritual expansion, and others from experiencing the human understanding and compassion which operate through all living beings in the form of understanding, compassion and caring. So if you suffer from the disease of egoism you need to practice the teachings of Sema-Yoga. You need to practice selfless service to humanity, study of the teachings, seeing God in other human beings, developing your inner gifts (joy, wisdom, encouragement, etc.), humility, and sharing these with others.

Economic, Social And Cultural Rights . United Nations, March 29, 2004, p. 6. Around 36 million people died from hunger directly or indirectly every year. .

[75] • Food and Agriculture Organization Staff. The State of Food Insecurity in the World, 2002: Food Insecurity : when People Live with Hunger and Fear Starvation . Food and Agriculture Organization of the United Nations, 2002, p. 6. 6 million children under the age of five, die each year as a result of hunger.

• Food and Agriculture Organization of the United Nations Economic and Social Dept. The State of Food Insecurity in the World 2004: Monitoring Progress Towards the World Food Summit and Millennium Development Goals . Food and Agriculture Organization of the United Nations, 2004, p. 8. Undernourishment and deficiencies in essential vitamins and minerals cost more than 5 million children their lives every year .

• Jacques Diouf. The State of Food Insecurity in the World 2004: Monitoring Progress Towards the World Food Summit and Millennium Development Goals . Food and Agriculture Organization of the United Nations, 2004, p. 4. one child dies every ve seconds as a result of hunger and malnutrition .

• Food and Agriculture Organization, Economic and Social Dept. The State of Food Insecurity in the World 2005: Eradicating World Hunger - Key to Achieving the Millennium Development Goals . Food and Agriculture Organization of the United Nations, 2005, p. 18. Hunger and malnutrition are the underlying cause of more than half of all child deaths, killing nearly 6 million children each year a figure that is roughly equivalent to the entire preschool population of Japan. Relatively few of these children die of starvation. The vast majority are killed by neonatal disorders and a handful of treatable infectious diseases, including diarrhoea, pneumonia, malaria and measles. Most would not die if their bodies and immune systems had not been weakened by hunger and malnutrition moderately to severely underweight, the risk of death is five to eight times higher. .

• Human Rights Council. Resolution 7/14. The right to food . United Nations, March 27, 2008, p. 3. 6 million children still die every year from hunger-related illness before their fifth birthday .

THE RIDDLE OF SOCIETY

What is the purpose of society? Think of a child who performs evil[76] deeds and is rude, disrespectful, selfish, etc. Most ordinary people would look at them and say that they are obviously receiving poor upbringing, that their parents are not doing a good job. Yet, why is it that when this child grows up people forget about the upbringing and see the person as evil or no good? All human beings have an innate goodness, because all of them come from the Self (God). This is why no group of people is all bad or all good. If they receive poor upbringing it is no surprise that they will tend to fall into negative company, ideas, desires, etc. They will fall prey to their lower nature. However, it is important to understand that just as a child needs proper upbringing, so do the masses of humanity. The leaders of society are like parents to society. If the leaders are promoting materialism, the lower desires and egoism, what can be expected of the ordinary person in society who does not know any better? The problem in modern society, which leads and promotes society to support unrighteousness in government, commerce and social organizations, is that the leadership is politically unethical and non-secular (without higher spiritual principles) and its goals promote power, greed and egoism. What is needed is leadership that is well-versed in high wisdom philosophy along with political science and economics. In a society where the leaders would follow the high wisdom philosophy, all people would be treated with respect and the resources of the world would be shared in such a way that people would not resent others or suffer the degradation of poverty which leads to despair and anguish leading to hatred and violence. This was the reason for the quality and longevity of Ancient Egypt. The leaders of society, the judges, teachers, doctors, warriors, etc., were experts in their area and also knowledgeable in the *Shetaut Neter* (Ancient Egyptian Religion). This is why the society lasted for **thousands** of years unlike others that based their society on greed, anger, hatred, desire, attachment and all other forms of egoism. The Ancient Egyptians recognized the unity underlying all humanity, and so they allowed peoples from all over the ancient world (Middle East [Asia Minor], Europe, India) to attend their universities (temples) and to study all subjects (secular and non-secular) so that they might bring the light of wisdom and civilization back to their own lands.

Generally speaking, human beings are organized in society so that they grow up within cultures where they are taught, directly (consciously) or indirectly (through unconscious impressions they pick up) about life and their relationship to society and the world. Ideally a

---

[76] For the purpose of this essay we may define evil as purposeful wrongdoing .

161

person should be shown how to relate to himself/herself as well as his/her parents, family, society, the world and spirituality. In modern culture, it is oftentimes society that teaches children who they are supposed to be. This information is usually carried on from generation to generation in such a manner that from the time of infancy the individual is bombarded with ideas from society [socialization]. These ideas are then reinforced by the immediate family or social groups who themselves have given into the beliefs of society at large, regardless of if those beliefs are rational, but also regardless of if those beliefs are denigrating or flattering to their own culture, other cultures, or humanity in general. In an ordinary society, which does not promote spiritual principles, the child learns that he or she is an individual human being, separate and distinct from others, and that he/she is part of a particular culture, group, country and nation in the world. Often, advanced spiritual matters are discussed superficially or not at all due to the ignorance of the leaders. When spiritual matters are discussed it is often in a perverted environment led by demagogues or an environment of ignorance, without the benefit of advanced guidance like that which could have been provided by sages. In the degraded environment the contextual focus is on discovering ways to attain the goals which society values highly: fame, fortune and all manner of sensual pleasures.

Those involved in the various psychological disciplines are well aware that if someone is repeatedly told information about themselves and their history, they will eventually begin to believe it. This is especially true the younger the person is, when the indoctrination begins and if the person does not have parents to rear them in their own culture. Therefore, if one grows up in a particular environment which espouses particular points of view, then the individual will tend to believe those points of view, and also support and defend them as well. This process is compounded and toughened if the negativity was reinforced in a previous lifetime as well.

If the society believes that it is superior or inferior to others, these ideas will be transferred to the individual through the process of social conditioning, childrearing, schooling, peer pressure, statements and actions from the leaders of society (in government, commerce and religion). At some point though, the individual develops an intellectual ability to rise above the pressure of society and to hold onto an elevating way of thought. She or he can begin to search for answers to questions which are deeply rooted in their mind, questions which relate to their very existence and to the condition of the world. They search for ways of understanding and coping with life. However, if the intellect is atrophied due to a life of pleasure-seeking, mental agitations and futile unfulfilled desires, the process of searching for answers to the important questions of life will be postponed and the life of that person will be degraded.

The wisdom ways include philosophies and ethical cultures that allow the individual to feel self-respect for him/her self. Once this process of ethical maturity begins, it is possible for the individual to develop a self-reliant ego structure which is interested in self-preservation and freedom, at first as an individual and then thinking globally, understanding that freedom is the highest goal of life and that, from a social/political/economic perspective, there is no abiding freedom for anyone if there is bondage somewhere in the world. At this stage the individual should be able to start looking inwards to the important spiritual questions of life. However, if the focus on self is distorted (egoistic), the individual becomes selfish and egoistic, providing for and seeking to satisfy him/herself alone (fancies of the mind and physical pleasures). Here feelings of attachment, desire, separation and segregation develop, wherein the individual clings to his/her individuality as a racial , ethnic or social member of a group and from this base seeks to include or exclude others. Feelings of intense emotions such as hatred, greed, lust, insecurity, and fear develop out of the ignorance of the deeper meaning of life, giving rise to racism, ethnophobia, sexism, capitalism, etc.

Ignorant of a higher form of thought, the individual identifies him/her self with the world and its apparent realities often without questioning or understanding them. The ignorance is sustained by desire and lack of reflection; desires and degraded feelings (based on ignorance of the Higher Self) cloud the intellect and lead to negative emotions that promote more worldliness, as part of the cycle of vice. In this manner institutionalized social systems that enforce injustice, social discrimination and materialism become perpetuated by robot-like human beings who do not have the capacity to think independently or act in accordance with reason, reality, facts or a higher purpose as they are led by ignorance, negative feelings and worldly delusions. This is the fate of the soul over many lifetimes until the individual is ready to perceive a higher reality, that is, a higher understanding of the deeper essence of him/herself. The higher form of thinking leads to true freedom and spiritual enlightenment which means going beyond an exclusive interest in individual concerns for well-being as a physical personality, but also emancipation from mental and spiritual slavery. Physical slavery relates to the antiquated ideas of society which label the individual and limit his/her opportunities. Mental and spiritual slavery is allowing those ideas to cramp the mental ability to perceive and pursue freedom to achieve worthy worldly goals and promote spiritual expansion in life.

The collective ego of society is useful and beneficial to humanity if it serves the purpose of uplifting its members through the higher ideals and values of life (truth, righteousness, honesty, compassion, benevolence, forgiveness and universal caring, understanding and love). However, if the power of society is used to control and exploit others, that society inevitably suffers the negative destiny it brings upon itself, due to it s actions, just as individuals bring a certain destiny upon themselves due to their actions. The seeds of unrighteousness which are sown will bring forth the fruit of unrighteousness, and that society will suffer from corruption and violence as well as many other social maladies. Anger, hatred and greed will flourish in society. Instead of doctors working to promote the health of their patients, they will persuade their patients to undergo surgeries they do not need just so the doctors could make more money. Even though certain products in society are documented as being harmful, either to the individual or the earth, these products will continue to be produced in society. A minority of such a society s members will hoard the majority of society s wealth, some of them gaining their money through overt unrighteous actions but all gaining inordinate wealth at the expense of other members of society. Very few of them are willing to assist those member s of society who exist in poverty. Mostly, they look down on the have-nots of their society as ignorant, lazy, drug-addicted leeches. Not realizing their own negativity, through their own complicity in creating and perpetuating the conditions in which lower income members of the society live, and the inherently violent nature of their greed, they are quick to condemn the violence of others, projecting upon them the transgressions that they themselves are, in great measure, responsible for.

Most advanced religious and spiritual traditions promote the values of non-stealing and non-covetousness, however these practices are not really understood or heeded by the majority of their members. Most people feel that stealing would be bold-facedly taking something from someone which did not belong to you. Nevertheless, a competing philosophy also exists, *caveat emptor* or buyer beware which may be extended to include any transaction. In the *caveat emptor* value system if one person can steal from another it is alright to take something (steal) as long as the person succeeds and does not get caught; in fact, it is not stealing, but just taking. Further, if a person (the owner of the object) can prevent the thief from stealing, then the owner won the struggle. This value system is predicated upon the idea that taking things that belong to others is a legitimate aspect human activity. Legitimate areas of human activity are those areas that have been agreed to by the society at large and promote the well being and integrity of society and do not cause pain, disease, stress or degradation.

Most people understand that coveting as desiring for something which another person has. However, the deeper, subtler philosophical implications of stealing and coveting are basically the same. They both refer to the hoarding of society s wealth and resources beyond that which one person needs for their personal use. When member s of society hoard, they are in effect stealing that which is needed by other members of society, because if they have resources tucked away somewhere, no one else can use them. They may not think that they are acting violently, but they are. Their greed forces others to do without, which causes stress and suffering, just like a robbery or burglary; sometimes they have to do without even the basic necessities of life. How does this happen? If there is a set money supply and the rich take most of it then there is less for the rest of the population, for their municipal services, medical services and to fulfill their personal desires. This is exactly what has happened in the last 30 years; the gap has become larger between the rich and poor because the rich have appropriated most of the income of the country. In other words, the income of the rich has gone up while the income of the rest has stayed relatively the same or has been reduced. The rich are acting out of their deep rooted violent impressions such as it is you against me, and me against the world or I got mine, you get yours . In addition, their hoarding of resources promotes violence in society. They are not upholding the spiritual as this foments competition among the masses for the limited resources that are left over, and as a result all affected by this problem are acquiring negative ethical unconscious mental impressions [negative *ariu*] for which they will pay the price as they live life, after they die and or in future lifetimes.

They do not realize that they too are here for the purpose of spiritual enlightenment, which in effect means, on a human level, becoming a caring, unselfish, loving, compassionate human being, and are not here to become rich and powerful so as to experience sense pleasures and also look down on other people [inflate he ego]. The people who are in destitute situations are not there simply to be stepped over, but are in the world, in part, to provide the rich and powerful with the opportunity to grow spiritually by showing caring and compassion, the height of which is sharing, protecting and helping them to meet their needs. So when they shun these people, they are in effect shunning their own Higher Self. Like the individual, if a society acts with vanity and injustice they will invite the condemnation from others and will suffer the consequences of their actions in time.

Most religions and ethical philosophies promote virtue and the folly of greed but from a practical perspective, the society, supported by religious, governmental institutions, political parties and commercial interests value greed sanitized with the hypocrisy of philanthropy. The rich are supposed to give to the poor, which makes them feel good about themselves and makes the country look generous; all of which maintains a fiction of altruism and righteousness. However, there would be no need for philanthropy if societies dealt with their populations and between each other in an equitable and just manner, sharing resources and technological advancements to make life better.

EVIL EXISTS BECAUSE THE MIND IS WEAK

Those who see only the human personality of others are only seeing the superficial nature, the ego (psycho-physical personality) and not the inner Self of that person. A person who only sees the exterior aspect of life is still caught in the ignorant ideas of self and other and about good and evil and usually sees him/herself as good and right while seeing others as bad or wrong. Yet they themselves will also do evil and not see it as such. People who do not commit crimes still support evil when they allow negativity to go on without impunity. Most people profess to be against violence and yet they support violence against groups within their own country or other countries when their government takes political, economic or military actions against others under the guise of altruistic or necessary actions or policies usually described euphemistically in statements such as to protect our way of life or we must defend our national interests. Those statements are in reality describing actions against other people that oppose the domination and exploitation that renders their economies weak and their populations susceptible to mistreatment and abuses that allow one country to be rich and the other poor. Violence in sports, television and the entertainment media promote a culture of intellectual dullness, stress and physical force of the strong over the weak as this inflates the ego and base feelings. When a person advocates violence such as meat eating (slaughtering animals), denigration of others by upholding stereotypes, intensification of the lower desires and pleasure-seeking, they are in reality supporting the mechanism that promotes ignorance, desire, greed, attachment, anger, hatred and violence in society. How is this possible? All of the egoistic pursuits outlined above weaken the mind and intensify the lower tendencies. This process intensifies the ego and reduces the capacity for rationality, reflectiveness, harmony, inner peace, forgiveness and compassion while increasing the capacity for emotionality, anger, hatred and greed which can manifest as callousness, apathy, misunderstanding, unsympathetic-ness, callousness, and even disdain when it comes to the well-being of others leading to cruelty towards others. Irrationality due to ignorance of the knowledge of Self leads to undue emotionality,[77] anger, hatred and greed that lead to further hatred and violence.

When a person feels misery because of what another has done to them or ascribes power to some group and feels powerless or stepped on, they are in reality displaying their ignorance as well as their lack of faith. They are ignorant as to the nature of Creation and to the existence of the

---

[77] emotions are defined here as the expression of inner feelings. Thus, normal emotionality is not to be confused with undue emotionality that expresses egoism, ignorance, sentimentality and other forms of feelings due to caring about incorrect things, things opposed by the wisdom teachings.

empowered Higher Self. They are fighting the world as individuals and as such they are in reality upset about their inability to acquire the objects and situations they feel will provide for their own happiness. This is egoism. If one is truly selfless and understands what it means to have insight, one would know that God [the Goddess, the Higher Self, the Universal Spirit, The Absolute, cosmic consciousness, etc.] is the true ruling factor in Creation and not some trilateral commission, government official, new world order, etc. In essence one is worshipping worldly people, objects and situations, placing these on pedestals instead of having faith in the Divine and in one s own spiritual gifts through inner spiritual awakening. In the higher perspective, the discovery of the Higher Self is the only really worthy goal in life since all else, including the social status, ethnicity, racial identities, political power, etc. as well as the distinctions of the body [male/female, black / white etc.] are perishable as all worldly life comes to an end.

When worldly objects and people are revered as powerful or when a person is worshipped, even with negative worship such as hate, one is in reality practicing idolatry, a negative spiritual movement which leads to worldly entanglements, stress and strain and away from the Higher Self, justice, harmony and peace. Believing that you are a victim of other people s actions, past or present, is like having a dream in which you are being chased by someone with a knife and saying that the person with the knife running after you in your dream is more powerful than you who are lying in bed having the dream. At any time you could wake up and realize you are perfectly safe, and escape from the entire dream, but instead you choose to become involved in the dream and the dream character. You begin to ask yourself, How can I escape? and Can I do something to hurt this person chasing me? Yet, the you in the dream and the person chasing you in the dream both came from your own consciousness. So, although no one is really chasing you, you become afraid. Similarly, this world is the Divine Self s dream and all personalities are essentially emanations of the Divine Self s consciousness. In reality, no one is persecuting you. You are essentially persecuting yourself by your negative belief system based on ignorance, manifesting as negative thoughts and actions. You can keep focusing and blaming others for your situation in your dream or you can wake up. This is what Sema-Yoga urges you to do, to wake up. What are you waking up from and to? You are waking up from your own egoistic desires which promote egoistic qualities in your personality (separation, differences, dualistic thinking, anger, hate, impatience, greed, envy, fear, etc.) to the desire for realizing your Higher Self (enlightenment) which promotes your embodying the spiritual qualities such as being peaceful, compassionate, loving, understanding, detached, dispassionate, equanimity [undisturbed by praise or censure] etc., by constantly practicing these disciplines in daily life.

Otherwise you are living like the personality in the dream who is running away from the person with the knife thinking that there is no escape. The running away from things out of fear, dealing with situations with anger and hatred, and the running towards things because of attachment lead a person to experience mental constriction and stress. All of these are due to misunderstanding and weakness of will. Agitation leads to mental distraction, forgetfulness, intellectual dullness and delusion. The higher reality, the knowledge that this life and the phenomenal world is like a dream, is lost by a person in favor of the egoism in them which accepts the dream with it s struggles, stresses and sorrows as the only reality. Thus, a person is caught in the situation of the dream (life), experiences brief periods of happiness when something they like happens or experiencing fear, anger and sorrow when something they do not like happens. The answer is to wake up from the dream of life, to mentally go beyond anything that can happen or not happen.

The process of waking up has been outlined in the various texts of Sema-Yoga from the time of the Ancient Egyptians. The problem is who will make themselves a qualified aspirant by preparing themselves to listen to, study and practice the teachings? Who will purify their heart by eradicating the negative qualities of the mind (anger, hatred, greed, etc.). Who will seek out an authentic wisdom teacher and take the steps which are necessary to study the teachings and then apply them in life? Who is ready to let go of human limitations and to grow into the peace and power of their true nature?

"To free the spirit, control the senses; the reward will be a clear insight."
Ancient Egyptian Proverb

A world renowned Indian Yoga spiritual master, once initiated a spiritual aspirant, who happened to be of African American descent, into the Indian order of Sanyasa (Swami monastic order based on renunciation of egoism). One day the aspirant came to him and told him that she was having trouble with life due to some issues related to racism . He told her that if she was not ready to renounce the world, that she should go back and be African American, but that when she is finished with that, she should then return to resume her spiritual practice.

He did not mean that she should forget she was African American, even after she would come back, but that she should renounce that as an exclusive identification preventing her from discovering her higher identity. In other words, black as a skin color identity, is, like brown or white or other color identifications, only related an illusory distinction; so it is not appropriate for someone who is seeking higher wisdom about the deeper aspects of human existence. Similar instruction would be given to an aspirant of Indian descent. So, this is not to say that racism and racial issues do not exist in the world or that they are not realities that affect life or that need to be confronted. It means that these issues are part of the world and exist due to ignorance on the part of those who perpetrate them and these socio/political issues cannot be allowed to stand in the way of higher spiritual evolution, discover what you are beyond your gender, race , ethnicity, nationality, etc. In fact the person who attains higher spiritual evolution will be better equipped to handle racial issues and work with those who are affected by it [perpetrators and victims] to promote real resolutions to the problem. It is important for all groups of people to understand the causes of hatred and disharmony well. Martin Luther King understood them. Malcolm X did also at the end of his life. What did Martin Luther King mean when he said he had been to the mountain top? What transformation occurred to Malcolm X upon his visit to Africa, Mecca and Egypt? Once he achieved higher wisdom, Mahatma Gandhi advocated for the freedom of all peoples and not just Indians; he also never advocated violence against the British who brutalized, enslaved and raped the Indian people for decades because he knew that the answer to hatred is not hatred but forgiveness, understanding, righteousness, education and love. The concept of non-violence, which first appears in the Wisdom Texts of Ancient Egypt, advocated the same teaching that was recently reiterated by King, Gandhi, Nelson Mandela and others. Yet, in order to be successful the strategy of non-violence needs to be universally practiced by the masses but with wise strategy to implement policies in a political arena. King was killed not before more than a decade of civil-rights protest but when he started a shift towards economic justice and political action. Non-violence is not just for marches or demonstrations unless these are on the way to the halls of government, with the intent to vote in wise leaders and just laws to protect the rights of everyone or if needed, to stop injustices, with civil disobedience. All must be prepared to work towards this end so that even if the head of an organization were targeted, the movement would be unstoppable.

It is also important to understand that tolerance is not the same as understanding. If you only tolerate people you have not practiced Sema-Yoga philosophy to the fullest. You can abstain from doing violence openly and still harbor it internally. This way of life allows a person to delude themselves, thinking they have evolved beyond racism or hatred but in reality they continue to be plagued by those scourges of humanity and their family and progeny will be similarly affected. This will still bring agitation to the mind, just as if you had acted out the violence in the physical world. When you understand the limitations and ignorance in your own past you can understand that of others, so learn to forgive yourself and them and be free of all internal animosity. Further, just by acting righteously you can help them to overcome their problem. The problem of racism is not only the problem of those who are practicing racism. It is the problem of humanity. It is the problem of every person who advocates truth, righteousness and justice. The problem of hate affects the hater as well as the hated. This entire situation is created by nature to allow souls to work out their spiritual evolution and to lead themselves to rise above anger, hatred, greed, etc., and attain enlightenment. The problem of hatred is not the hater or the hated but hate itself.

The Past, the Present, Hate and the Illusion of Body Awareness

Think of all of the past instances of racism in the history of humanity before the African slave trade. When the Aryans invaded India (1500 B.C.E.) they subjugated the indigenous people of African descent there. What would the Indian Sages have told the people and what would they have told the spiritual aspirants back then? When the Muslims invaded India (1200 A.C.E.) and imposed Islam, there what would the Indian Sages have told the people and what would the Sages have told the spiritual aspirants? They said the same thing any truly enlightened teacher would, that all evil comes into humanity due to ignorance, and that action should be taken to oppose the unrighteousness, not by retaliation in anger or revenge, but through steady righteousness (acting out of correctness and duty instead of egoism) will prevail in the end. Look at history; when has righteousness not prevailed in the past? People lose sight of this when they get caught up in the pain and emotions of the experiences that lead to the sustained anger and hatred that foments the pursuit of revenge which maintains the cycle of hate. What happened to all those people who were discriminated against hundreds or thousands of years ago? According to the philosophy of reincarnation, their bodies have passed on into the devouring abyss of time. But their souls have reincarnated into the present in order to work out the issues which keep the soul searching for peace. Beyond the individual, the society carries on the wounds of past violence, the trauma of those who were hurt or killed, and the trauma of those who perpetrated the hurting and killing; this is especially true of war, where the scars on the perpetrators last for the rest of their lives in the form of physical disabilities, and or mental illnesses like *Post Traumatic Stress Disorder.* A spiritual aspirant needs to recognize that human life is transient and that what seems so important at present will become little in time, a footnote in history and eventually it will be forgotten. So what is really important in life? Enlightenment is the only important aspect of life and **NOTHING** else: waking up from the dream of the world process.

This world and all of the embodiment possibilities (Chinese, European, African, Asian, etc.) in it have been prepared to provide each soul the varied experiences it needs for its evolution towards attaining enlightenment. How would you feel if you were to see your previous embodiments as a European man, a Chinese woman, a Native American man, a Hebrew woman or an Ancient Egyptian man? It would shock you out of your attachment to your present personality as well as the ideas in reference to personalities of others and the fallacy of gender, ethnicity and their related social, and political complications. You would realize that the body is just a vehicle for the soul. Just as in your life you may once have owned a red car, then perhaps you sold it and bought a car of another color, similarly, the soul incarnates in different colored bodies. Each incarnation offers different experiences, to allow the individual consciousness of a human being to expand beyond the confines of identification with one sex or one culture or ethnicity. If people were to have this experience, it would pull the rug from under the notion of racial identities and the ignorant pride and vanity by which most people live. This is the reality but people negate this teaching due to ignorance, delusion and lack of reflectiveness and philosophical inquiry. They are more interested in pursuing worldly goals rather than unraveling the mysteries of life. So they get caught up in the snares of their own desires and the disappointments and frustrations of their own egoistic pursuits.

Human beings have been given all the tools they need; all the experiences they have gone through and will go through have been inspired to lead them to attain enlightenment. Whatever the color of one s skin and the experiences one has been through related to the ethnicity of one s body, it was what one needed at the time to grow towards discovery of the Higher Self. Now that you are reading this book, you have come to a level of maturity in life where you know deep down that you need to move beyond body identification to identify with your true human and spiritual essence which encompasses all humanity. This is your only purpose of life, and as it has been said, You cannot serve two masters. You cannot be a higher being whose essence is universal and also belong to a specific gender and or ethnic group, nationality, class, etc. On a practical basis you may acknowledge the association that your body has with a specific ethnic group, but internally you know this is not your true and ultimate identity. Identifying with a specific ethnic group would be like identifying with your car. It would be like calling yourself red because your car is red, and a Toyota because your car is a Toyota. That would be ridiculous. Likewise, from a higher perspective, identifying yourself solely with the color and make (cultural/ethnic ancestry) of your body is actually equally ridiculous. Your body is merely a vehicle for the soul on its journey to attain enlightenment. Just as you take care of your car because you expect it to take you someplace important, you should take care of the body, but not identify with it as the only essence of who you are. However, for practical purposes (to function in the practical world) you could say that you have a red Toyota, knowing that you are not your red Toyota. Likewise, for practical purposes you may find it necessary to recognize and describe the color of your skin and the cultural ancestry of your personality for the purpose of interacting with others who operate on that level (viewing other personalities in terms of their race and or ethnicity), however, you should not really feel that you are describing the real you or the only aspect of you and definitely not the essential nature of who you are but rather, only a description of what you are, or more accurately, what you are manifesting as right now. It is in this way that a sage allows him/her self to be identified with a particular ethnicity or culture. At all times the sage knows he/she is beyond both ethnicity and culture, yet he/she allows him/herself to be identified with his/her birth culture and ethnicity because this serves to inspire people of that culture and ethnicity to grow beyond their egoistic identifications into truly human wisdom and spiritual enlightenment. People who have not yet opened themselves up to envision the universality of all creation are usually initially more receptive to someone they can identify with at the physical level. So sages are born into cultures and are members of varied ethnic groups. Yet, they do not limit themselves to only inspiring those who belong to their own birth culture and ethnicity. In their speeches, writings and other communications they espouse this same universal view of humanity and if they were in each other s company they would not need to espouse cultural or ethnic distinctions. Their inspiration is universal, affecting all people of all cultures and ethnicities who are sensitive enough to receive the teachings.

There is ample documentation to prove that reincarnation is a reality experienced by the soul; so why do most people refuse to believe it? Because this would mean giving up the illusions and attachments of life. Weakness, due to mental agitation, and the reduced capacity for serious thought, due to a life based on believing in self-serving cultural and egoistic ideals, running after desires and cravings, reinforces spiritual ignorance, human suffering and animosity. Therefore, the eradication of egoism and spiritual ignorance should be the true target of everyone s efforts if they want to promote peace and fulfillment in life.

Just as activities in one corner of the world have repercussions in the rest of the world, the actions of an individual have repercussions for all humanity. Those who want to improve human relations need to work on relieving the underlying cause of hatred in themselves, ignorance of their true nature. Only then will they have the higher positive effect on their community and the world at large. Nothing will be more effective in eradicating violence and injustice than removing ignorance and all of its ramifications in your own heart. One who aspires to high wisdom must begin by removing egoistic desire, attachments, expectations and greed from their own heart. Then they will be examples for others to follow and they will be able to show others how to live as human beings instead of as animals led by their lower instincts, desires, cravings and ignorance. Thus, the answer to hatred among people is the same answer to the question of how to end human misery of any kind, to eradicate ignorance and promote the teachings and way of life which leads to health, wisdom and enlightenment. Sema-Yoga is the science of discovering the mysteries of life and of transcending all obstacles and all limitations which separate a human being from the Higher Self, the source of all that is true, beautiful and good.

Most people who do not practice Sema-Yoga cannot control the clamoring thoughts of the mind and because of this, do not experience inner peace or clarity of purpose in life or the underlying unity that binds all humanity and is the higher experience that allows a person not only to intellectualize about the unity of humanity but also feel it and thereby truly act and cause others to act in accordance with this higher human principle when interacting with each other. Others, beset by intensely negative thoughts succumb to these and commit acts against their conscience and suffer the consequences of a self-defeating way of life wherein painful situations and disappointments in life are increased while happiness and contentment are decreased, producing hellish conditions not only after death but even while a person lives. The mind is weakened due to the mental energy being tied up in useless endeavors which only serve to further entangle one in neurotic relationships, desires and expectations that lead to frustration and more unrest. The most important cause for the weakening will-power is the susceptibility to negative emotions, thoughts and feelings, which are, again, due to the underlying ignorance about the true nature of life. Negative emotions such as anger, hatred, greed, gloom, sorrow, and depression as well as excessive, inordinate positive emotions such as elation serve to create mental agitation and desire which in turn drain the mental energy and cloud the intellectual capacity to make correct decisions in life. Therefore, spiritual life is directed at living a balanced life, in accordance with the wisdom teaching, taking care to refrain from extremes of any kind.

WHAT IS FORGIVENESS?

From a Sema-Yogic point of view forgiveness is a highly advanced spiritual discipline when it is practiced to the fullest extent. Many times in society people externally forgive others but they harbor internal resentments and animosities. When a practitioner of Sema-Yoga forgives a wrong he or she does so with a higher understanding. He or she feels compassion for that person who is suffering the ravages of anger and frustration so much so as to not be able to feel the oneness of humanity to the extent of hating or hurting others. A Sema-Yoga practitioner remains free of the emotions of the ego and is thus able to feel the peace of the Self within. Those who hate are in reality in a state of suffering and so the Sema-Yoga practitioner feels compassionate towards them and seeks to alleviate their pain. Those who engage in egoistic emotions such as hatred are as if in a hell of their own making, founded in degrading self-hate due to the degradation of life lived in futility, disgust and delusion, which prevents them from experiencing the wisdom and peace of higher consciousness. Thus, a spiritual aspirant should strive to act like the Sema-Yoga practitioner who forgives all out of the goodness of their heart and the knowledge of the Higher Self.

There are three stages in forgiveness. At the first level a person forgives but feels resentment and does not let go of the anger. At the second level a person forgives a wrong and forgets the wrong. At the third and most advanced level, the Sema-Yoga practitioner does not even recognize that a wrong has been done since he or she sees all human beings as expressions of the same human family and higher origin. It would be like saying that the teeth have done wrong to the tongue by biting it inadvertently. Should the teeth be punished or forgiven or neither?

Forgiveness is a highly evolved expression of love. But what is love from the spiritual point of view? Most people confuse love with attachment and passion. They feel that if you love someone you must touch them and feel passion all of the time. Passion may be understood as a form of intensified infatuation with certain forms in nature as well as the belief in the illusion of pleasure which is thought to be derived from them. It is an expression of a superficial desire to experience sensual pleasures whereas love implies knowing your own faults and realizing that others have the same concerns, fears, stresses, etc. which sometimes cause them to act in negative ways. Understanding means being aware that you yourself have committed transgressions, also due to ignorance, and therefore, you should be able to understand the transgressions of others and be working to promote justice as you try to help others to find their way without animosities, hatreds, grudges or resentments, but with resolute will against ignorance, that is the true enemy of peace and harmony. True understanding allows you to have patience with others. Love also means looking beyond the personality and having an awareness of the divine essence of every human being and not becoming attached to their transient body and personality. True love means understanding, even if you may not agree, and assisting humanity to see a better way. True love is universal and not confined to a particular family, ethnic group, country, etc. This form of love is uplifting to all relationships. The ordinary form of attached love is degrading as well as the basis of untold miseries, pain and sorrow, due to maladies such as jealousies, unrequited love, betrayals, loss and disappointments. Attached love is egoistic and you cannot truly care for others when you are always concerned with your own ego. You will be trying to satisfy your own desires through them and you will not be able to help them to your best capacity. Therefore, live selflessly and love universally. If you think you cannot rise to this important discipline reflect that there have been people in the world who have been hurt just as you or worse and they were able to find the way; the way is discovered through the practice of the disciplines enjoined in this volume. Essentially you are no different from those other personalities; so you to have it within you to discover the way.

THE GLORY OF CONTENTMENT

Contentment is that wonderful feeling that there is nothing needed, nothing left to desire. In the state of complete contentment the mind of a human being subsides into the true nature to which it belongs like a wave receding into the ocean. Contentment is that serene place where the ideas of happiness and sorrow are both far away from the mind. Consequently there are no worries or concerns about the future or regrets about the past. Contentment is such a lofty goal that all spiritual traditions from around the world have extolled its virtue as an ideal for humanity. This is because true contentment allows a person to see the divine essence of Creation and to discover the Divine in one s very own heart.

From The Shetaut Neter (Ancient Egyptian Mysticism)

"They who revere *MAAT (truth, righteousness, justice)* are *long lived*; they who are **covetous** have no tomb."

"Do not be **greedy** in the division of things. Do not **covet** more than your share. Don't be greedy toward your relatives. A mild person has a greater claim than a harsh one. Poor is the person who forgets their relatives; they are deprived of their company. Even a little bit of what is wanted will turn a quarreler into a friendly person."

"MAAT is great and it effectiveness lasting; it has not been disturbed since the time of Osiris. There is punishment for those who pass over it's laws, but this is unfamiliar to the **covetous** one....When the end is nigh, *MAAT* lasts."

"To be satisfied with little is the greatest wisdom; and they that increaseth their riches, increaseth their cares; but a **contented mind** is a hidden treasure, and trouble findeth it not."

Contentment is the key to unlocking peace and happiness in the heart of a human being. It is cultivated by understanding that money is not the source of happiness. It is promoted by having a profound understanding about the nature of the soul and Creation. It is nourished by the practice of serenity of mind and it blossoms when there is sharing and caring for others as oneself.

Contentment is a profound and dynamic spiritual discipline of understanding that everything you desire is contained in the Higher Self and that Higher Self is the innermost reality of your heart. Therefore, there is no need to desire worldly objects or to worry over worldly situations. It means abiding in the Higher Self and experiencing a life of inner peace and continuous spiritual expansion, joy and abiding love for all humanity. All of the energy that would have been directed towards illusory pleasures and unnecessary conflicts and attachments can now be directed towards discovering your real mission in life. Your life will be more satisfying and you will discover great fulfillment in your chosen line of work because you will pursue it not for personal gain but because this is the true calling of your life. It will give something beneficial to humanity and you will derive from it a heart-felt satisfaction, knowing that you have given of yourself and have allowed the divine flow of love to work through you to serve all people.

Mystical Spirituality *and* Sema-Yoga

How is it possible to overcome hatred and ignorance in life? Religion and Sema-Yoga were originally created to address this very issue. However most people have a mistaken notion about what religion is as well as what Sema-Yoga Philosophy is and how they can help a human being. Many people do not understand spirituality and have turned away from the mention of religion and others are afraid of Yoga practices in general because they have been told that it is an occult practice. These notions are due to ignorance as well as to the negative examples given by many over the years who called themselves preachers or gurus but who were only trying to deceive others for their own personal gains. So you need to re-learn what philosophy, religion and Sema-Yoga are all about. When you do, you will discover that there is a marvelous treasure awaiting you if you understand how to unlock the mysteries of the soul and transcend the negative aspects of the mind.

The word *religion* comes from the Latin Relegare which means to link back." This implies, to link the individual human soul back to its original source, the Universal soul. The Sema is an Ancient Egyptian word meaning Yoga, to join individual consciousness to universal consciousness. While it is true that Sema-Yogic practices may be found in religion, strictly speaking, Sema-Yoga is a set of disciplines used to make religion effective, to make it work. It should be thought of more as a way of life or discipline for promoting greater fullness and experience of life. It was developed, thousands of years ago, by those who wanted more out of life. Sema-Yoga is the practice of mental, physical and spiritual disciplines which lead to self-control, self-discovery and self-mastery by purifying the mind and body so as to discover the deeper spiritual essence which lies within every human being and object in the universe. In essence, the goal of Sema-Yoga practice is to unite or *yoke* one s individual consciousness with universal or cosmic consciousness. Sema-Yoga is not an escape from life but a more profound way to understand life so as to succeed in life. Therefore, Ancient Egyptian religious practice, especially in terms of the rituals and other practices of the Ancient Egyptian temple system known as *Shetaut Neter* (the way of the hidden Supreme Being), may be termed as a Sema-Yoga system: *Egyptian* Sema-Yoga. Religions that lack the mystic disciplines [Sema-Yoga] cannot be considered as effective religions and their deficiencies will lead to limited practice of religion and therefore limited capacity of their followers to access higher consciousness and higher virtues, such as compassion and understanding others, thus leading society to more conflict. In this sense, religion, in its purest form, is a Sema-Yoga system, as it seeks to reunite people with their true and original source, God, Goddess, Higher Self, Great Spirit, etc.

Religion encompasses three levels, *myth, ritual* and *mystical philosophy*. Many students of Ancient Egyptian religion have focused on the religious stories of Ancient Egypt as mythical fables or superstitious rantings from a long lost civilization. In the *Egyptian Yoga Book Series*[78] we successfully show how the teachings of mystical spirituality and the disciplines of Sema-Yoga philosophy were carefully woven throughout Ancient Egyptian Mythology.

> Body to earth, Soul to heaven.
> Ancient Egyptian Proverb

Ancient Egyptian Religion centers on the understanding that every human being has an immortal soul. Further, it holds that creation and the human soul have the same origin. How can this momentous teaching be proven and its reality experienced? This is the task of High Wisdom Philosophy and Mystical Spirituality (religion in its three phases and the practice of Sema-Yoga disciplines).

What is the deeper meaning of Sema-Yoga?

In a broad sense Yoga is anything that brings you closer to your Higher Self. Sema-Yoga is a spiritual way of life which has been practiced since the time of the Ancient Egyptians in Africa. The disciplines of Sema-Yoga fall under five major categories. These are:

---

[78] see the book *Egyptian Yoga The Philosophy of Enlightenment* by Muata Ashby

Sema-Yoga *of Wisdom,* Sema-Yoga *of Devotional Love,* Sema-Yoga *of Meditation, Tantric* Sema-Yoga and Sema-Yoga *of Selfless-Righteous Action.* Within these categories there are subsidiary forms which are part of the main disciplines.

So, from a broad perspective, the practice of any discipline that leads to oneness with the Supreme Consciousness, the Higher Self, can be called Sema-Yoga. If you study, rationalize and reflect upon the teachings, you are practicing Sema-Yoga *of Wisdom.* If you meditate upon the teachings and your Higher Self, you are practicing Sema-Yoga *of Meditation.* If you practice rituals which identify you with your spiritual nature, you are practicing Sema-Yoga *of Ritual Identification* (which is part of the Sema-Yoga of Wisdom and the Sema-Yoga of Devotional Love of the Divine). If you develop your physical nature and psychic energy centers, you are practicing *Serpent Power* Sema-Yoga (which is part of Tantric Yoga). If you practice living according to the teachings of ethical behavior and selflessness, you are practicing Sema-Yoga *of Action* (Maat philosophy) in daily life. If you practice turning your attention towards the Divine by developing love for the Divine, then it is called *Devotional* Sema-Yoga or Sema-Yoga *of Divine Love.* In this manner, Sema-Yoga has been developed into many disciplines which may be used in an integral fashion to achieve the same goal: Enlightenment [attaining the knowledge of self]. Therefore, the aspirant should learn about all of the paths of Sema-Yoga and choose those elements to concentrate on which best suit his/her personality and practice them all in an integral, balanced way.

Enlightenment is the term used to describe the highest level of awakening. It means attaining such a level of spiritual awareness that one discovers the underlying unity of the entire universe as well as the fact that the source of all creation is the same source from which the innermost Self, within every human heart, arises. It is a state of ecstasy and bliss which transcends all concepts and descriptions and which does not diminish and is not affected by the passage of time or physical conditions. It is in the state of Enlightenment that the absolute proofs of the teachings of mystical spirituality are to be found and not in books, doctrines, compelling speeches or dogmas. This is because intellectual knowledge is only the beginning of the road which leads to true wisdom. There are two forms of knowledge, intellectual (theoretical) and absolute (experiential). The teachings of Sema-Yoga and the advanced stages of religion can lead a person to experience the truth about the transcendental, immortal and eternal nature of the Soul and the existence of higher consciousness. This is what differentiates Sema-Yoga from intellectual philosophies and debates, cults or religious dogmas. Sema-Yoga means going beyond simple faith. In Sema-Yoga faith is required to begin the journey of self-discovery but there is no exhortation to believe in anything other than what you can prove through your own experience. In order to do this, all that is necessary is to follow the disciplines which have been scientifically outlined since many thousands of years ago.

All forms of spiritual practice are directed toward the goal of assisting every individual to discover the true essence of the universe both externally, in physical creation, and internally, within the human heart, as the very root of human consciousness. Thus, many terms are used to describe the attainment of the goal of spiritual knowledge and the eradication of spiritual ignorance. Some of these terms are: *Enlightenment, Resurrection, Salvation, The Kingdom of Heaven, Moksha or Liberation, Buddha Consciousness, One With The Tao, Self-realization, Know Thyself,* etc. Also, many names have been used to describe that transcendental essence: *God, Allah, Osiris, Isis, Krishna, Buddha, The Higher Self, Supreme Being* and many others.

Integral Sema-Yoga

The personality of every human being is somewhat different from every other. However the Sages have identified four basic psychological factors which are common to all human personalities. These factors are: Feelings, Reason, Action and Will. In order for a human being to evolve, all aspects of the personality must progress in an integral fashion. Therefore, four major forms of Sema-Yoga disciplines have evolved and each is specifically designed to promote a positive movement in one of the areas of personality. The Sema-Yoga of Devotional Love enhances and harnesses the emotional aspect in a human personality, by purifying the inner feelings, and directs it towards the Higher Self. The Sema-Yoga of Wisdom enhances and harnesses the reasoning aspect in a human personality and directs it towards the Higher Self. The Sema-Yoga of Action enhances and harnesses the movement and behavior aspect in a human personality and directs it towards the Higher Self. The Sema-Yoga of Meditation enhances and harnesses the willing aspect in a human personality and directs it towards the Higher Self. All paths of Sema-Yoga lead a person to promote purity of heart. Purity of heart means purifying the Emotion, Reason, Action, and Will aspects of the personality in order to eradicate anger, hatred, greed, jealousy and ignorance which are preventing a person from experiencing higher forms of consciousness.

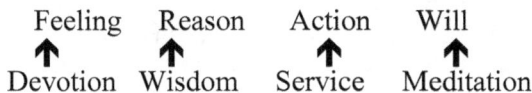

Feeling	Reason	Action	Will
↑	↑	↑	↑
Devotion	Wisdom	Service	Meditation

Thus, Sema-Yoga is a discipline of spiritual wisdom living which transforms every aspect of the personality in an integral fashion, leaving no aspect of a human being behind. This is important because an unbalanced movement will lead to frustration, more ignorance, more distraction and more illusions leading away from the Higher Self. For example, if a person develops the reasoning aspect of personality he or she may come to believe that they have discovered the Higher Self, however when it comes to dealing with some problem of life, such as the death of a loved one, they cannot control their emotions, or if they are tempted to do something unrighteous, such as smoking, they cannot control their actions and have no will power to resist. The vision of Integral Sema-Yoga is a lofty goal which every human being can achieve with the proper guidance, self-effort and repeated practice. There is a very simple philosophy behind Integral Sema-Yoga. During the course of the day you may find yourself doing various activities. Sometimes you will be quiet, at other times you will be busy at work, at other times you might be interacting with people, etc. Integral Sema-Yoga gives you the opportunity to practice Sema-Yoga at all times. When you have quiet time you can practice meditation, when at work you can practice righteous action and selfless service, when you have leisure time you can study and reflect on the teachings and when you feel the sentiment of love for a person or object you like you can practice remembering the Divine Self who made it possible for you to experience the company of those personalities or the opportunity to acquire those objects. From a higher perspective you can practice reflecting on how the people and objects in creation are expressions of the Divine and this movement will lead you to a spontaneous and perpetual state of ecstasy, peace and bliss which are the hallmarks of spiritual enlightenment. The purpose of Integral Sema-Yoga is therefore to promote integration of the whole personality of a human being which will lead to complete spiritual enlightenment. Thus Integral Sema-Yoga should be understood as the most effective method to practice mystical spirituality.

The important point to remember is that all aspects of Sema-Yoga can and should be used in an integral fashion to generate an efficient and harmonized spiritual movement in the practitioner. Therefore, while there may be an area of special emphasis, other elements are bound to become part of the Sema-Yoga program as needed. For example, while a Sema-Yoga practitioner may place emphasis on the Sema-Yoga of Wisdom, they may also practice Devotional Sema-Yoga and Meditation Sema-Yoga along with the wisdom studies. Further, it must be understood that as you practice one path of Sema-Yoga, others will also develop automatically. For example, as you practice the Sema-Yoga of Wisdom your faith will increase or as you practice the Sema-Yoga of Devotion your wisdom will increase. If this movement does not occur your wisdom alone will develop only into dry intellectualism or your faith alone will be blind faith. So when we speak of wisdom here we are ultimately referring to wisdom gained through experience or intuitional wisdom and not intellectual wisdom which is speculative. If you do not practice the teachings through the Sema-Yoga of Action, your wisdom and faith will be shallow because you have not experienced the truth of the teachings and allowed yourself the opportunity to test your knowledge and faith. If you do not have introspection and faith in your wisdom and actions you will be externalized, agitated and distracted. This level of mind will not produce true understanding or enlightenment, but instead, entanglements in the world of time and space where a person may even seem to be accomplishing many things but without inner peace and the quality of their accomplishments will also be lower. Your spiritual realization will be insubstantial, weak and lacking stability. You will not be able to meet the challenges of life nor will you be able to discover true spiritual realization in this lifetime or even after death. Therefore, the integral path of Sema-Yoga, with proper guidance, is the most secure method to achieve genuine spiritual enlightenment. See chart of spiritual paths.

THE EFFECTIVE WAYS TO OVERCOME ANGER, DISLIKE AND HATRED

The most effective way to overcome anger, dislike and hatred is to strengthen and develop every aspect of your personality (emotion, intellect, action and will). This can be accomplished through the path of authentic religion [comprised of the three steps] and or through the various disciplines of Sema-Yoga (Devotional Sema-Yoga, Wisdom Sema-Yoga, Action Sema-Yoga and Meditation Sema-Yoga).

It will become apparent to anyone who practices introspection, self-examination and self-awareness, that ego sentiments such as anger, hate, lust, greed, etc., cannot exist at the same time in the mind when conscious awareness is present. When egoism exists in the mind, thoughts about the Self cannot enter and likewise when total immersion into the experience of the divine presence occurs, egoism cannot exist. Through continued practice of ego sublimation techniques, the patterns of egoism whereby the thoughts of anger, hate, desire, etc., which used to immediately enter the mind and be accepted are now consciously examined and rejected in favor of remembrance of the Divine Self.

Also, when you remember your true nature, you immediately become aware that the true essence of the person you are angry at is the same Self, that the other person is ignorant about as they engage in egoistic actions based on egoistic thoughts and feelings. This remembrance allows you to replace the anger with compassion and understanding. You will remember that those who have angered you have performed

181

whatever actions they did out of their own ignorance and further, you will realize that your anger is due to your own lingering ignorance. You must strive to be like the sun who shines on all, good or evil, without discrimination or regret, abiding in its own glory and ever detached, transcendent.

So a person can overcome all of the defects within by strengthening their intellect through the study of and reflection upon the teachings (Sema-Yoga of Wisdom). This study will allow them to understand their shortcomings and the reason for their desires, cravings and longings as well as the correct way to seek fulfillment and happiness in life. They can strengthen their emotions by harnessing their feelings and directing them towards what is truly worth loving: God (the Sema-Yoga of Devotional Love). They can learn to control their actions and discover happiness not in the fruits of their actions but by discovering the joy of serving humanity and allowing the divine essence to flow through them (Sema-Yoga of Action). They can discover true mental peace and strength of will through the practice of concentration and meditation (Sema-Yoga of Meditation).

When you succeed in the practice of this philosophy of life you will discover of what great benefit you can be to humanity as well as the depths of inner peace which can be experienced through service to humanity. Thus, anger dies down, and even though you are in the midst of strife and conflict, you will utter words of peace and understanding which will bring harmony and stability to yourself and others. This practice of reminding yourself of your true identity allows the illusory ego identification you have built up over many lifetimes to dissolve. When this level of philosophical practice takes hold in your unconscious, you will notice a profound transformation in the way you see the world and all those around you.

How is this wisdom applied to the understanding of min and its control? The process of spiritual life means turning away from the negative aspects of consciousness and turning toward the positive or lucid aspects which lead to enlightenment. The waking state is the most concrete state. As such it acts to anchor the soul to a physical form (human body) over an extended period of time, and through it, the soul derives various experiences which will provide pleasure and pain. Thus, the waking - physical state is the field in which the thoughts, desires and actions of a human being can be played out in an extended format of time and space, unlike the dream world in which an entire world can come into existence and vanish in a flash. So the task of spiritual disciplines is to engage in practices (virtues) which will promote a movement towards lucidity (wisdom-enlightenment) and move away from the activities, thoughts and feelings which promote agitation, distraction, discontent and ultimately lead to dullness and ignorance of the intellect. This process entails controlling anger hatred, greed, etc. and promoting effacement of the ego through righteous actions, simplicity, truthfulness, patience and other virtues.

Once an aspirant has worked on promoting lucidity in the waking state, it is possible, with a mind that is calm, lucid and strong willed, to practice formal meditation on the inner Self. When this level of practice is reached such a person is considered to be advanced on the spiritual path. Their powers of concentration, fortitude and inner peace they have gained through intellectual knowledge has allowed them to develop real faith with which they can understand the goal of spirituality and exert the necessary self-effort needed to realize the objective. Already they are far elevated from the masses of people who live only to satisfy their desires for the enjoyments which the world can bring. This constantly agitated state of mind precludes reflectiveness and inner peace, without which it is not possible to discover the deeper meaning of spirituality. Their understanding is shallow, intellectual and theoretical and their willpower is weak, so they do not desire for spiritual emancipation. They too are caught up in the activities, desires and longings of modern society.

Out of ignorance of the deeper Self, most people (the masses) are caught between the dualistic thoughts of their mind. They have not yet discovered the transcendental peace, so therefore they are caught up in the waves of positive and negative emotions and the desires for acquiring something which they perceive will bring happiness. Ignorant people live life in a state of delusion. There is a constant belief that the world will somehow bring them happiness, despite the relentless disappointments and frustrations that abound in life. It is like gambling. There is a constant expectation that one will win, even though the odds are stacked against it. Even if there is a win, it is not really a win because the winnings will be used to strengthen the belief in the world and will set up the winner for an even bigger disappointment later on. Spiritual life does not mean that there is no fun or experience of pleasure due to objects of the world. It means that there is no dependence on the world for happiness; instead there is indifference. If pleasure is experienced a Sage accepts it. If pleasure is not experienced a Sage also accepts this. At no time does the absence or presence of pleasure due to worldly objects or situations affect the deeper experience of peace and joy which comes from the inner Self. Therefore, the experiences of pleasure and pain remain in the enlightened state, but they are transcended with the ever-present knowledge of the innermost Self within. It is like standing on the shore and looking at the ocean. Even though the different waves are there the ocean cannot be missed, and furthermore, the waves cannot exist without the ocean. Likewise a Sage looks at the pain and sorrow of life as waves but never looses sight of the Self which surges like an ocean in every corner of Creation.

Thus, the abiding presence of wisdom and Divine awareness in the mind overpowers all disturbances of the outside world even though those movements, changes, sounds, situations, the passage of time, emotions, waking, dream, dreamless sleep, etc., may continue. For the enlightened Sage these waves are seen as transient forms which will pass as they give way to new ones, which will also eventually pass away. So there is no mourning over, attachment to or leaning upon the past, present or the future for anything that is fleeting, uncertain and unstable. Of course, the Sage harbors no desires or longings for anything that is not real and abiding and so experiences constant peace, contentment and bliss internally even while carrying out the various duties of life or performing the most dynamic work in the service of humanity. Due to a sage s resolution of the original problem, ignorance of the knowledge of self, there is capacity and ability to sidestep the pitfalls of human existence in the form of anger, hatred, greed, pain, sorrow, lack of egoistic desires, etc. and the consequent freedom from delusions about life allows a Sage to conserve energy and attune the mind to the heavenly realms where it Is possible to gain intuitive communion with the Higher Self (God), and in so doing, bring the marvels of spiritual wisdom to humanity through literary works, and teaches humanity through various means which require a high degree of stamina and resiliency. This is the art of living which a Sage embodies and teaches to others for the purpose of leading them to spiritual realization, a process which will promote peace and harmony in the world.

The Practice of The Teachings

The practice of the teachings is the most important part of Sema-Yoga after the teachings have been received and understood. Many aspirants and lay people believe that the mind may be transformed by simply reading a particular book or some special exercises or secret techniques. This would be like discovering a map for a buried treasure, but then not putting in the effort to follow the directions of the map to find the location or just having the map and not digging for the treasure. While many breakthroughs can occur wherein the subject may experience bursts of enlightening experiences, the process of psycho-spiritual transformation leading to full Enlightenment and transcendence of the karmic process requires many small strides which together amount to a force which cleanses the mind of all illusions and all egoism.

As a developing aspirant on the path of Sema-Yoga, you must learn how to determine when you are progressing and when you are falling back into the old ways. Patience is an essential quality to develop because transformation takes time. You will know how to recognize your progress on the path by your level of increasing peace and harmony within yourself. However you should not place overwhelming

184

importance in day to day assessments of yourself since the battle between the higher and lower self often fluctuates from day to day. Some days you may feel harmonious and at peace while on other days you may feel troubled and agitated. You should look at your life in a much more holistic fashion and on a broader scale. Ask questions like: Am I slower to anger than I was a month ago? Six months ago? A year ago? These questions will give you a better indication of your current stage of spiritual development. Most importantly, be honest with yourself and never be afraid or too full of pride to ask for help and advice from more advanced personalities. When the troubles of life are no longer insurmountable, when you become slow to anger, when you begin to discover feel more compassion and empathy and desire for selfless service to humanity instead of disdain and impatience with or prejudices about others, when you begin to discover a higher vision of yourself which goes beyond any mental concepts, that is when you are moving towards self-discovery. This is the art and practice of Sema-Yoga in Life.

The process of Sema-Yoga may be divided into three major sections: *Listening, Reflection and Meditation.* Most of what you have learned up to this point falls under the phase of learning about the teachings. In the book *Introduction to Maat Philosophy,* we presented the value of Maat in action and the basics of the inner implications of Selfless Service and Action for Purity of Heart rather than for exterior gains. Also we saw how finding an occupation which is in line with your karmic personality allows the divine will to flow through you. This will lead to purification of the heart. In this volume we will practice exercises which will serve to begin the process of reflecting on and practicing the teachings in your day to day life. This will lead you to attain the purity of heart which will allow correct reasoning and feeling to develop in your being.

It is easier to deal with the negativity of the ego (anger, hatred, greed, etc.) when they are just passing thoughts in the mind. However, if a person holds onto the negative thoughts they gradually accumulate and become deeply rooted in the mind to the extent that a person will not accept anything else as the truth, even incontrovertible evidence disproving their notions. So negativity in the mind should be dealt with even as it arises in the mind just as a spark can be put out easily before it grows into a raging forest fire. Whenever an angry thought rises, take a deep breath, realize what is happening and take a time out to remember the teachings and neutralize it with understanding. This is the spark stage that, if left unchecked, can lead to hatred and violence. As soon as you realize that you are becoming aroused with anger, before the anger runs its course and leads to harsh thoughts, words and deeds, remain silent and allow reason to flow into your mind. Understand that your ego is angry, then look at it and the motive of its anger from a detached point of view. Reflect that the deeper you is the immutable Soul and that the reason for anger is bogus since there is no point to being angry at the world or people who have done something you find upsetting given that you have engendered the situation through your ignorant desires of the past and others are acting out of their own ignorance.

In handling anger, reflect upon the idea that whatever has happened to bring on the anger is only a test of your ability to separate from your hurt ego. Go to a quiet place and recall the teachings. Anger can only be experienced when you associate with the mind and its worries, fears, likes, and dislikes. Disassociate from the mind, through breath, reflection and you can be immediately released from mental pressures so you can handle the situation with maturity and wisdom instead of emotion and irrationality. Remember who you really are, the supreme abode of peace and bliss, and allow this idea to flow. Take deep breaths so that you can concentrate on the Life Force energy and keep it in the body instead of venting it through negative or evil thoughts, words and deeds. Controlling the energy allows you to retain mental strength instead of weakening yourself and making yourself more susceptible to the foibles of the personality and the desires of the ego. Concentrating on the breath allows you to take the mind away from the flow of thoughts to the situation and events and bring it into the here and now. The situations that provoke worldly feelings occur in time and space while the higher peace and freedom are discovered when transcending time and space. Practicing coming into the here and now, through stopping what you are saying or doing or involved with, that is making you angry, is the first step in moving towards the transcendental experience. Focusing on the breath and channeling the flow of mind towards the wisdom teaching brings one into the present moment instead of getting caught up in the rush of feelings and emotions that lead to regrettable occurrences. In this manner you can control the body and mind at the same time. When you are in control, then tackle the problem or respond to the situation with reason, in greater control of yourself. This practice will become more and more automatic and eventually you will not be as affected by situations which in the past would have caused you much anger.

Whenever a greedy thought comes in, remember that your goal is Enlightenment and realize that all objects are attained that are needed for life so there is no need to hoard and in the end all are fleeting anyway and do not bring abiding happiness even when attained. When you attain the higher realization you will become One with all objects in consciousness so there is no need to pursue external objects which you do not need for your practical reality and which in the end are perishable anyway.

Bhagavad Gita: Chapter 16
Daivasur Sampat Vibhag Yogah--The Yoga of Division Between the
Divine and Demoniac Qualities

21. There are three gates to hell which are the destroyers of the soul.
They are Lust, Anger, and Greed; these three must be renounced.

Whenever a thought of selfishness arises, substitute it with a thought of charity and reinforce it with acts of charity and selfless service with a spirit of honesty and without seeking for rewards or praise in return. The mind entertains greediness and selfishness because it has learned to believe it is an individual among other individuals and that it can be happy by acquiring objects, or through worldly relationships with others. Therefore, any thought of giving up or losing an object of attachment evokes feelings of selfishness and aversion to loss. You feel you are giving up your chance for happiness, and indeed you are because you have linked your happiness to the idea of possessing that object or having a particular situation. Through the force of the wisdom and the practice of the teachings you will discover that you are giving up something little in comparison to what you are gaining. In fact, you are giving up your hell and gaining heaven.

"To be satisfied with little is the greatest wisdom; and they that increase
their riches, increase their cares; but a contented mind is a hidden
treasure, and trouble find it not."
-Ancient Egyptian Proverb

Popular culture holds that individuality and egoism are natural and desirable features in the human personality. The advertisements on television, the movies and the leaders of society [secular and non-secular] in general promote the idea that people should have desires and seek to pursue the fulfillment of these by buying consumer goods as if the more a person can get the more they are adding to themselves or getting religion by buying the church [tithes, volunteering, donations, etc.]. If this were true why is it that there are fabulously rich people in the world who attain all they wanted and then feel so empty that they need to get more, or having attained what they thought they wanted they commit suicide or become addicts (drugs and alcohol) and there are others who give large sums to the church and may even attend services every day but find no abiding satisfaction or resolution for their condition. These are not signs of happiness or contentment, but the masses of people continue to delude themselves with these ideas presented before them by the media and other people around them. People become so proud of their ignorance and egoism that they proclaim it loudly for the world to see and hear: I like this and I don't like that;   This makes me sad and that makes me happy. This is my personality and that is who I am and that s that so I can change, etc. These kinds of statements denote a personality that is either satisfied and comfortable with its own egoism or ignorant to the possibilities for change through purification of heart but either way this person is unaware of how this way of accepting life or determining what life limits the possibilities, reinforces egoism and leads to untold disappointments, frustrations and miseries. All they are doing is reinforcing the ignorance of their minds and leading themselves to dissatisfaction and contributing to the pathologies of society at large. The practice of Sema-Yoga allows a person to see the folly of egoism and allows them to integrate every aspect of their personality so that they will not have to rely on the weak ego desires in order to feel happy and fulfilled. As this process of personality integration moves forward, the aspirant develops fulfillment through inner experience of expanding self-awareness rather than through externalization. The individual s feeling of inner contentment increases in direct proportion with the level of effacement of the personal ego.

Through the incorporation of these teachings in your daily activities and by incorporating the practice of reflection and meditation, it is possible to intuitively discover real inner fulfillment, contentment and abiding happiness which is not affected by the outer conditions of the world. One who understands this teaching would act because he or she wants to, out of the "goodness" of their heart, not because they are looking for happiness expecting something in return; such persons act as the sun, which shines and gives life to the earth without asking for anything in return and yet is splendorous, full and content within its own being even as it shines on sustaining life without being dependent upon it s action. Outside factors are always variable and therefore illusory. In a higher sense though, since all is the connected in the Higher Self, when one acts in the interest of others or the world, one is acting for the Higher Self. One's contentment with oneself and one's acceptance of one's actions as virtuous and the relinquishment of the outcomes, favorable or not, leave little room for mental agitation, anguish or frustration. Thus, full enjoyment of the world and happiness are best achieved with a mental attitude of detachment, living in a way which promotes purity of heart: decreasing mental disturbance (agitation) and increasing peace. Growing into the discovery of one s true higher nature means growing out of the pettiness and the other forms of negativity of the lower self. This is real growth and real maturity. Otherwise a human being is, as if, retarded. True success in life means growing beyond hate and all of the negative repercussions that go along with it. This is possible only for those who set out to practice the teachings which allow a person to develop the virtuous qualities of the soul, detachment and inner contentment. When this movement occurs, the negative aspects of the lower self are eventually defeated and eradicated from the heart. This movement culminates in the enlightenment of the heart.

""Knowledge derived from the senses is illusory, true knowledge can only come from the understanding of the union of opposites."
Ancient Egyptian Proverb

The Spiritual Search and the Riddle of Causality

WHO AM I?

Who am I? Where do I come from? Where am I going? And Why am I here? are perhaps the most important questions to every human being. These questions are at the heart of the high wisdom philosophy that leads to contentment, inner peace and freedom from hatred. Some people believe that there is a God who created humanity and the universe. These people are called *theists*. Others believe that there is no God and that Creation occurred by chance. These people are known as *atheists*. The theists rely on faith in what they cannot see or experience while the atheists say that nothing outside of what the senses can perceive is real, and that anything that is perceived outside of the senses represents imagination or insanity. The *agnostic* believes that there can be no proof of the existence of God but does not deny the possibility that God exists. The *Gnostic*[79] on the other hand believes that there is a spiritual basis for all existence and that this essence can be experienced; this process of achieving the experience is called *mysticism*.

The ideas outlined above have shaped the way in which people view themselves and nature as well as the spiritual possibilities or lack of spiritual possibilities in life. The views have been the source of controversy and conflict because many of the groups view the others as being inherently wrong. Modern psychology has shown that the human psyche is much more complex than previously thought. However, parapsychology studies have expanded the view of the psyche, showing that there is a deeper level of a human being, which transcends the physical nature. Modern physics has shown that matter and physical reality are not physical and real at all, that they are illusory projections, which are relative, depending on the sense instruments, which are used. A hawk can perceive much more with his visual organs than a human being can. A bat can hear things which a human being cannot, etc. If all of this is true then why would it be so far fetched to believe that there is something beyond ordinary human perception?

In human history, the first powerful systems of Religion and Sema-Yoga were developed in Ancient Egypt as a means to lead people from ignorance of the spiritual reality to self-discovery, inner peace, and harmony with nature and unity with that which transcends physical

---

[79] (Ancient Egyptians and Greeks who practiced Sema-Yoga and Mystical Spirituality before and during the early Christian era)

189

reality. The goal of Ancient Egyptian Religion is an exalted vision of individual and societal enlightenment.

THE POWER OF SEMA-YOGA

T he power of Sema-Yoga to enhance all forms of spirituality is derived from its universality. The power of Sema-Yoga is increased when it is taught in an integral fashion as a blend of all forms. The human personality is composed of four main aspects (Emotions, Intellect, Action and Will). Therefore, an effective system of spirituality needs to accommodate and develop all of these aspects so that a person may achieve an integral spiritual movement. If this integral movement does not occur there will be imbalance and failure in the overall progress. A person may become highly intellectual but not become enlightened. Another may do a lot of meditation and still fail to achieve high wisdom. One technique or system may suit one personality over another and a spiritual teacher needs to know how to direct an aspirant to practice the teachings, according to their level of spiritual evolution and their particular karmic basis. They need to have a spiritual program, which is best suited for them at that time. So the most effective method of spiritual practice is not any one system or technique but an integral spiritual practice with the correct guidance.

Sometimes people get caught up in the orthodoxy of a particular wisdom writing or a particular spiritual scripture because they believe that from just reading they have understood a teaching and do not need further explanation or instruction, having received all they need from the reading alone. Swami Satchidananda once said: If it were possible to learn from a book there would be no need for universities. There are two forms of knowledge. The first comes from information and the second is from experience. Books are only the beginning of knowledge. The teacher brings life, relevancy, context and meaning to the text. There is no other way for real and abiding wisdom knowledge to be imparted and correctly understood. As you begin to bring the teachings into focus and see how you already have the tools needed to succeed in spirituality, you will then be able to move forward towards inner spiritual realization enlightenment. For more on the teacher-disciple relationship consult the book *Initiation Into Egyptian* Yoga and Neterian Spirituality.

So mystic spirituality is the discipline of discovering the deeper essence of life and these disciplines have been referred to as Sema-Yoga Philosophy. The big difference between mystical spirituality and Sema-Yoga and the practice of religion as it has come to be known in modern times is that while ordinary religion offers places of worship, myths and rituals, Sema-Yoga and Mystical Spirituality offer a way to realize the transcendental truths behind those myths and rituals. In essence real spirituality is the art of proving what is held as faith based on one s beliefs or intellectual knowledge; faith or intellectual knowledge are not the end or objective and are not enough to produce a wise person. So in Sema-Yoga and mystical spirituality there is no question about whether or not there is a God or Goddess. The objective of Sema-Yoga practice is to discover that deeper essence of self and in so doing achieve supreme peace and abiding happiness for oneself and justice, harmony and peace for society. This is enlightenment. Its attainment is your only purpose in life. This is the only purpose of everyone s life, whether or not they are aware of it. Going through life without an awareness of this higher purpose would be like someone sending you into the world to look for something with the following instructions: Look, I know not where, for I know not what. You would endlessly wander through the world leading a meaningless life. However, if you understand what you need to accomplish in a given situation and are given a road map of how to accomplish it, you will be able to consciously put forth effort in that direction and be able to accomplish the task faster and with more precision than if you did not know what you were trying to do. Similarly, once you understand that the purpose of your life is to attain enlightenment, you can put forth self-effort in that direction.

The practical realities of a person s life are specifically designed by the Higher Self to lead that individual to greater and greater awareness and growth. This is called the higher plan. You are constantly being challenged by life to act righteously, to be understanding, forgiving, loving, compassionate and express other virtuous qualities. To the extent that you are able to identify with your spiritual nature and overcome the negative sentiments of your lower egoistic nature (anger, hatred, greed, envy, fear, insecurity, etc) you mature spiritually and are able to experience peace and joy in life. When you choose to be egoistic rather than spiritually altruistic, you are going against the flow of the river of life, and consequently you will experience agitation, frustration, pain and suffering in life.

On the journey to the truth, one must stay on the path of love and enlightenment.
The heart filled with greed and lust will be overcome by its selfishness.

Ancient Egyptian Proverb

So, through your actions in daily life you lead yourself either to the experience of peace and happiness or to agitation and suffering. Thus, you and you alone are responsible for the condition of your life. If you find yourself experiencing a negative condition, you brought it on yourself by your past negative, thoughts, desires and actions. In this sense, negative actions refer to actions, which go against the purpose you are here for, attaining enlightenment. Likewise, positive situations in life which permit you to study scriptures and practice the teachings of Sema-Yoga to lead yourself to attain the supreme peace and joy which is unaffected by any happening in life (enlightenment) occur as a result of your past (this and previous lifetimes) good actions. Such actions should therefore be promoted in your life.

Everything we do is sowing, and all of our experiences are harvests

Ancient Egyptian Proverb

The above proverb is referred to as the law of sowing and reaping, the law of cause and effect. The implication of the proverb above is that every person, even those who are seemingly being victimized by others, are really responsible for their situation. In reality they are reaping the negative fruit from the negative seed that they had sown, either in this or a past lifetime. This does not justify the negative action of those persons who are doing the victimizing. They too are failing the test being presented by the universe to be kind and loving to their kin [humanity]. They too are creating their own bed of nails to sleep on in the future, either in this lifetime or a future one. The eyes of this justice system which is based on cosmic law are truly blind, unlike the eyes of human beings, which often apply egoistic sentiments, prejudices or other biases. It doesn t discriminate on any basis. Everyone is judged equally. The law is best stated in the following Ancient Egyptian Proverb:

Every cause has its effect; every effect has its cause.
Everything happens according to the law. Chance is a name for the law unrecognized.
There are many planes of causation, but nothing escapes the law.

As the law of cause and effects states, those people who are not aware of this law attribute its effects to chance. It is by chance that their car got stolen or got a flat tire on the way to the football game. They believe that it is by chance that they moved next door to people who do not like them. They believe that it is by chance that they won the lottery, etc., etc. They believe in chance because it seemingly offers them excitement and or hope that somehow they can escape their current situation, maybe by winning a lottery, clear out of the blue, by doing nothing but buying a ticket. And perhaps even more importantly, they do not have to accept personal responsibility for the situation since they believe that it was by some stroke of luck that it happened to them. Chalking things up to chance however has a detrimental effect on the mind. In other situations they can blame someone or something other than themselves. Ultimately, it leads to a sense of powerlessness whereby people feel that they have no control over the events transpiring in their lives or the world. This promotes the development of procrastination, laziness and complacency as well as apathy, acquiescence and feelings of futility in their personalities. The effects of apathy, futility and acquiescence can produce an insensitive, callous, unfeeling, malicious and cruel personality. Since such feelings and thought processes do not require that the individual accept responsibility for their current negative situation, statements like It wasn t my fault and the world is going to hell, everybody else is doing it, why shouldn t I? become the mottos of choice. It is someone else s fault, someone else s responsibility. It is the government s fault. I m in this condition because the man controls everything. It is their fault, they are oppressing us. It is anybody s fault but mine. The individual looses their sense of power and feels like a helpless victim. They feel that their actions have no bearing on their condition, so why try? Thus, not recognizing that you, through your actions (and even thoughts are subtle actions), are the one who is really responsible for the situations in your life, both good and bad, is the next obstacle to be overcome, a step away from the thoughts and feelings that helped in becoming a degraded human being, the first step of course being ignorance of their true higher nature. If you do not understand that you created your current negative conditions, how can you feel that you have the power to also overcome them? And if you attribute the good conditions of your life to chance or some external agency [God, Jesus, the man, my spouse, etc.], what incentive is there for you to strive to work for more good situations to develop in your life?

What confuses the issue further is that people see tragedies and atrocities occurring to people they consider to be innocent or good, especially children. They cannot envision anything these people could have done in this life to have deserved it, especially when it happens to babies who did not even have a chance in this life to do wrong. But as the proverb above states, there are many planes of causation, and nothing escapes the law. What this means is that even if you did a negative deed in a past lifetime and died before you could experience its repercussions in that lifetime, the effect (repercussions) will carry over into some future lifetime. The same holds for good deeds. This becomes a problem when the law is not understood. Because the cause (action) and the effect (result) are not always linked in the same lifetime, people do not recognize the effect (result) as occurring because of something that they did. However, the cause is always equal to the effect, and the effect is essentially the cause transformed. For example, suppose you planted a lemon seed and after some years it grew and bore fruit. The seed is the cause; the lemon is the effect. Although the seed and the fruit do not look alike, essentially they are the same. Similarly, if you plant negative seeds through your thoughts and actions, you will reap negative fruit, and if you plant positive seeds, you will reap positive fruits. So, if you don t want to have a certain negative effect occurring in your life, the solution is simple, don t initiate that negative causative action. Likewise, if you want positive situations to occur in your life, perform positive virtuous actions in life. Furthermore, when you perform truly virtuous actions,

193

you are promoting your spiritual evolution towards attaining enlightenment because you are operating in harmony with the flow of life and the laws of the universe (Maat, God).

So, realizing that you are the architect of your destiny, work to change your thoughts to become positive and in harmony with your spiritual goal of life, and as a result your actions which are based on those thoughts will also become positive and lead you to positive (uplifting) situations. You, through your own self-effort to promote righteous action (Maat) will lead yourself to transcend all negativity in your life. Therefore, instead of seeking to blame or praise anything or anyone outside of yourself for your circumstances, look within your own very thoughts and actions for the cause of your current condition. Search your own thoughts with a pure mind and seek to uproot the egoism (anger, hate, greed, racism, sexism, and all other negative isms that lurk in the human heart) that grows there. It is this egoism that had led you to the negative situation you are experiencing, and until you understand its erroneous basis and eradicate it, you will continuously perform the same ego-based actions and keep leading yourself to the similar negative experiences, again and again.

Most people want others to stop directing negative emotions towards them rather than looking within themselves to effect a change in the situation. They don t see the root cause of the problem as being within themselves. Since you cannot control others, and others may not desire to grow in wisdom, you have a choice. You can either continue to let their spiritual immaturity upset and control you, seek to revenge it, or you can choose to act in a spiritually mature manner, promoting virtuous behavior and not allowing yourself to fall into the pit of egoism. You can choose to view the situation as a test designed by your Higher Self to challenge you to act wisely. Furthermore, the other person is probably content for the moment to be egoistic. Just as a mother will expect more from the older child than a younger one since the older child should know better, more is expected of an aspirant or initiate (student of Sema-Yoga seeking enlightenment) than an ordinary person. They are not aware of their deeper nature and purpose in life, but an aspirant has been instructed as to his/her purpose and goal of life, therefore, like the older child, an aspirant should know better and therefore should try to act better. As an aspirant or initiate, your only quest in life should be to rise above your lower nature. This should be your primary concern and focus, and not how other people are acting. They too are bound to the law of cause and effect and will suffer consequences for their actions in due time. Their destiny should not be your concern since you have not secured your own destiny.

One cannot force another to grow beyond their capacity.

194

Why do you seek revenge, O man! For what purpose do you pursue it?
Do you believe that you will cause your adversary pain by it?
Know that you yourself will be the one to feel its greatest torments!

Ancient Egyptian Proverbs

In his book *Stolen Legacy,* George G. M. James listed the Ancient Egyptian precepts of Initiatic life. Two of these are of special interest to those who have experienced hate and or persecution in life and the way in which it is to be handled from a spiritual (initiatic) point of view.

> *(7) "Be free from resentment under the experience of persecution"* (Bear insult)
> *(8) "Be free from resentment under experience of wrong,"* (Bear injury)

If the resentments, anger and animosity are not eradicated from within your heart, the possibility for wisdom or spiritual evolution will be limited. This does not mean that you should allow yourself to be physically injured. Of course take common sense measures to deal with the practical reality, removing yourself from physically being harmed if that is a possibility. However, it implies that after taking whatever practical measures are necessary to ensure personal safety, you do not continue to harbor ill will or hold a grudge towards the person or persons you perceived as persecuting you or doing you wrong. Remind yourself that it is your own past egoistic thoughts and actions that led you to your present predicament, that you and not they are responsible for the situation, [they are responsible for their own lives and egoistic desires] that you are being given an opportunity to move closer to your Higher Self through virtuous thoughts and actions, to actually put your intellectual knowledge into actual practice, and if anything, be grateful for the opportunity to grow spiritually. Other people, who manifest as agents [vehicles of pain or things you dislike] who do you wrong are actually playing out the effect of your negative cause. They have consequences they will suffer for taking part in the action [due to their own ignorance and egoism] but those are their business, not yours.

Be always more ready to forgive than to return injury;
They who watch for an opportunity for revenge lieth in waste against themselves, and draweth down mischief on their own head.

Ancient Egyptian Proverb

THE NATURE OF THE SOUL AND THE HUMAN CONSTITUTION

So what is the nature of the human body and what is the purpose for the differences among human beings? How are these differences to be understood and reconciled or even transcended? Also, what is the underlying basis of the mind and body? What is a human being? People see themselves as different but are they really? Don t people all over the world desire love, happiness, peace and joy? These are similarities are they not?

> The soul belongs to heaven, the body belongs to the
> earth
> Ancient Egyptian Proverb

A human being is a complex entity composed of a soul or spirit, a mind and a body. The mind and body constitute the psychophysical personality of a human being. The soul is the eternal part while the body/mind is the transient part of a human being. However, when human beings forget their eternal nature, they identify with the body and the mind with its desires, complexes and ignorance and this causes the soul to become entangled in a web of illusions about the world and about its own nature; they become entangled with the worldly illusions and the misconceived notions about the nature of the Higher Self. A person sees him/her self as the physical body only and the underlying essence, the spirit becomes as if veiled. Nevertheless, a human being has an innate desire to discover his or her true nature, but due to ignorance, does so through the limited mind and body only and many times gets caught up in the illusions, misconceptions, prejudices and cravings of the mind and body.

In addition, the individual soul of a person is in reality one with the universal Soul, God, just like each wave in the ocean is essentially one with the whole ocean. The goal of Sema-Yoga is to realize that you are not an individual, but in fact, that your true nature is universal. When you realize this goal in your own life, you will have attained enlightenment. When enlightenment dawns, all virtuous qualities will bloom in your personality. You will become the embodiment of supreme peace and bliss (unconditioned happiness). You will realize that you were always the abode of peace and bliss, even when you were ignorantly identifying only with your psychophysical personality. The ego in a person develops as a result of this identification with the psychophysical personality as being who you are. Instead of realizing your true nature to be like the blue sky, expanding into infinity, you identified yourself with a small patch of blue sky created by clouds of mental delusion and ignorance. Identified with that little patch of blue, when the clouds darkened around you, you felt gloomily. When the clouds were soft and fleecy, you felt happy. When the clouds drifted apart a little, you felt expansion and became peaceful and less stressed. When the clouds contracted, you felt unsettled and miserable. Your inner experience was always conditioned by the clouds of ignorance surrounding you. However, even then, you were really always the entire blue sky, completely unaffected by the clouds.

So it is with the Higher Self which sustains your psychophysical personality and is the reality behind it. This innermost Self within you is completely unaffected by any condition which affects the psychophysical personality of an individual. It experiences no pain, sadness, and sorrow. It remains always completely blissful and peaceful. It always exists in the awareness of its universal nature. So, the goal of true mystical spirituality is to identify more and more with your true nature, and less and less with your ego-personality. When you do this, you will be able to go beyond all the egoistic concepts which you have tied to your existence as a psychophysical personality. This includes anger, hate greed, envy, jealousy, fear, insecurity, and attachments. Instead you will bathe in the elixir of virtuous qualities such as compassion, universal love, understanding, peace and bliss. You will truly Know Thyself.

Gods are immortal men, and men are immortal Gods.
Ancient Egyptian Proverb

It is very important to understand that the Soul within you is not affected by any happening in this world. To understand this, think of yourself when you are dreaming. The *you* that you consider to be real is ever asleep on the bed, safe, peaceful, calm. The dream *you* experiences all kind of situations, some very painful and some pleasurable yet, the *you* asleep on the bed is not really experiencing any of these situations of pleasure or pain. Likewise, the real you, the Self, like that sleeping personality, is always resting on that bed of peace, bliss and absolute existence, remaining ever unaffected by the experiences of the psychophysical personality. And just as if a lion is chasing you in your dream, though seemingly you have several choices of what to do such as running away, finding shelter to escape it, picking up a stick to fight with it, there is only one real choice which will take care of that problem for you, that is, to wake up. Likewise, the only way you will be able to deal with the problems in your life right now is to wake up from the dream of yourself being a psychophysical (ego) personality to realize your higher nature. Otherwise, trying to battle the forces of egoism afflicting you in life by reinforcing your existence as an ego-personality would be like deciding in your dream to turn yourself in to a lion in order to beat the lion chasing you. Even if you become a bigger lion and even kill it, you will still have suffered injury in the battle. Why go through all that pain and suffering when you could just wake up?

So, your efforts to overcome negative sentiments within your personality or even being directed at you from another personality, which is nothing but egoism stemming from ignorance of one s true nature, is not to attack it with more egoism, but to realize that none of the negativity of the world, which in the end is illusory anyway, touches your deeper essence. When people experience hurt from others, they feel the need to retaliate because they feel that they have personally been violated and hurt. Yet, this is not so. It is only their psychophysical personality which has been insulted or hurt. The real them is totally unaffected, resting on the bed of consciousness, absorbed in peace and bliss. The real you cannot be hurt.

Something is added to you unlike to what thou see;
Something animates thy clay higher than all that is the object of thy senses.
Behold, what is it? Thy body remains still matter after it is fled;
therefore it is no part of it; It is immaterial.
Ancient Egyptian Proverb

So your experience of being hurt only belongs to the unreal you, the dream you, the ego-personality, and as long as you identify with this lower aspect of who you are, you will be bound to all egoistic emotions (anger, hate, etc.) and not able to experience the deeper aspect of who you are, the embodiment of peace and bliss. If you look at your own life, you will realize that all you have ever been really searching for in life through all your various actions is to be happy and peaceful. Yet, you have been searching for it in the realm of egoism where it does not exist as a permanent condition or to the extent that it is experienced in the state of enlightenment. If you really want to find true peace and happiness which remains unaffected by any condition or circumstance of life, there is only one way. You must wake up to the knowledge of your Higher Self. This process of waking up is the goal of the disciplines and practice of Sema-Yoga.

The wickedness of the soul is ignorance; the virtue of the soul is knowledge
Ancient Egyptian Proverb

PART III: QUESTIONS AND ANSWERS

Question: Does Neterian religion & philosophy promote forgiveness of enemies – Part 1?

Greetings Dr. Muata Ashby,

This question is based on a lecture I recently attended. Overall I think your presentation was positive. We would certainly be better off, if we practiced much of what you are saying.

Dr. Ashby, you spoke about forgiveness and peace. Of course, I have to put everything in a political context, and what I heard made me think of Malcolm X s wake up, clean up, and stand up program, minus the stand up, at least a clear call for standing up.

Wake up to your divinity.
Clean up--practice Maat, eat right, etc.

But as I see Kemetic history, they stood up and fought (physically and spiritually) to maintain Maat, against internal and external enemies--the dynamics of *Isfet*[80]. Had the Maatian dynamics not been able to dominate the dynamics of Isfet, Kemet would not have lasted so long.

We live in a world dominated by the dynamics of Isfet--primarily the European power structure/White Supremacy Dynamic and their cronies of color.

How do we restore Maat without challenging the dynamics of Isfet-- within and without? Surely, reciprocity is one of the cardinal virtues of Maat.

---

[80] unrighteousness

I also think their concept of forgiveness is more Euro-Christian than it is Maatian. South Africa is going to hell, largely because Mandela forgave the Europeans before demanding repentance. Repentance always precedes forgiveness, but most Christians want to go straight from the commission of a sin/ crime to forgiveness, bypassing repentance. Hey, you have to repair the damage first. In the Maatian context, Khun-Anup says the following:

"Punish the robber and save those who suffer."
"Punish those who deserve punishment and none will equal your righteousness."
"If you turn your face from violence, who will punish wrongdoing?"

But, by no means is he saying be like the Europeans-- "answer not good with evil and put not one thing in the place of another." I would say, answer evil with righteous (Maatian) justice. That assumes that we are a Maatian people.

I also heard a bit of abstract humanism in your lecture that I would challenge.

Most often I don't like to confront positive people in public forums. All too often, when there is a serious challenge, we lose focus of the positives.

Your message was too valuable to do that.

Answer by Dr. Muata Ashby

Greetings,

Your comments are very much appreciated.

The question of meting out punishment and retribution and how it relates to Maat Philosophy has been asked previously. This is an extremely important question which deserves much discussion and reflection.

I would also like you to know that you are not the first person to make such comments in private or otherwise. I do not see these comments from serious people as impediments to the upliftment of the community since they bring out important issues which need to be dealt with and understood. Further, I do not see these comments as challenges but as honest attempts to understand the teachings. Since Kemetic Philosophy also promotes humility and selflessness, I do not cultivate egoism and therefore do not have an ego to bruise. Listeners are free to agree or disagree. Freedom of speech is a hallmark of Maat Philosophy as long as it is honest and true speech. Rhetoric and confusion are Western principles and they should not be allowed to get in the way of authentic discussion of philosophical principles. Sometimes people hold back on their comments because they know the answers to the questions but do not want to hear them due to fear of having to listen and adhere to these. Therefore, it is unfortunate that you chose not to bring these up at the meeting.

Sometimes listeners of any spiritual tradition tend to highlight certain teachings that agree with their own predilections as opposed to others that challenge their world views. Perhaps you did not attend the entire three days of the seminar since we dealt with the issues you are inquiring about within the framework of Maat Kemetic Philosophy. Certainly the Kemetic teaching advocates punishment from a social political point of view in order to maintain order in society. But it does not advocate grudges or revenge, neither against individuals or other countries. It does however advocate justice and not just punishment.

> "Be always more ready to forgive, than to return an injury;
> they who watch for an opportunity for revenge, lieth in waste
> against themselves, and draweth down mischief on their own
> head."
>
> -Ancient Egyptian Proverb

While promoting truth and righteousness, Maat Philosophy also advocates forgiveness and understanding. Read the writings of Sage Ptahotep, Sage Ani, etc. (excerpts below). Sometimes honest seekers on the path fall into the error of focusing on certain teachings to the exclusion of others because some teachings support their egoistic sensibilities at a particular time or another. This often happens to those who follow secular cultural values and or orthodox religions like Islam or Christianity. They end up meting out punishment to everyone who does not believe as they do. The teachings of Maat must be viewed in a context as a whole and they are to be applied to all equally. However,

201

one cannot practice any philosophy entirely intellectually. One must practice and live the philosophy in order to discover its inner wisdom. The Ancient Egyptian Story of the Eloquent Peasant that you have cited deals with a peasant, Khun-Anup, who is seeking redress for a wrongdoing. He is seeking justice and not revenge. If punishment is necessary to teach a lesson, that punishment can be justified. But if a lesson is learned, the punishment is not necessary since the goal of learning and growing that will prevent future injustice has been achieved. If an injustice has not been acknowledged or redressed and no justice has been served, does that mean that the person who was wronged should maintain a grudge indefinitely? Would that not make the victim a perpetual captive to the original injustice? And would that not impair the capacity of the victim to heal and grow by learning from the injustice and promoting her/his own strength to prevent that injustice in the future, instead of focusing energies on the perpetrators and not employing them towards elevating their own conditions?

Those in the African-American community who choose not to forgive the European community for past and or present and future wrongdoing will continue to doom themselves to a life of limitation and unrest because their recrimination and resentment will draw them into the same fire of delusion, weakness and hatred which leads not to heaven but to hell. It is curious that those who say they are Africentrists and or students of Kemetic philosophy conveniently overlook the precepts which deal with these issues and hold up those proverbs which speak of upholding laws or exacting punishments. Why is that? This is indeed a hard pill to swallow. But it is our own wisdom which says this, not Muata Ashby.

If there is any question about this, perhaps it should be directed at the ancient Egyptian Sages who established Maat Philosophy, the same basic concepts of ethics which are also the basis of every authentic (mystical) world religion of modern times? If there is any abstract humanism in the philosophy which resembles European philosophy, it is perhaps a remnant of Kemetic philosophy embedded in European philosophies which some Europeans have tried to uphold, recognizing its intrinsic practical and spiritual values.

In Kemetic Culture, it was the Per-aah s (i.e., Pharaoh s, King s) first duty to protect the land from Isfet (Unrighteousness). However, this unrighteousness was not just referring to attacks from outside the country, but also corruption from within. While most people like to assign blame on other groups or cultures, they seldom apply the principle internally; they do not like to chastise themselves for eating meat, doing drugs, overindulgence in sex, smoking, spending too much money, etc. Those are isfet also.

In Ancient Egypt, all actions, including wars, police actions and the discharge of law and order in the court system were to be based on Maat Philosophy, and judges were priests of Maat. This means that the carrying out of justice is to be done without resentment or passion, since these cloud the intellect and lead to favoritism, nepotism, sexism, etc., which lead to the disintegration of individual morals, spiritual strength, family cohesiveness, community harmony and cultural decay. The following proverb *"Punish firmly and chastise soundly, then repression of crime becomes an example. But punishment except for crime will turn the complainer into an enemy,"* does not say punish with resentment, recrimination, vengeance, etc., but only for crime committed.

Therefore, what is needed to practice Maat to its perfection is mental peace and purity, freedom from passion and resentment, wisdom, integrity, non-violence, forgiveness, etc., even while upholding the laws and discharging justice. Maat does not play favorites, nor does she allow wrongdoers to escape the universal laws of life which all human beings must observe. This means that even those who seem to get away with murder cannot. That is one of the main teachings of the Story of Hetheru and Djehuty also known as the Story of the Golden Cow. It is not necessary for any human being to take on the burden of being God s instrument of retribution as if God could not handle her affairs! This is a sign of lack of faith in the Divine and it is rewarded with anguish, strife and adversity.

However, she also does not advocate hatred and resentment towards evildoers or their descendants. This is the culture that leads to more misunderstanding and violence. Is this not the same culture that led us to where we are today? How can this kind of culture lead to prosperity and success?

The road to greatness is hard since it requires the giving up of long held notions which comfort the passions and are hard to relinquish. Even Malcolm X, towards the end of his life, realized that the philosophy of hatred towards white people was misdirected. In reality there is a political and economic force, sustained by a plutocracy composed of a small group that may be referred to as a power elite, controlling the masses of white and black people through dogmas and ignorance, such as the notion of race and faith-based religion, and that is where the true problem is to be found and that is what needs to be combated. To hold ignorant people responsible for actions they do not understand misses the more important point of stopping those politicians, captains of industry and religious leaders that use dogma, fear and ignorance to perpetuate unending pain and suffering and conflict between the masses, making them think they are rivals, when in reality it is the politicians who are vying amongst each other (using the masses as cannon fodder) for control of the world economy, which requires the confusion and subjugation of the world populations.[81]

However, the rewards of success on such a journey are inner peace, contentment and success, both personally and as a community and humanity as a whole. This is the lofty vision which lifted up Kemetic society and allowed the culture to persist for over 5,000 years.

Below are some teachings that directly relate to your question of how to handle wrongdoing. I believe they speak for themselves and clearly advocate justice, but not unrestrained or uncompassionate punishment, and certainly not unnecessary punishment. If a person is hurting others, then justice is required and punishment may be warranted. If a person has learned their lesson or ceases the wrongdoing, there is no further need for the punishment; then understanding and forgiveness are in order. The objective is to reach peace and understanding and not just to administer punishment. When would we ever punish a child without explaining why and trying to reach understanding? If the child realized the mistake, what is the point of punishment except revenge? Realizing the mistake here means understanding the error and pain caused as well as the fault in the thought process that led to it, and a sincere personal desire to avoid that error ever again in order to prevent that suffering to self and other. And even if we fail in our duty to punish when punishment is due, is there escape from the great judgment administered by God?

---

[81] For more detailed analysis see the book *The Collapse of Civilization and the Death of American Empire* by Sebai Muata Ashby (2006)

GOD PUNISHES THE EVILDOERS

"MAAT is great and its effectiveness lasting; it has not been disturbed since the time of Osiris. There is punishment for those who pass over it's laws, but this is unfamiliar to the covetous one....When the end is nigh, *MAAT* lasts."

"Indeed they who are yonder (those who live righteously will join GOD after death), will be living Gods, punishing anyone who commits a sin. Indeed they who are yonder will stand in the boat (boat of RA) causing the choicest offerings in it to be given to the temples. Indeed he who is yonder will become a sage who will not be hindered from appealing to GOD whenever they speak."

"O think not, bold man, because thy punishment is delayed, that the arm of God is weakened; neither flatter thyself with hopes that the Supreme winketh at thy doings; Its eye pierces the secrets of every heart, and remembered are they for ever..."

ON FORGIVENESS

Sage Ptahotep:

"If you meet a disputant who is not your equal or match, do not attack, they are weak. They will confound themselves. *Do not answer the evil speech and give in to your animal passion for combat by venting your self against them.* You will beat them through the reproof of the witnesses who will agree with you."

"If you are angered by a misdeed, then lean toward a man on account of his rightness. Pass over the misdeed and don't remember it, since GOD was silent to you on the first day of your misdeed."

"Why seeketh thou revenge, O man! With what purpose is it that thou pursuest it? Thinkest thou to pain thine adversary by it? Know that thou thyself feelest its greatest torments."

"Be always more ready to forgive, than to return an injury; they who watch for an opportunity for revenge, lieth in waste against themselves, and draweth down mischief on their own head."

"The root of revenge is in the weakness of the Soul; the most abject and timorous are the most addicted to it."

"One cannot force another to grow beyond their capacity."

ON NON-VIOLENCE

"If you meet a disputant who is more powerful than you, fold your arms and bend your back. Confrontation will not make them agree with you. Disregard their evil speech. Your self control will match their evil utterances and people will call them ignoramuses."

ON THE BEHAVIOR OF INITIATES

(7)"Be free from resentment under the experience of persecution" (Bear insult)
(8)"Be free from resentment under experience of wrong," (Bear injury)

FROM THE PRECEPTS OF MAAT

(3) "DO NO VIOLENCE (TO ANY ONE OR ANYTHING)."

(30) "DO NOT ACT INSOLENTLY OR WITH VIOLENCE."

Peace and Blessings!

Sebai MAA

Question: Follow-up: Does Neterian religion promote forgiveness of enemies – Part 2?

Hotep Dr. Ashby,

I welcome the opportunity to respond to your email. The Friday lecture was the only one that I attended.

I did not raise these issues Friday night, because the Q&A session on that evening was not conducive to dialogue.

While I recognize that Maat is the foundation for cosmic and social order, when I use the term I'm primarily referring to a philosophy of social ethics based on the Seven Cardinal Virtues--Truth, Justice, Harmony, Propriety, Reciprocity, Balance, and Order.
Maatian Ethics, like any other philosophy with various contributors over long periods of time has apparent contradictions, and different interpretations, as you well know.

No one can say that Ptahotep is more correct that Khun Anup, and vice versa. Dr. Kwame Nkrumah says that "each historical situation produces its own dynamics." Their writings and the writings of the Sebait in general, reflect the history at a particular juncture.

Ptahotep was writing during what was probably the pinnacle of African freedom, power, and productivity. Tranquility and peace were the dominant aspects of his day. Had he been writing during a time of either internally driven Isfet, or a time of foreign invasion and domination (Hyksos period) his views may have been different. We see this in the writings of later Seba.

Sometimes we make the mistake of trying to apply our traditions wholesale to our current conditions without critical analysis of those conditions. Ptahotep was not dealing with a people who have suffered a Maafa[82] at the hands of the white supremacy dynamic. A people who Diop says needs their personalities reconstructed. He didn't live in a world dominated by the Yurugu syndrome--spiritual retardation which

---

[82] calamity

infects life-sustaining institutions. Dr. Karenga's Kawaida Theory helps us understand why tradition must be informed by reason, and tested by practice.

My objective is to synthesize knowledge from a variety of sources. This is necessary because the problems that African people face today are so complex that no one source can provide all of the answers. Synthesizers have no room for exclusion based on egoistic sensibilities. Critical thinking does not allow for such. That which is not currently applicable is filed for later, relevant usage.

You've written an epistle on forgiveness without dealing with my fundamental point--repentance precedes forgiveness. The Sebait write extensively about justice, and balance--right measure. X-amount of damage, requires x-amount of repair. For African people, European repentance for their crimes against humanity requires reparations for us. You expect us to forgive them before they repent. Brother, they haven't even apologized. That's why I say your concept of forgiveness is more Euro-Christian than Maatian. African life is just as valuable as the others who have received reparations.

If you got hatred, resentment, and revenge out of what I wrote, you've misread me. That's why I added the quote from Khun Anup. Surely, we must pursue justice without revenge and hatred.

Certainly, the Niswt (King) was the living embodiment of Maat. But Ahmose and Nefertari did not wait for God to send a strong wind to drive the Hyksos from Lower KMT. They were divinely inspired to physically liberate their land and restore Maat   righteousness and order. Within the context of our historical situation we need Maatian consciousness and similar Heka (effective action).

Abstract humanism is most often used by liberals who want to avoid using race as the basis for dealing with issues. I should mention that I believe race to be a pseudo-scientific concept, but it has become such a powerful force and farce that discussion of it cannot be avoided. I don't quite understand what you are saying about abstract humanism being in Kemetic philosophy, but if it's there it's hard to imagine that it's pertinent to the psychodynamics of the current historical situation.

I see the fundamental problem of African people as one of powerlessness. Without power-the ability to either control or significantly influence life-sustaining institutions, people cannot hope to live in peace. We must strive to develop a moral people, and a moral community, and that community must be ready to stand up and fight on every level to make Maat a reality.

Answer by Dr. Muata Ashby

Greetings,

I appreciate your interest and comments.

First, I would like to point out once more, that there is a deficiency with this exchange because as you have said, you did not participate fully in the program that we presented last weekend. This places us all at a disadvantage because the depth of the philosophical issues involved in this discussion were dealt with at some length during the presentation as well as afterwards in separate conversations with the attendants and should have been dealt with at that time. Sometimes honest seekers of knowledge err in not delving deeply into a subject before coming to a judgment. Many times people seek to hold on to their concepts and do not approach the teaching with the openness required to benefit from the teachings. Here we mean by approaching the teaching to include the practice of the disciplines such as worship, meditation, diet change, etc., and not just reading the philosophy since understanding the depth of the philosophy cannot be achieved simply by reading the writings of the philosophers or doing historical researches into political events or legal precedents. Having partial knowledge, these seekers believe they have understood a teaching while in reality they have colored it with their own interpretation based on their background, history, desires or concepts. Sometimes seekers make excuses as to why they cannot attend lectures and seminars. If the struggle of liberation (physical, mental and spiritual) is supposed to be paramount, what should come in the way of receiving the nectar of spiritual wisdom? If a man was told he will win a lottery if he only goes to a certain place to receive the ticket, what other appointments would be more pressing? Those who arrogantly dabble in this philosophy are like the unsuccessful well diggers. They dig here and there but never in one place and deeply to discover the depths, because in their minds they think they already know what will be said and in the process, they belittle the teaching and maintain themselves and the community in an ignorant state.

Those who are truly concerned with good speech should consider that the manner or intent behind a question is the determiner of its righteousness or unrighteousness. Should not the ignorant ask ignorant questions, or should they remain ignorant for fear of not adhering to some notion of propriety based on ignorance? All questions are valid if they are honest attempts to learn and reach understanding. A true seeker of truth will not allow impropriety or embarrassment to stand between them and truth. However, true seekers humble themselves to those who merit respect and do not challenge them with concepts based on passion and ignorance of the teaching only to cause argument and confusion so that they themselves to not have to make the important changes they know, deep down, that are necessary in their own lives.

Mystical Philosophy is not like academic study of an ordinary nature. It requires more than intellectual knowledge to be comprehended. It requires that the person reflect upon and practice it in order for it to bear its real fruits. Otherwise, there is no real frame of reference for the higher aspects of a teaching to be given or understood. Not until that point is reached wherein a student is well versed in the intellectual as well as the practice of a philosophy, should that person venture to enter into judgments either condemning or affirming it. How can a calculus teacher explain calculus concepts to an arithmetic student and how can the arithmetic student judge the value or lack of value of calculus without undergoing the rigorous discipline of study and practice algebra, geometry and then of calculus? For someone like this, no amount of proofs or arguments will suffice because their mind is made up to the way they want to feel, think and act based on their closely held concepts about the world. They would then say that calculus is too hard or the teacher is too idealistic or in error, or perhaps calculus is useful for others maybe but not for me. How can a teaching be imparted if there is lack of regard for the teacher or the teaching as a whole? You indeed added the quote from Khun Anup but you neglected to add the other teachings, presumably because as you stated they seem to be contradictory. However, perhaps you did not consider that the teachings are not absolute instruments to be applied in every situation indiscriminately but meant for certain situations and not others; for example, the injunction for not telling lies does not imply one should not lie in every situation; what if lying would save someone s life, certainly saving a life is a higher truth than telling the truth in that situation is it not? Yet that does not mean that the injunctions are invalid. Furthermore, the principles of the Maatian teaching are valid whether or not they are able to be applied. In other words, just because a maatian injunction cannot be followed does not mean that it should not be followed.

> "MAAT is great and its effectiveness lasting; it has not been disturbed since the time of Asar. There is punishment for those who pass over it's laws, but this is unfamiliar to the covetous one....When the end is nigh, *MAAT* lasts."

In your letter you said that No one can say that Ptahotep is more correct than Khun Anup that statement implies that the philosophy expressed in either parable is mutually exclusive. Ptahotep s writings extolled injunctions for wisdom and good conduct; the Story of the Eloquent Peasant expressed, through parable form, the need and importance of seeking justice and standing up for oneself in that process. Seeking justice and achieving justice actually have the same effect in terms of elevating the personality whether or not justice (however that is defined in terms of an outcome) is achieved. Furthermore, justice may involve punishment of a wrongdoer, but what if the injustice occurred due to an accident or an error or misunderstanding? If you killed someone by accident for example, if you were driving a car and did not see someone and hit them, or by misunderstanding instructions for setting up a machine that later blew up and killed someone, should you be killed? That is blind justice and not wise justice. Justice should be blind to egoism, coercion, bias, etc., but not to mitigating circumstances or to the true goal that the legal system should have, to maintain balance in society so that the needs of all will be met and not to maintain perpetual enmity, conflict and hatred amongst peoples.

Secondly, many seekers make the mistake of formulating the idea that somehow, their plight is different from all people who have come before. You stated: Tranquility and peace were the dominant aspects of his (Ptahotep) day. Had he been writing during a time of either internally driven Isfet, or a time of foreign invasion and domination (Hyksos period) his views may have been different. This statement seems to imply historical relativism, if not moral relativism, meant to absolve our responsibility to follow the instructions of our ancestors with the idea that if we have different challenges then we can ignore their own teaching and do what we want, etc. People have been known to utter comments such as Jesus did not suffer as much as I suffered or things were easy in the times when Buddha was born but I am too oppressed by the world to think about philosophy right now. They believe that certain wisdom teachings are for past ages when things were supposedly different, easier, and not as complicated or rough. This is one of the most misguided notions on the spiritual path and it is recognized as a great obstacle to attaining spiritual enlightenment. During one of the several struggles throughout Kemetic history, Kemetic culture was threatened with extinction. This is pointed out in the writings of *IPUWER* wherein the extent of civil disruption rivaled the condition of any modern country ravaged by war, disease, rampant corruption and civil unrest as well as the complete breakdown of social and government institutions, i.e. total chaos:

> Lo, the face is pale, the bowman ready,
> Crime is everywhere, there is no man of yesterday.
> Lo, the robber --- everywhere,
> The servant takes what he finds.
> Lo, Hapy inundates and none plow for him,
> All say, "We don't know what has happened in the land."
> Lo, women are barren, none conceive,
> Khnum does not fashion because of the state of the land.
> Lo, poor men have become men of wealth,
> He who could not afford (S) sandals owns riches.
> Lo, men's slaves, their hearts are greedy,
> The great do not mingle with their people [when they rejoice-].
> Lo, hearts are violent, storm sweeps the land,
> There's blood everywhere, no shortage of dead,
> The shroud calls out before one comes near it.
> Lo, many dead are buried in the river,
> The stream is the grave, the tomb became stream.
> Lo, nobles lament, the poor rejoice,
> Every town says, "Let us expel our rulers."
> Lo, people are like ibises, there's dirt everywhere,
> None have white garments in this time.
> Lo, the land turns like a potter's wheel,
> The robber owns riches, [the noble] is a thief.
> Lo, the trusted are like ------
> The citizen [says], "Woe, what shall I do!"
>
> Lo, the river is blood,
> As one drinks of it one shrinks from people
> And thirsts for water.

Lo, doors, columns, cofferS2 are burning,
While the hall of the palace stands firm.
Lo, the ship of the South founders,
Towns are ravaged, Upper Egypt became wasteland.
Lo, crocodiles gorge on their catch,
People go to them of their own will.
'-The land is injured",
One says, "Don't walk here, there's a net,"
People flap like fish,
The scared does not discern it in his fright.
Lo, people are diminished,

In those times of strife the sages recognized one central problem, the lack of Maat in society. With the restoration of Maat (implying, order, punishment of wrongdoers, reconciliation, forgiveness and justice for all equally) there was a return to harmony and balance in society which allowed it to resume the greatness that was temporarily lost. Therefore, the argument that those who created Maat Philosophy did not have to cope with hard times, social strife, respond to violence or that they were living in an idealistic abstract humanist dream world must be rejected as a misunderstanding of history and a consequent misinterpretation of the theory and purpose as well as the manner in which Maat Philosophy is to be applied to modern times; nowhere in any Ancient Egyptian text do we find it written that Maat is to be suspended when Egypt is under attack. It is a wonder that after 50 years of independence in many African states, the conditions for many African peoples have worsened. Therefore, it is the application of modern philosophies, theories and theories of government that should be suspect and scrutinized. For example, you mentioned Dr. Kwame Nkrumah and his philosophy. What happened to him and his country (Ghana)? While he was well meaning and suffered to liberate his country, he fell victim to mismanagement and internal corruption, dissent and social disorder. Granted, much unrest was fomented in Ghana by western forces, but still Ghana succumbed politically due to internal weakness and lack of an ethical basis due to loss of cultural cohesion through the slavery and colonialism periods.

While the statement by Mr. Nkrumah may be correct, that "each historical situation produces its own dynamics," it is also true that there are some universal constants in human social order, just as there are constants in the physics of the universe. In fact, truth (Maat) is always the same in the past, present and future. Otherwise, how would we know it to be true? That which changes cannot be true because it is inconsistent; it can only have relative value, conditional significance and therefore relative usefulness in terms of determining correct social principles as a basis for authentic social order and prosperity. Therefore, this argument must be rejected in light of Maatian injunctions. It is exactly this principle which needs to be applied in our times. Is there any wonder that there is unrighteousness in the society generally and there is a lack of Maat? Why not try speaking of the "outdatedness" of Maatian principles once they have been tried, implemented and failed as opposed to judging these without understanding, or practicing them?

"The closer you get to the truth, the simpler it is"

One of the problems of Africentrism is its close affiliation with Western paradigms of thinking, theorizing, conceptualization and philosophizing.

"The Greek tongue (Western language and thought process)
is a noise of words, a language of argument and confusion."

In this error, some Africentrists often use Western paradigms for determining what the African culture is and the best answers are for themselves, instead of looking to themselves and discovering their own rich heritage of philosophy, principles and standards. I ask here is that not the way of western culture? Ideas such as making war by claiming that war is necessary in order to have peace is a typical example of a Western paradigm that many people around the world have adopted, which has led to the perpetuation of wars. It seems akin to we must have an apology before we can forgive and this also means before one can be free from the another who has done wrong which keeps one tied to and disturbed by the object of hatred or resentment and that also ties up the capacity to grow beyond the unrighteous occurrence that led to the disturbance. Due to confusion in the agitated mind, there is always an impetus to discover some complex formula to deal with the problem which is in reality a self-created and self-imposed web of concepts based on ignorance. You stated that some teachings should be filed for later, relevant usage. That perspective also seems Western, just as Christians or Muslims worried about conquest first, and then promoting civilization and Biblical values later, like destroying Native Americans or the atrocities of the African slave trade and then worrying about the ethics, justice and the moral implications later. This view is incorrect.

Ethics are relevant always, especially when one is under attack or persecution, otherwise one becomes as cruel and lawless as the attacker, and both the attacker and the victim go to hell together. You also stated X-amount of damage requires x-amount of repair. Here again, that sounds like an eye for an eye and a tooth for a tooth which is again, a Western paradigm and not an African-Kemetic one. This follows the idea of fighting fire with fire instead of fighting fire with water. But fire burns everything. Thus, hatred is countered most successfully with understanding and not with more hatred. Justice cannot be an end onto itself in the absence of understanding, because without understanding more unrighteousness and injustice will always arise.

These ways of thinking often lend themselves to a picking and choosing (like at a salad bar salad bar spirituality) of those aspects of the philosophy which go along with the subjective sensibilities, and thereby promote degradation in the teaching and its understanding, and consequently its practice. You have brought up the teachings of Khnun-Anup, but not those of the other Sages because you believe that this supports your argument, but in reality your selective application of the teachings is deficient due to the aforementioned reasons. Therefore, the theory of the uselessness of Maatian principles for modern times must be rejected in light of history. Maat philosophy withstood the onslaught of invasions, breakdowns in Kemetic society, etc., for over 5000 years. Therefore, we should look to a breakdown in the practice of Maat in its complete form, and the development of ignorance as the source and cause as well as the solution for the problem of not only racism, but also, sexism, hunger, disease, hatred, violence, and all other imbalances in society.

The very idea that the human plight is complicated, requiring a plethora of ingredients to forge some new solution because we are dealing with a new situation that no one ever had to deal with is a very modern concept indeed. Why not the logic that if it is confusing, then it is an incorrect form of reasoning? Mind you, simple does not necessarily mean easy. The sages of old recognized that time moves on, but human nature stays the same, and no matter how much new technology may emerge, the faults and virtues of human nature remain the same, and therefore require the same treatment from age to age. Therefore, the mystical psychology of the Ancient Kemetic teachings is especially able to cope with the psychodynamics of the human being, especially the psychosis of those who identify with the African experience. In fact, the philosophy of righteous living, Maat, is simple when a person resolves to give up the egoistic and sentimental attachments as well as the negative aspects of the personality which are Setian (demoniac) in nature (anger, hatred, greed, lust, envy, jealousy, etc.), but most of all ignorance of the true nature, the higher Self. Until this lofty but attainable goal becomes the main objective of life, the unenlightened mind will always find a way to convince one that one must struggle or blame others or punish others first, and then worry about higher spiritual issues when the times are calmer or easier. The easier times never come, and a person wastes their opportunities all due to ignorance and egoism (Setian behavior). Therefore, indulging in the disease of hate cannot lead to the cure of peace and harmony, but will lead to more strife and disharmony and a doomsday mentality of impotence and slavery. How can such a person, beset with a deficit of self-awareness and virtue, succeed righteously in any struggle?

Continuing to push for punishment of evildoers and or their descendants at the exclusion of opening the door to forgiveness and reconciliation is in effect the perpetuation of hatred and resentment. While outwardly those efforts (push for punishment of evildoers) appear to be righteous or justified, at a subtle psychological level they are based on the goal of revenge, and this is referred to in the scriptures as physical, mental and spiritual bondage. However, reconciliation without the recognition of what is a just outcome will be incomplete. Forgiveness does not require reconciliation and can occur in the absence of reconciliation and it does mean that the one forgiving has moved on from the emotional and psychological obstruction of hatred and resentment so they can become whole and be powerful in their life again.

In closing, I will repeat once more that Maat does not preclude self-defense or other actions when necessary to respond to certain kinds of injustices, and at the same time the promotion of non-violence and humanism (which is defined here as concern with the interests, needs, and welfare of human beings) is not negated by the need to practice self-defense or the struggle to liberate oneself from injustices.

Therefore, the teachings of Khun-Anup ("Punish the robber and save those who suffer") do not conflict with those of Ptahotep (from the Ancient Egyptian Wisdom Texts), but Ptahotep modifies and refines the concepts:

36. Punish firmly, chastise soundly,
Then repression of crime becomes an example;
Punishment except for crime
Turns the complainer into an enemy.

The teaching from the Instructions of Merikara (also from the Ancient Egyptian Wisdom Texts) is also instructional:

(3) May you be justified before The God,
That a man may say of you even when you are absent,
That you punish in accordance [with what is just for the crime].

The practice of self-defense without a philosophy of righteous action (ethics) is like driving a car at night without headlights. It is very difficult to see the way and the journey is perilous and full of anxiety as well as confusion. Any social philosophy devoid of humanism will degrade to the level of the base egoistic tendencies of the human character with its worst manifestations, hatred, selfishness, and greed, which are based on ignorance of the higher unity of humanity and constitute the sources for all social maladies. However, the use of violent action is to be entered into only on the last resort, and not under the urging of passion for revenge, but out of necessity of duty in self-defense. Revenge is not a divine principle nor is hatred a virtue. Reconciliation and understanding are better than revenge and recrimination. Does anyone knock out their teeth when the teeth bite the tongue? Then why harbor resentment and recrimination, which only serve to prevent positive action and promote self-pity, self-doubt and dependency?

Those who hate, regardless of the reason, whether one was wronged by the other and regardless of who is right or wrong, all go to the hellish condition of miserable existence, while alive, and then also after death, because the vibration of hatred has shaped the mind and that is a form of torment that atrophies the intellect and prevents spiritual evolution. Should a battered woman wait until her husband, the batterer, apologizes or makes restitution, before she picks herself up and gets on with her life? Should she spend the rest of her time blaming him for her miserable state and sit around complaining about how bad life is? Or should she move on and make her way, strengthening herself so as not to allow the battery to occur again, commanding respect instead of begging for it like a panhandler who is lost in the wilderness of life with no direction except

217

the illusory dreams of a corrupt culture based on greed, sexuality, drugs, poisonous diets and pleasure seeking? How can this person be expected to understand her plight if she does not purify herself from the negative thoughts, foods and lifestyles of the corrupt culture? So she stays and continues to accept the battery, and this is her own doing for she chooses not to allow herself to change because it is comfortable where she is. The future away from her hellish condition seems even more fearful because she has no inner fortitude due to a life of unrighteousness, and so the cycle continues.

If people are to be lifted up it cannot be with the rhetoric of hatred and false pride. These are the failings of the unrighteous leaders that become social diseases affecting the masses. Rather, Maat is what endures and while it is hard to practice Maat in the midst of temptations and injustices, the answer is not to excuse the wrongdoing on our own part by blaming its cause on others. When those perpetrating injustice are gone those practicing Maat will remain. Otherwise, the oppressors and the oppressed, both practicing unrighteousness, will perish in the cauldron of mutually assured destruction due to the evil of vice.

If it is true as you have said you saw: the fundamental problem of African people as one of powerlessness, then we need to know where true power is to be found. With paradigms and customs of the conquerors that lead us to live and think in ways that dis-empower us spiritually, mentally and consequently materially, or by discovering the true essence of our own traditions that made our ancestors great and have made any people great throughout history, and which are universal principles applicable to all historical periods? Perhaps the next time I visit your area you will be able to attend a full session in order to draw a fuller understanding of the teachings as they constitute a science of life and cannot be disseminated entirely through books or letters. In order for an individual or a group to learn an advanced discipline, they must spend the time and develop sensitivity to the subtle meaning of the teachings. This is true in ordinary disciplines of life (medical science, engineering, law, etc.), and it is more important in the study of mystical philosophy. In the meantime I hope this letter may assist you in your quest.

May the Blessings of Maat be with you.
Peace and Blessings!
Sebai MAA

Same Question Answered now by Sba Dja Ashby

Greetings,

I have not had an opportunity to reply to your initial letter or communications with Dr. Ashby with regard to his response to your initial letter, until now. Please know that although we appreciate your expression and willingness to communicate at this time, we do not mind so-called challenges. It seemed that you feared that somehow we cannot or would not be able to support what we espouse, and therefore your questions would have somehow had the impact to point out the holes in our work, which would then have a deleterious effect on our credibility and people would become so disillusioned that they would not want to have anything to do with us, and therefore, you felt it best to keep your opinion to yourself, except to comment to another member of our following, for fear of the public losing focus on the positives. Innate in your presumption is that you are correct in your views and we are wrong and would have been left helpless that we would be discredited, and your not challenging us was to spare us the disgrace. It seems that you presume your intention to be a lofty one, however, it is based on closed-mindedness, which limited your perception to the persons with whom you were dealing. Perhaps more homework was needed on your part before placing pre-mature judgment, and in addition, a humbler approach, where perhaps you informed our associate that you had some questions related to the lecture which you would like to address to Dr. Ashby directly. But you did not do this. Rather, you wrote another member of our following, not even asking her if you can discuss this point that you did not agree with with her or Dr. Ashby, but instead, with self-righteous comments, leaving no room for the so called dialogue that you say is so important to you.

In addition, in your second letter to Dr. Ashby, you made a comment in response to what Dr. Ashby had said in his first reply letter about freedom of speech. You made the point that you were concerned about good speech (Mdw Nfr) rather than free speech, yet, Dr. Ashby had qualified his definition of freedom of speech, which is complimentary to your point of good speech. I refer you to re-read that section of the letter. I also urge you to reflect on what you consider to be good speech in light of the comments remarked in reference to the tone and content of your letters, above. Sage Ptahotep*: "If you examine the character of a friend, don't ask other people, approach your friend.*

Deal with them alone, so as not to suffer from their anger. You may argue with them after a little while. You may test their heart in conversation. If what they have seen escapes them, if they do something that annoys you, stay friendly with them and do not attack. Be restrained and don't answer them with hostility. Do not leave them and do not attack them. Their time will not fail to come. They cannot escape their fate."

If Dr. Ashby and I had egos to bruise, we would have written back to the person in our organization that you initially directed your comments to, and offered a short remark about you and ended it there. However, we feel that the basis of your comments is important, because many within the African American community hold a similar view, and it is important that they be addressed, as this is the arena that the Divine has put us in to share his/her wisdom in order to lead these souls back to their true home, to Enlightenment, that is, oneness with the Divine. Dr. Ashby specifically addressed such issues in a recent lecture on *Pan-Africanism in the Light of Kemetic* Sema-Yoga *Philosophy* and the video is available. We also felt that it was important to open a dialogue, because it is also said, When the student is ready, the teacher will appear, and as the person you originally contacted chose to forward your letter to us, it is important that these issues be properly addressed, as she is considered to be a student of Dr. Ashby. Only you can decide to be benefited from what is said here, or to further resist and reject it. Kemetic proverb: *"One cannot force another to grow beyond their capacity." "The lips of Wisdom are closed, Except to the ears of Understanding."*

And to the contrary, you are not the first person to pose this same so-called challenge, and it is certain that you will not be the last. In the past, such challenges have only served to promote deeper insights an understanding into the teachings, for those who are ready and capable of being open to receive them. I refer you to an audio tape we have called: Race Relations in the light of Sema-Yoga philosophy, which came out of a previous seminar challenge in 1997. I don t know about how other speakers / lecturers operate, but we stand firmly by what we say, because of our own personal practical and spiritual experiences. Just because someone may not fully comprehend the workings of gravity, or even deny the existence of gravity, does not mean that gravity does not exist, though, it cannot be seen with the physical eyes. So too the spiritual teachings are understood at many levels as the spiritual aspirant or initiate continues to grow, and they soon realize that what they thought they understood at a lower level, they really did not. Therefore, though thinking they were following the teachings, they were not they were doing so only to their capacity, without the benefit of the preceptor s guidance. However, with continued sincere practice, and with an attitude of surrender to the teachings and spiritual teacher, and with humbleness, they remain open and continue to grow spiritually. Their capacity continues to increase, until the teaching is understood in its most subtle form. This is why one of the 10 precepts of the Initiate states that one must: "Have faith in your master's ability to lead you along the path of truth." Initially, it is this faith in following the advice of the teacher and teachings that must be one s guidance, and there must be surrender, even when it seems contradictory to what your ego tells you, otherwise, the student will fight against the teacher and teachings and continue to maintain themselves in the state of limitation, trapped by their own concepts. Faith in the teacher and teachings implies trust in that guidance, otherwise the teacher-disciple relationship will be limited and one s success in practice will be limited.

Imagine a child whose parents tell her/him that he/she must give up these baby toys to grow into an adult, but that he/she will be given new grown up objects to replace the baby toys, such as books, computers, etc. Suppose that that child is not ready to grow up and give up its stuffed animal toys and baby games and toys. That child will seek to hold onto the toys, and cry and fuss as the parents try to take them away, and may even lash out and injure the parents, believing the parents to be wrong and not to understand what they are doing. Likewise, those who are not ready to grow spiritually resist giving up the notions related to the lower self, even to gain something greater in knowledge of the Higher Self, focusing on the lesser loss rather than the greater gain.

However, if a child is ready to grow, they will gladly let the parents take the toys, though feeling some sadness or discomfort about giving up that which is familiar, but trusting in the parents that something better will come along. As they act this way, the new objects will come and their own experience will lead them to see that the parent s words were true, that as they continue to grow up, they will not miss the baby toys. So faith and trust in the teacher and teachings is needed in the beginning of the spiritual journey, but with practice of the disciplines and teachings, faith becomes personal experience. Then faith is no longer needed. Initiatic Precepts: *(4)"Have faith in your master's ability to lead you along the path of truth," (5)"Have faith in your own ability to accept the truth," (6)"Have faith in your ability to act with wisdom."*

Many people feel that the teachings can be read and understood without the benefit of an authentic spiritual instructor, but as Dr. Ashby pointed out in the lecture, who would want to be operated on by a doctor who read about how to do the surgery in a book. The initiatic path implies a teacher disciple relationship. For more on this subject, I refer you to the book, *Initiation into Egyptian* Sema-Yoga, and a 6 cassette series on the Initiatic Process, where this subject has been dealt with in depth. This is why there is a Kemetic proverb that admonishes: *"And now that thou hast learnt these lessons, make promise to keep silence on thy virtue, and to no soul, make known the handling on to you the manner of Rebirth, that we may not be thought to be calumniators."* The implication of the teaching is that those who have not been initiated into the teaching will find fault with it and its presentation. This is why the Friday night lecture, though it was given to all publicly, it was with the presumption and assumption that those who were there would also attend the Saturday or Sunday seminar. Questions and doubts such as you have posed also came up throughout the seminar, and answers were given.

Another important Kemetic proverb which must be reflected upon is: *"Such words as these have few to give them ear; nay, probably they will not even have the few. They have, moreover, some strange force peculiar to themselves, for they provoke evil unto even more evil."* The implication is that though there are many people who do not know of Maat philosophy, there is also concern for those who study or listen to the teachings, but having not fully understood them, nonetheless believing that they did, use the teachings and espouse the teachings as they continue to perpetuate un-Maat [unrighteous] actions and even worse, lead others along the path of so-call Maat while really promoting un-Maat, all the time blaming others for their lack of effectiveness in the task they are trying to accomplish, all the while there are their own worst enemy. Hence the Kemetic Proverb: *"He who is wrong fights against himself."*

So, there is no question about fighting against injustice, but unless one understands how to fight, so one s soul is not wounded in the battle, but rather, moves closer to its true essence, one is creating as the general comment has become now, bad karma for oneself. One is tripping oneself up, creating future hardships which must be unnecessarily dealt with. The most important Kemetic Myth is a battle of good and evil, the Asarian Resurrection Myth which was discussed Sat and Sun morning. So the question is not if to fight, we have already established this, but how to fight: Kemetic Proverb: "On the journey to the truth, one must stay on the path of love and enlightenment.

I also appreciated the example Dr. Muata Ashby used in his second reply to you about the battered woman, and wanted to expand on this further, as it related to the situation of the African Americans. Dr. Ashby asked the question, after the wife leaves the husband, should she spend the rest of her time blaming him or should she move on and strengthen herself so as not to allow a similar situation of battery to occur again. Which choice is victory? In addition or instead of *strengthen,* one could also use the word *heal*, which implies that she will be able to go on with her life, independent of her husband, of what he does or does not do i.e. regardless of if he apologizes or not, regardless of if he goes for counseling or not. Can she be victimized by him or anyone else if she deals with herself?

If she decided that his actions were wrong and chooses to take action to make him accountable for his actions, what should her reasons be? Because she wants to hear him say he s sorry. Only then can she forgive him and move on? What if he goes to his death bed without saying he s sorry? Should her reason be because she does not want him to do this to anyone else, as he is likely to (concern for humanity-humanism)? Or because she cares for him as a human being, and knows that he is acting that way because he is somehow in pain himself, somehow battered himself, and he too needs help to be released, plus she does not want him to do this to anyone else, as he is likely to (concern for humanity-humanism)?

The subtle power of forgiveness, as you have not realized, lies not in so called **letting the other person off the hook...**but in **LETTING YOURSELF OFF THE HOOK!** Recently, during his televised series on racism and the church, a pastor gave a beautiful example where he threw a folder on the floor and stepped on it. He made the point that when you try to keep someone down (European-Americans trying to step on African-Americans and keep them down), you are really keeping yourself down also. Not only can they not move, but the one who is doing the stepping on also cannot move. Just like in jail, yes inmates are locked up, but aren t the guards and all the people that run the prison also behind bars. And though in the physical realm, you may say, but the guards get to go home, therefore they are not affected to the same degree as inmates, but, based on the laws of Maat of cause and effect (karma), they are equally affected in their mind, the deep unconscious mind. And though in their conscious minds they may delude themselves to feel that they are not prisoners themselves, there is a different story going on in their unconscious, as will be expounded on in the next paragraph below. So, as long as racism exists, both sides are trapped, caught, affected.

Now suppose the suppressor decides to take his foot away, but the one being stepped on is so upset that he grabs a hold of the foot and does not let him off the hook, does not let him move away, that is, until he apologizes, then what? What if the one who was suppressing (doing the stepping on) does not want to apologize? Then what? They both will end up staying locked in a stale mate, neither moving on, neither getting ahead, neither healing. Who benefits? What is not realized, again, because of the subtlety of the teachings, is that by holding to this notion that they do not deserve forgiveness until they have said they are sorry, or until repentance is demanded, as you put it, is that you are karmicly linking (binding) yourself to them, sowing seeds of egoistic impressions (having an individual view of self) in your deep unconscious mind, even if your conscious mind does not realize it. Kemetic Proverb: ***"Everything we do is sowing, and all of our experiences are harvests."*** It will come bear in the future, as will be discussed below.

So what, you demand forgiveness, as does the battered wife. There is not a response. Then what? The mind is continually dwelling on how they have not asked for repentance, how bad they are, how they . they they they . they   The mind becomes agitated and bogged down with they. And the they   the teachings tell us is none other than other souls who all come from the one Mother-Father God (or whatever name you chose to call the Supreme Being), which means spiritually, they are our spiritual brothers and sisters   albeit they too are ignorant of their spiritual kinship with African Americans and people of other so-called   races, so ignorant that they hurt their own kin.   There is no peace of mind. There is no Maat in they.   They is separate from you.

They is different from you. The Higher Self is only revealed in a peaceful mind. Spiritual growth and gaining insights into the teachings only occurs when there is peace in the mind. Maat can only be revealed in her depths when there is peace in the mind. With forgiveness, there is at least one less thought related to them and your mind will be a little calmer, and therefore you will be closer to the experience of your Higher Self. From this vantage point, any situation will be dealt with from a higher perspective of purity and truth Maat.

Forgiveness with repentance is good. But forgiveness, without repentance, is even better from a spiritual point of view. It allows one to practice the teachings of being free from resentment. The teachings of Sema-Yoga are not to make one a normal human being going along with the mass mentality, but to make one super-normal, an enlightened Sage. In Sema-Yogic discipline, what others may consider adversity, one considers as prosperity, because they realize that they will gain spiritual strength in dealing with the situation and keeping themselves centered in Maat. You have yet to prove to me how demanding that repentance always precedes forgiveness; forgiveness does not = holding resentment. Superficially you may feel that you have no resentment, but your words say otherwise, so if you feel that you are truly without any trace of resentment, it is possible that it is being harbored in your deep unconscious mind, and if so, it must be cleansed through forgiveness and letting go. There is a higher reason for this which will be discussed later also. **The Ancient Egyptian Precepts of Initiatic Education: (7)"Be free from resentment under the experience of persecution"** (Bear insult), **(8)"Be free from resentment under experience of wrong,"** (Bear injury). In Sema-Yogic practice, these are regarded as the highest form of Sema-Yoga thus, they are not easy to do, but necessary for sprititual growth.

The holding onto this repentance before forgiveness concept is not conducive with spiritual growth. Also, perhaps the person who was stepping on you did move on and did repent, as the European-American lecturer Marianne Williamson has done and espouses to her mostly European-American audiences and encourages them to do with respect to African Americans. Will you hear their one or two or three voices amidst the large crowd of silent European-Americans, and forgive them? Or is it necessary for every European-American to apologize? And if only one European-American has apologized, then do you stop lumping all European-Americans in the same category? What do you now say to the European-Americans who have not apologized   and to whom must they apologize? To you? On local TV or an international broadcast? Or on the internet? Or in Congress? Suppose they apologized to the African-Americans they have had contact with, but you are not aware of this, then what? Are they still on your list since they have not apologized to you personally? What about those European-Americans who try to help African-Americans? Do you consider that actions speak louder than words, or do you just deal with them by negating their actions, saying,   They are just trying to get rid of their guilt ? If one reflects deeply as the teachings of Aset (Isis) urges the initiate to do (listening, reflection and meditation on the teachings), one will see things are not always so black and white as people would like to believe.

If you want to fight, fight for Maat, for righteousness. The thing with Maat, as has been pointed out, is that sometimes Maat is with you, sometimes against you. If African Americans persist in wrong actions, Maat will always be against them, even if their wrong actions are in response to a wrong being currently perpetrated or that had been perpetrated on them. And the biggest un-Maatian act is to see them as   them rather than holding that vision of oneness and underlying unity of creation. The importance of this was elucidated in the morning lecture series by Sebai MAA on the Asarian Resurrection Myth, where attaining this vision was the only way that Heru (Horus) was able to defeat the evil Set.[83]

Kemetic Proverbs: *"The wickedness of the soul is ignorance of the Higher Self; the virtue of the soul is knowledge of the Higher Self." "If you are angered by a misdeed, then lean toward a man on account of his rightness. Pass over the misdeed and don't remember it, since GOD was silent to you on the first day of your misdeed."*

So, in effect, you are upset at them for not understanding their true nature, their spiritual nature as being all-encompassing, and thereby acting incorrectly, yet, you too, in withholding forgiveness, are acting out of this same ignorance of your Higher Self, yet you want to hold them responsible, but not yourself. Again, He who is wrong fights against himself.   To truly understand this point, an in depth study of Maat Philosophy as it relates to the laws of cause and effect and reincarnation is needed   more than there is time for in this letter. There is an in depth 2 or 3 audio tape lecture series on the two Precepts of Being Free from Resentment when wronged or persecuted which I presented last year.

---

[83] (audio cassette available from lecture, as well as video from a previous lecture).

We also have a whole series of audio tapes on Maat Philosophy, as well as two books on Maat, one following with the tape set, if you wish to proceed further with more study. There is a saying, that when you point a finger at someone, three fingers are pointing back at you!!! In other words, the accuser is often times a perpetrator of the same type of injustice. It is possible that you may consider this next statement to be too Euro-Christian, but it is in harmony with the second Kemetic quote above about passing over a misdeed. Jesus said, Let he who is without sin cast the first stone. Then there is the general statement, Two wrongs don t make a right.

Then, rather than a fight, black against white, it becomes a fight to establish greater levels of right-ness, of Maat, and with the understanding of them being spiritually connected to you, it becomes like teaching your baby brother or sister that an action they took was wrong and what must be done to correct it. Would you or do you also withhold forgiveness from your children (if you have any), or your family s children, for something they did to you, like kicking you, until they have said they are sorry? Would you even develop and harbor ill-will or demand repentance from a European-American infant for smacking you in the face while you were holding them? Would there even be a discussion of repentance or forgiveness? People who do not understand the spiritual nature of humanity and the purpose of life being to become an enlightened personality, do not understand how to properly relate to negative people in society, emotionally. The assumption is that because people are adults, they are spiritually mature. Spiritual age has nothing to do with physical age. Children can be very young and more spiritually mature than an old person. That is why the teachings says, one must: *"Strive to see with the inner eye, the heart. It sees the reality not subject to emotional or personal error; it sees the essence. Intuition then is the most important quality to develop."* So one must develop an eye to judge the spiritual maturity of the person, and when dealing with a spiritual child, have the same patience, openness, detached love and letting go ability that one would have in dealing with a physical child.

Embrace all European-Americans who wish to fight alongside with you. If you want them to apologize to you personally, face to face, and you will then utter words of forgiveness to them, before they can join your team, tell them that, but be ready to forgive and move on. This will be your true test of whether not resentment was being harbored in your unconscious mind, unbeknownst to even you. You may find that you may even have European-American supporters. If you have led your

African-American followers along the path of Maat, truth, none of them should have any problems with this.

Don t you realize that with the situation with the battered wife, that if she insists on bringing him to a point where he understands his errors and begs forgiveness, that she has help to save his soul from a hellish afterlife, that she has brought about his spiritual upliftment. Regardless of if she did it with resentment in her heart or with wishes for him to be saved in her heart, he will be benefited. She too will be benefited by his repentance, however, if she had bitterness in her heart, she experienced being distanced from her true essence, the source of peace and joy within her, her Higher Self all the time from when she left him until he repented. In addition, her capacity to heal herself would have been limited, as some of her mental energies were being diverted towards him. There are penalties for the physical body and mental body for stressing them out that way, and there are consequences to one s spiritual evolution, as was discussed in the Saturday and Sunday afternoon lecture. An audio cassette is also available from this lecture.

Similarly, anyone who makes efforts to heal the rift between African Americans and European Americans, from any angle, Marianne Williamson teaching European Americans or you or other African Americans teaching African Americans, will allow both parties to evolve spiritually, and society will be benefited. Therefore, it is important that one does not fight against anyone else, but rather, to promote universally based justice only. In this capacity, one needs to cease making generalizations against the European American community. Read Marianne Williamson s books Illuminata where she (European American) has a prayer towards this and her book The Healing of America, where she specifically gets into this issue and politics.

The only caution, is again, what if you never gain enough apologies to satisfy you, or from the specific person or persons you want to apologize and act rightly, then what? Will you destroy yourself stewing in your own juices even as you go about trying to bring so called justice? The discipline of detachment must be intensely studied and applied. Again, we have audio tapes discussing this subject. I presented a lecture on this subject, a 2 or 3 tape set, that goes into this in detail, and this relates to the subject I alluded to that I would discuss later.

These are teachings which we did not address there because of the time limitation, and they are even more difficult for the uninitiated to accept, if one is not properly instructed with the basic teachings. That is, first, the teachings say that what one focuses intense emotions on in life, one becomes: *"When an idea exclusively occupies the mind, it is transformed into an actual physical state."* and *"The choice of the earthly condition is made by the soul itself, and very generally it differs from what it has been in the preceding term of life in this world. The cause is in him who makes the choice and the divinity is without blame in the matter."* The choice the soul makes is based on the impressions, alluded to above, that become stored in the unconscious mind which survives the death of the physical body. Thus, the souls of some African slaves would have reincarnated as European Americans and vice versa. So, genetic lineage and spiritual lineage are two different things. Those who you are fighting against based on color, and those who you are fighting for based on color are most likely not the same slaveholders or slaves, respectively. Something to consider... therefore, it is safest to fight for Maat which is a fight for all humanity. African Americans will benefit from this fight, and even though this may be your main area of concern, it will also have far reaching ramifications for humanity as a whole, and European Americans will also benefit.

Furthermore, as implied in the proverb above, the soul has something to do with the situation into which they incarnate: *"The choice of the earthly condition is made by the soul itself, and very generally it differs from what it has been in the preceding term of life in this world. The cause is in him who makes the choice and the divinity is without blame in the matter."* There is personal responsibility for one s condition in Yogic culture. It is all within the realm of the divine plan for the spiritual growth of that soul. This is another difficult area of acceptance when the teachings are not understood in depth. Initially this is often taken as blame and taking the responsibility off of the evil doers. Rather than being seen as blame, it should be looked upon as opportunity for spiritual growth, based on what that souls/those souls needed to go through. Who knows what souls were inhabiting those black bodies. Black souls? This could not be since souls are sex-less and race -less. Teachings of Aset to Heru in the *Asarian Resurrection*:
"Souls, Heru, son, are of the self-same nature, since they came from the same place where the Creator modeled them; nor male nor female are they. Sex is a thing of bodies not of Souls." And from the Hymns of Amun in *Egyptian Yoga Volume II*: *"Thou art The Supreme Being, who didst create beings endowed with reason; thou makest the color of the skin of one group to be different from that of another, but, however many may be the varieties of mankind, it is thou that makest them all to live."* You may read about these more in depth in *The Mystical Teachings of the African Religion Vol. 4 Asarian Theology* book and the *Egyptian* Yoga

Volume II book, respectively, as well as there are audio tapes available.

Regardless, these souls need to learn the righteous path to go back to their true home, not to Africa, because that is not their true home, but to the Universal Self (God, Higher Self), and this is Sema-Yoga, by whatever name you choose to call it. Kemetic Proverbs: *"The impious Soul screams: I burn; I am ablaze; I know not what to cry or do; wretched me, I am devoured by all the ills that compass me about; alack, poor me, I neither see nor hear! This is the Soul's chastisement of itself. For the Mind* (the deep impressions held in the unconscious mind I spoke about above) *of the man imposes these on the Soul."*

"Suffering in search of truth gives true meaning to the truth."

"To suffer, is a necessity entailed upon your nature, would you prefer that miracles should protect you from its lessons or shalt you repine, because it happened unto you, when lo it happened unto all? Suffering is the golden cross upon which the rose of the Soul unfolds."

Furthermore, when one wakes up to their true essence, one discovers this physical world with its so called pressing realities to be no more than a dream world. So Enlightenment is to this physical world, what this physical world is to your dream world. This is the source of ultimate detachment to understand the relative unreality of the world. For an enlightened person, having achieved oneness with the Higher Self, this world is nothing more than a dream in which they have woken up, even as the dream continues, and the substratum of the dream world is discovered to be the Higher Self. Thus, when the world is discovered to be an illusion, and God, the Self, is discovered as the only reality behind the world, then there is no need to discuss repentance or forgiveness, for these become non-issues. If someone in your dream did everything the Europeans did to Africans in terms of slavery, and in your dream you were an African or European, what does it matter when you wake up and discover that it all happened in a dream? The duality of white and black dissolves upon waking up. However, the catch is, that the way to find out this supreme wisdom, is to practice Maat, that is, developing detachment from the idea of victim and victimizer. Kemetic Proverb: *"The half wise, recognizing the comparative unreality of the universe, imagine they may defy its LAWS."* Thus, one cannot come to this point of ultimate detachment without embracing Maat. So, even though an enlightened person understands the relative unreality of the world, they also understand the importance in dealing with the practical realities and adhering to the spiritual laws, setting positive examples for their students. These laws actually become integrated into them, so they don t even have to think as the initiate does, constantly reminding themselves to see with the inner eye, the illusoriness of the world, etc.

The goal of human life is not to save the world, but to become Enlightened. In the path to attain Enlightenment, self-less service and righteous action is promoted. Kemetic Proverb: *"There is no life for the soul except in knowing, and no salvation but doing."* Therefore, through this action, what ever project you choose to take on, i.e., insisting that European Americans repent and beg forgiveness, or insisting that they do as they promised, with respect to reparations, this project is to be engaged in with the understanding that it is only a means to an end and not the end in itself. It should be understood that its primary divine purpose is to give you an opportunity as it were, to practice what you are learning and offer you challenges to see how established you are in the teachings, if you will be able to keep your vision of unity, or if like Heru in the battle, you will lose it, and how long after losing it will it take you to regain it.

So, the intense practice of Sema-Yoga is the most selfish as well as the most self-less act that you can undertake. You are pursuing your goal of life, and at the same time, setting a positive example for those around you to follow, so they too will be led to Enlightenment, as well as making a difference in the world, for if you get one European American to see the error of the ways of this country, you have changed the world for the better. Likewise, if you get one African American to release hate and anger or to forgive without the need for repentance first, again, you have changed the world for the better. But even if you don t do this, then still, you get your spiritual enlightenment and are setting a positive example to lead those around you towards enlightenment. If your divine task was to work in the arena of souls who are incarnated into African American bodies, then these will be that much closer to true Liberation...Enlightenment.

This is what people really are seeking in life, abiding joy and peace, unaffected by all external conditions Enlightenment, also called Liberation. All the actions people do in life, all people, all actions...good and bad, are because they are trying to secure this goal. But this is a grave error because it is an impossible feat. And this notion is the true cause of all strife, of all evil-doing in life. It is connected to ignorance of one s true spiritual nature. Therefore this is what must be remedied in the hearts of all human beings. It is a grave spiritual error to think or lead people to believe that their experience of profound and abiding happiness depends on anything in this world. Kemetic Proverb: *"There is no happiness for the soul in the external worlds since these are perishable, true happiness lies in that which is eternal, within us."* True happiness does not depend on getting forgiveness from others or needing others to ask for forgiveness, or on getting 40 acres and a mule, or on others treating you with what you consider to be respect or kindness or fairness. It lies in discovering the source of happiness that is your very soul, your very essence, which is unshakable in any external circumstance or situation. This is how you truly liberate yourself and others, by showing them how to get to this destination, this discovery.

This is a profound study of Kemetic philosophy, espoused in the book *Egyptian* Yoga *Volume II* and the audio tape series on Detachment previously mentioned, audio tapes and the book on the *African Religion Vol. 3 Memphite Theology.* This gets into the illusoriness and limitation of the sense organs in judging and experiencing reality as it really exists (that the Divine Self is the only reality that in-fact exists) and the modern findings of quantum physics that are consistent with ancient Kemetic and Eastern wisdom and teachings.

It is easier considering harming or killing someone you feel different from and when holding antagonism towards them, but with true detachment, born of being established in truth and righteousness, one must **philosophically**, just as easily be able to kill their mother, father, brother, child, etc., if they act unjustly as well. How many African Americans who promote harming/fighting or killing Europeans would be also able to do the same to their family if their family stood across them in opposition of Maat? How many African Americans would jail their own family for breaking the laws of Maat and not excuse them on the basis of racism, slavery, etc?

This was the predicament of Arjuna in the Indian Mystical Epic, the *Mahabharata (mahabarata or mahabharatam),* out of which the *Gita,* a spiritual text which deals primarily with Arjuna s plight, emerged. Arjuna told Krishna (an incarnation of God and his teacher in this story) that he would rather give up the land and kingship, than have to kill his family members, but Krishna reminds him, he is a warrior and as such, his duty is to uphold righteousness, and if his evil family takes over the rule of the country, all will suffer. Of course they tried to avoid war at all cost, but the evil family was so evil that they did not want reconciliation. They wanted power and wealth and to rule.

The main inciter to the war was a cousin who would have been heir to the throne as his father was the oldest son of the grandfather king, and should have been crowned king after the grandfather died, but that did not happen because his father was born blind, so the grandfather had given the throne to the younger son. This always stuck in the craw of the father, and he passed on this resentment to the son, so now after the younger brother who was king died, the son of the blind brother felt justified that he should be king, instead of the son of the younger brother (much like the Asarian Resurrection story). But the son of the blind brother was of an evil nature, unlike the son of the king that died who was virtuous and deserving of kingship. Moreover, God, in the form of Krishna, wants justice done and righteousness established. So, Arjuna, known for his valor, is now being compelled to fight in this battle of good over evil, but weakens as he sees his grandfather whom he loves and his teachers and relatives before him those whom he must kill to establish righteousness. This story is about ultimate detachment in performing one s duties. The metaphor is that life is a battle, and one must always fight for righteousness, even if it feels uncomfortable. But not only that, Krishna, in order to get him to fight, arms him with all the major precepts of spiritual wisdom and evolution that Yoga includes, especially about the oneness, and about all of the things discussed above, and many more that fill the many books, audios and videos that we carry. This is much like in the Asarian Resurrection story, of Ancient Egypt, Africa, where Heru had his eyes gouged out by the evil Set, implying that during the course of the battle he got frustrated and lost his spiritual vision. The goddess Hetheru and the god Djehuty came to restore his vision, meaning giving him full spiritual vision. Only then could he defeat Set.

Krishna therefore, used this battle which Arjuna would have to fight anyway, because that was his duty as a warrior, as the means to lead him to spiritual victory. This is the glory of a spiritual teacher and the teachings. They cannot lead a person who is a warrior, whose duty is to fight for justice, to stop being a warrior, and should not. Neither should they try to make one who s path is not to be a warrior, but perhaps, a businessperson, or a spiritual teacher, or a regular working class member of society, into a warrior in the physical world. People must act according to their grain, not against it.

However, everyone should be a spiritual warrior, regardless of which field of expertise they may be involved with or what their duties are to perform, seeking always to uphold Maat. Before you fight, you must be sure you have this wisdom, because as the proverb says, *"Be always more ready to forgive, than to return an injury; they who watch for an opportunity for revenge, lieth in waste against themselves, and draweth down mischief on their own head."* And again, the Kemetic Proverb: *"He who is wrong fights against himself."*

Hetep

Sba Dja Ashby

Question: Is Ancient Egypt the source of the caste system and capitalism?

Greetings,

This question comes from a discussion with someone who was regurgitating some information they read regarding the state of the current capitalist society. It was suggested that the Ancient Egyptians hierarchical way of living and worship was the predecessor of the caste system and of current elitist capitalist exploitation.

While I believed that this is a misunderstanding I didn t really know how to respond.

Could you please help me clarify this? Thank you.

Peace

Answer by Dr. Muata Ashby

Greetings,

Such a comment as you have relayed may be similar to someone comparing the Ancient Egyptian Sage Ptahotep to a personality like President George W. Bush Jr., the former a philosopher, sage and humanitarian, and the latter an avowed war President. These kinds of statements denote ignorance and lack of diligence in reflection and study of history and philosophy while making assertions that are at best infantile, and at worst dangerous to one s own welfare and that of one s culture. For, knowing history prevents others as well as one s own egoistic notions from pulling the wool over one and enslaving one. Nevertheless, such questions are to be answered if asked in the lecture hall by sincere aspirants, however, as you have brought them to our attention I will reply briefly, though I would not entertain such otherwise.

In contrast, the two cultures follow different philosophies of government. While it is true that Ancient Egypt made use of a hierarchical system of government, it is not true to say that Ancient Egypt had an absolute

235

monarchy like Europe.[84] It is also incorrect to say that Ancient Egypt had a capitalist system.[85] The Ancient Egyptian government is often referred to as a Theocracy, but a more accurate term would be Ethiocracy [Ethical-Theocracy]. In fact, the pre-Late-period (Late period is when Egypt was conquered by Asians and Europeans) system of government in Ancient Egypt, going back to the Old Kingdom Period (5000 years B.C.E), may be termed **hierocracy"** ({hiero = clergy} -government by priests or religious ministers), since the leaders were priests and priestesses and the Per-aah (Pharaoh) was considered to be a priest(ess) as well.

In terms of economics, Ancient Egyptian Maat philosophy required a socialistic arrangement.[86] One of the reasons for their success (lasting for thousands of years) is that the Ancient Egyptian culture was founded and governed by an ethical philosophy that discouraged and prevented government excesses and economic frauds, unlike a capitalist market economy or fiat currencies that promote fraud, depletion of resources and a winner takes all mentality that promotes corruption and vice. Ancient Egyptian government followed Maat[87] as its foundation and the concept of Heka-Hekat (Shepherd-flock) it is the concept from which the Christian usage of the appellation of Shepherd for Jesus came. Maat philosophy, when applied to social order, demands the Per-aah was the Shepherd (Heka) who had a fiduciary relationship to the people (Hekat). The Per-aah was responsible primarily for, but not limited to, taking care of the basic needs of the people (food, clothing, shelter/opportunity)[88] and protecting the Holy Land (Kamit-Ancient Egypt), which included safeguarding the land from pollution.

As far as has been demonstrated by USA and European history, the current capitalist globalization system of present day Europe and the USA is an evolution of the previous systems of government and economics (conquest, enslavement, colonialism, serfdom), which has the main goal of protecting the wealth of the rich and if necessary, using people as cannon fodder to accomplish that goal.[89] The current system is

---

[84] See the book *Egyptian Mysteries Vol. 3, DVD Lecture How to Build a Spiritual (not necessarily religious) Civilization* by Muata Ashby
[85] See the book *The Collapse of Civilization and the Death of American Empire* by Muata Ashby
[86] See the book *The Collapse of Civilization and the Death of American Empire* by Muata Ashby See the book *African Origins* by Muata Ashby
[87] See the book *Introduction to Maat Philosophy,* See the book *Egyptian Mysteries Vol. 3* by Muata Ashby
[88] See the book *Egyptian Book of the Dead* by Muata Ashby
[89] See the book *The Collapse of Civilization and the Death of American Empire* by Muata Ashby

not concerned with protection of the land if protecting it is an obstruction to profits. The USA government began as an aristocracy (a group or class considered {by themselves} superior to others.), and developed to an oligarchy (a wealthy class that controls a government.), which is what we have today.[90]

At no time in recorded history is there any record of aristocracies or plutocracies operating in Ancient Egypt- except when dominated by Asians or Europeans. Such forms of government would have been contradictory to the foundation of Maat, the concept of *Heka-Hekat* and the code of the clergy who were after all the true power. Therefore, the notion that Ancient Egypt was the foundation of modern western capitalism, or modern western aggression and imperialism must be rejected absolutely. While there is evidence that the Ancient Egyptians recognized different ethnicities and hues of skin they did not assign those differences to a concept of race or caste. This is akin to recognizing people who are of different occupations, doctors, lawyers, carpenters, etc. There is no evidence that the well-defined social divisions of Ancient Egypt, royalty, farmers, civil servants, army, clergy, were used as rigid castes, preventing people from moving between them or intermarrying, like the practices of the Indian or the European racist social systems. If anything, there are contrary evidences from Ancient Egyptian writings and letters demonstrating interaction between all peoples and aspiration for good positions from all segments of society. There is no evidence of apartheid and no evidence of racism in Ancient Egypt or in ancient Greece for that matter. Again, there is contrary evidence demonstrating intermarriage and absence of any notion of skin color as a criterion of human worth or as a basis for social segregation. People from Nubia as well as Asia and Europe, even when taken as slaves through war, were accepted and naturalized (accepted/adopted) as Ancient Egyptians unlike the modern Western and Arabic culture that forces perpetual segregation of peoples by the color of skin, favoring rule by the lighter skinned members of the population. While the caste system of India may have originated as a means to organize the population, it apparently devolved into a system of segregation by skin color. Later on in the Western countries and the United States of America it further devolved as a system of slavery and domination of one race over all others. Nothing like that has been observed in Ancient Egypt. After all, racism is a form of mental illness, a product of extreme egoism, fear and greed

---

[90] ibid

237

caused by spiritual ignorance, stress and unethical unfettered desires for power and pleasure-seeking. Additionally, there is no evidence that Ancient Egyptian culture, when controlled by Ancient Egyptians and their traditional governing systems, initiated or perpetrated wars of aggression or conquest, only self-defense.

While it is one of the greatest failings of human nature, the ability to develop illusory belief systems of one s own or agree with those of others who can speak well or with influential arguments without presenting any evidences is both breathtaking and damming. Such behavior is not allowed even in authentic universities   except for those places that want to perpetuate dogmas at the expense of truth, like schools that teach Creationism as an event that occurred no more than 6000 years ago even though there is ample evidence to the contrary. Thus, an aspirant should learn the difference between opinions and wisdom. Wisdom is based on knowledge gained, tempered by experiences learned. Wisdom is valuable as it is backed by the evidence of the lives of the wise and their substantiation of the facts and the authentication of their proven insights. Opinions are based on egoistic desires and partial or total ignorance which may or may not be influenced by others or misunderstanding experiences in the world. Opinions are worthless-without proof. For this reason, potential aspirants or honest seekers are admonished to come in contact with authentic teachers.

The present question we are dealing with here falls in the realm of history, but I am not aware of any history class which would make such an assertion as your acquaintance has made, and if they did I wonder what evidences they would present to back it up? Sometimes people are ignorant because they never had the opportunity to study history or were never instructed on the importance of history, and also how to discover the truth through primary sources instead of relying on books written by peoples from other cultures who have a vested interest in maintaining the ignorance of the masses or reflecting some cultures in less than admirable light, or from television documentaries designed to cause controversy, greater viewership and higher profits. Sometimes people prefer to engage in prejudice or bias or outright willful ignorance (purposely not investigating) so that they may retain their preconceptions and thereby not have to come to terms with their own ignorance and change their belief system AND their behavior. Whatever the case may be, such ignorance continues to be perpetuated and conflated with history and social studies books presently used in schools. Therefore, our role in countering such lack of knowledge is a substantial task, but only those who are truly interested in wisdom will hearken to the answer when it is given and proven. Thus, we are forced to reserve our energies for such ones who display the qualities of virtuous seeking and diligent aspiration for self-discovery and self-mastery.

Peace and Blessings!
Sebai MAA

Question: What Should Neterians do about 'racial' Violence and Suffering?

Are Neterians to observe our ethic group being murdered "Wholesale" using many methods by the "so called" elite and do nothing or is that an illusion also? I am requesting your insight on this issue as to why the onslaught of killing is being committed on the black or darker poor uneducated people by the white lighter rich educated people in time and space and what can be done to stop this type of activity?

Answer by Dr. Muata Ashby

GREETINGS,

Neterians like others are sensitive to and can be affected by the realities of the world of time and space. However, just because there are realities to be acknowledged it does not necessarily follow that those realities must be accepted or confronted either physically, mentally or psychically. Consider that when you sleep you are confronted with many realities and why do you not act on them when you wake up? The answer is because though they are real they are not true. Something that is real but not true may also be referred to as an illusion. Why? Because the reality is of the nature of a transient dream. Yet, even in a dream people can suffer until they wake up. In the case mentioned here the dream is of race, there are no races, but yet people act as if there are; in reality all are the same souls encased in watery containers [bodies]. Not all Neterians are of a particular ethnic group but all do belong to the same race , the human race, which originated in Africa, and should feel universal human compassion for the suffering, and righteous indignation towards those who cause pain, when that response is appropriate. So Neterians should work to promote the welfare of all human beings and all nature. The other illusion is that of death, there is no death, but from a relative standpoint there can be suffering and who wants to suffer or see others suffer? Perhaps sadists and the psychopaths but definitely all of the ones who have intensified their egoistic beliefs to the extent of caring only about their desires and not the welfare of others, who they see as different and repugnant. Nevertheless, to the extent it is possible to relieve pain and suffering and ignorance it is appropriate to assist whenever possible to alleviate pain and suffering-this is an expression of ethical culture and divine conscience; so we are also instructed to do by the *Pert M Heru* teachings, especially Chap 33 but also the Sages of the wisdom texts exhort us to extend a helping hand. One can help physically, mentally or psychically depending on the situation;

physically through physical action, mentally though thoughts and elevating reasoning; and psychically through harnessing subtle energies that move cosmic forces and peoples hearts. But that help is to be tempered with wisdom and also we cannot completely fight other peoples battles for them since as soon as we stop they will again falter and fall under the misery of life all over again. So, what are we to do? We are to assist others to help themselves, to help us all, working to teach them, working to provide the necessities of life for all and opportunity to succeed; we are to promote justice. But realize that in order to be successful in changing the world of human society our efforts need to be combined with the efforts of others and if there are insufficient numbers the change will occur very slowly and many people will suffer in the mean time. Nevertheless, to the extent that people suffer before we can relieve their pain, that suffering is dictated by their delusions about the world be it from past actions or present ones and fated by their destiny due to their actions of the past. So, it is mandated by their soul; thus we should feel compassion but not feel anger, hatred or depression over it since it is in the Divine plan; and one day it will end and all will wake up. But in the mean time we should render assistance with this philosophy in mind and we will remain free of resentment, hatred, fear and depression so our actions will be more dynamic and powerful to help those who need uplifting. Many times some people of an ethnic group, that has been wronged, understandably take to resentment, anger, hatred and violence, which perpetuates the cycle of vice, ignorance and war. While there are some situations where war may be justifiable or appropriate [even by Kemetic standards] it is also real that there are situations where war is futile or impossible or undesirable and reason and or civil disobedience are a more plausible solution, and saving that, surrender is not an option. However, in a struggle such as this, where most people are overwhelmed with and debilitated by their own ignorance, desires, resentments, etc. it would be impossible to organize them for a war, for example, such as was depicted in the movie [*The Spook Who Sat By The Door*], so one should not expect the massive torrent of ignorance in the world to respond positively to the wisdom of life but one s mission should be to radiate health, right reasoning and peace as an example; one should provide righteous speech to teach by word and one should provide pure thoughts, desires and prayers to influence the environments, hearts and minds of others about the way of peace, light and truth that leads to harmony, reconciliation and enlightenment.

Peace and Blessings!
Sebai MAA

Question: Is Neterian religion and its priesthood only for black/African people?

Greetings,

I have a question about your priest/ priestesshood. Is the priest/ priestesshood in your organization Ancestrally inherited, meaning strictly for those who are Black/African, or can whites be initiated as priest/ priestesshood as well?

Thank you...

Answer by Dr. Muata Ashby

Greetings,

The Kemetic (Ancient Egyptian) priesthood is for those who follow the culture of Kemet (Ancient Egypt). For instance if you wanted to be a Buddhist priest, you do not follow Western culture and religion (Christianity, Judaism or Islam) and be a Buddhist priest. You must follow the culture associated with Buddhism to be a Buddhist priest. As Buddhism is primarily either Indian, Tibetan, Chinese or Japanese, you would follow one of those cultures. There is no Western independent development in Buddhist culture. Other examples, to practice Islam you follow Arab culture, to follow Taoism you follow Chinese culture. If you fully follow Chinese culture (language, customs, rituals, etc.) and Taoism tradition, you are effectively Chinese. Further, while Buddhism began in India (with association to Ancient Egypt) one could conclude that the primary source of Buddhism should be in India and not in Japan, Tibet or China. However, while it is true that the Japanese, Tibetans and Chinese brought forth positive developments in Buddhism, they were following a culture that it came with (primarily Indian) to them. If we might be able to say that Zen Buddhism from Japan is a distinct form of Buddhism, can we say that it is different, that is, a different religion altogether? Further, could we say they are practicing something in contravention with the original Buddhism of India? It is all Buddhism, but with its distinct cultural nuances that have developed over centuries. If Buddhism were to come to the West (as it has), can we say that a distinct western form of Buddhism has developed there? No, what is practiced are the styles brought there from the East, the cultures of the East.

Likewise, if Kemetic religion is practiced in the West, it comes there with its associated culture. There is no independent development of Neterianism (Kemetic religion) in the West; it developed in Africa, therefore the specific African culture should be practiced with it. Even if over time the Kemetic religion or the Buddhist religion were to develop in the West, could they ever say they are originally Western developments? No, they would always have to say they are looking to their sources just as Zen Buddhism in Japan and Tibetan Buddhism in Tibet would ultimately have to say they are looking to India. The same may be true for the so-called Western religions (Judaism, Christianity, Islam) since these originated in Asia Minor. However, those religions have been altered from their original forms and the adulterated and co-opted forms have been associated with Western culture by the Western rulers and masses.

As Kemetic religion is based in African culture, the practitioner must follow an African perspective. Since African culture, and especially the Kemetic tradition, do not recognize the concept of race and its degraded sociopolitical application (racism), Kemetic culture does not recognize or condone segregationist or racist policies. In fact, the teaching is the opposite, that all human beings have the same source and same kinship as well as the same Divine heritage. Therefore, whether or not the person is of recent (black people) or distant (white people) genetic African descent [all human beings are Africans either recently or anciently], the person should follow Kemetic-African culture. The great teachings of Sage Akhenaton as well as that of other Kemetic sages, enlightens us to the fact that all human beings, regardless of their skin color, originate from the same Spirit and the same physical creation. So we, as Neterians, cannot and do not recognize the human fabricated concept of race or the practice of racism. We do however recognize the cultural basis of religions and the need to follow and practice the philosophy as well as the culture of a tradition in order to experience the fullness of a religious process. Therefore, as long as the practitioner wants to adopt Kemetic/African culture, they may be accepted freely, regardless of the ethnicity (not race) or culture from which they come.

However, while the efforts of many people in different cultures to adopt Kemetic religion are appreciated and to be encouraged, the process of cooptation and delusion that they may keep Western culture and practice an African religion needs to be challenged because that process of adopting the religion without the culture facilitates cooptation and the adulteration of the Kemetic principles with alien cultural values that are incompatible with Kemetic tenets, as well as African values. One example is the Kemetic injunction against pollution of the land and water (found in the 42 precepts of Maat). The question would be how can a person who follows the practices of Europe, Japan or Australia of polluting and co-opting the cultural elements of other peoples, adopt Kemetic teachings but also support the right of Western countries to pollute the world with greenhouse gasses and other pollutants? If a non-African person in a Western country should adopt the Kemetic principles and not support the pollution agenda of the West, that would mean they are rejecting the pollution principle of Western culture and adopting the Kemetic/African, and thus, can be accepted into the Kemetic culture. Another example, Neterian/African religion/culture holds that religion is *Henotheistic*-There is a Supreme Being and lesser gods and goddesses. If a Western person should adopt that tenet, they are putting aside the monotheism of the West and adopting the African paradigm, and can be accepted into the Kemetic culture. Most importantly, if a person adopts a religion/culture fully they would also adopt its concept of Holy Land.

Can we imagine a Jewish person looking to South Africa as their Holy Land ? Why not? Those who practice Christianity, Judaism, Islam, Baha i, Sikhism, Buddhism, etc., look to either Palestine, India, etc., as their Holy Land. In addition, they look at these places as special, as the source of their tradition, the place of their spiritual pilgrimage, and even where they want to be buried. A person who adopts Yoruba religion, for example, but wants to continue believing in Jesus as their savior and Jerusalem as the Holy Land and or be buried with their family in the hills of Tennessee or the family mausoleum in Scotland or Jamaica because they see that as their special place, etc., is not fully following the Yoruba religious culture and its traditions. Likewise, those who want to be considered Kamitans and never want to go to Egypt and want to stay with their families in Georgia or be buried back home in Barbados are not following Kamitan culture, but rather a self-styled hodgepodge of religious practices and name-only vows based on their own desires and not on history or the reality of the practice of the culture; in other words, what they have done is a self-created religion that facilitates their remaining part of their present culture while giving them psychological cover so they may continue making themselves believe they are something else.

But also, there are many levels of following. People follow in accordance with their capacities. Nevertheless, if you are an avid follower of a tradition, that is the culture that should inform every aspect of your life, including the place where you would want to make the final journey of life. That is of course something to work on; but the principle is to be understood. Much failure in following religion occurs due to the misunderstanding of this principle of culture of religion, especially when there is a dominant religion in the environment of human society affecting most aspects of a society and the economy.

Peace and Blessings!

Sebai MAA

Question: Is violence ever justified in the name of righteousness?

Greetings,

I have some comments and some questions. What are Sufi dervishes and what deity(s) preside(s) over the internal life force energy?

Is violence ever justified in the name of righteousness? I understand that Jesus and Gandhi were proponents of nonviolence but I am under the impression that any sage would defend themselves through violent means if Someone (wild animal, criminal, etc) were attacking them. Is this so? My question stems from reading the Indian book Bhagavad-Gita. When Krishna urges Arjuna to fight for the sake of righteousness, even though he will violently kill many humans, is this just? I understand that the Gita should be understood as a metaphor for resolving an inner battle, but if we take the events in the Gita as factual, can the Pandavas kill the unjust Kauravas and be justified?
Please help me understand this, for I am having difficulty with it.

Answer by Dr. Muata Ashby

Greetings,

In reference to the first question, the Sufis are supposed to be the mystical sect of Islamic religion. The Dervishes are a sect of Sufis who practice a famous dance as a meditation and communion with God in the form of Allah. Some Sufis, like Rumi, have recorded highly mystical philosophies. However, there have been some instances of Sufis who have engaged in spiritual terrorism, like the destruction of Ancient Egyptian religious monuments throughout history.

The Kamitan Divinities who preside over the Life Force energy are Aset, Nebethet and Maat. Looking at the caduceus with the shaft intertwined with two serpents, the central shaft is Maat and the two serpents are Aset and Nebethet.[91]

There are two perspectives on the question of the justification of violence, one is worldly and relative and the other is transcendental and

---

[91] See the book *The Serpent Power* by Muata Ashby

enlightened. Violence can be justified in the name of righteousness in reference to the world but not in reference to an enlightened Sage. If a car is going to run a person down another has to violently push them out of the way. If a person is beating another to death another has to violently restrain him or her. If a person is insane and wants to make war on another they should be restrained by force if necessary. However, if one country exploits another, thereby fostering anger, injustice, hatred and resentment it is their own *ariu* (karma) that will bring retribution. However, war alone will never resolve the issues of injustice and unrighteousness that provoked the conflict since the true source of the problem is egoism, desire and greed. This is why understanding, righteousness, fairness, sharing and caring for others are the sure ways to prevent violence and disharmony. Also, that is the way to heal wounds caused by previous unrighteousness.

A sage is not concerned for his or her personal survival and therefore will not do violence to preserve his or her life for the sake of living as a human being who clings to life for life s sake. If a Sage sanctions violence it is for the good of the world as described above. For this reason, the Bhagavad Gita enjoins war, but there is also another war, to protect the order of society and war against the lower nature (unrighteousness) within oneself.

So there is another war; in Ancient Egyptian religion the conflict is the war of Heru and Set, the war between the lower and Higher self. In the inner spiritual struggle, we are also not to kill our enemy, the ego, but we are to subjugate it and transcend it. In society as well as between societies and countries, we are not to promote killing, but reconciliation and understanding. However, if understanding is not possible and the society is attacked, then it is within the right of the culture to repel that attack. In the same way Ancient Egypt had to go to war, and we find no writings from the sages against war for the protection of Ancient Egyptian society, but they do enjoin not killing and of course not making war, meaning, no murder for personal gain and no wars of conquest, but only for self-defense.

The sagely logic for war and social self-defense is that while sages have transcended physical life and its purpose, to attain enlightenment, the unenlightened still remain in need of physicality. Therefore, they need a proper place to live in peace and practice the spiritual disciplines. Therefore, such a place is to be created and protected to the extent it does not cause violence to the environment (pollution) or hurt other people and their societies. This also means that one society does not have the right (as in might makes right) to conquer or exterminate another society for the sake of their own survival -that is the law of animals, which exist on instinct. Humans have the capacity for intellect and should therefore comport themselves with greater ethical conscience. When intellectual capacity is employed to justify wars of conquest or capturing the natural resources of others for one s own benefit or enrichment at the expense of others or the environment, that is a sign of a degraded culture and of a degraded ethical conscience in the leaders and followers of such leaders within a society. So to the extent that a people can promote peace and prosperity without injuring others or attacking others, they have a need and therefore practicing higher social culture and have a right to seek the necessary conditions for living a fruitful life (a life that includes the necessities of life and can lead to spiritual enlightenment).

On the other hand, at the same time, even though the perpetrators are indeed wrong for their unrighteous actions, the people who are enslaved or otherwise abused, are abused to the extend their *ariu* has led them to that condition and they have a right to seek better conditions, but that will only be possible to the extent that they are able to improve their *ariu*. The way to improve *ariu* is through righteousness, ethics, devotion of purpose, right worship (practicing the three steps of religion) which all promote powerful culture, strong cultural identity and clarity of social justice, leading to physical social liberation and inner spiritual enlightenment. It is natural to defend yourself, this is a God given ability, and also attacking is a God given ability. A Sage s actions to protect himself or herself are for the good of the world and not for personal gain. However, what makes people different from animals is the ability to choose forgiveness and understanding as opposed to hatred and revenge.

In the Hindu story of the Mahabharata as well as in the Ancient Egyptian story of the Asarian Resurrection, violence is promoted when there is no other solution. The stories have an inner reference as well as an outer. The inner is that there is a battle between the Higher self and the lower self within a human being. The outer is the battle of righteousness versus unrighteousness between human beings. In Ancient Egypt, there was an army and police force. And in ancient times, they were used as a force to preserve the country from danger. This is a noble cause (the purpose of armies and police), but only if it is based on righteousness and truth. Likewise in ancient India, the Kshatrya caste (warriors) were given the duty of preserving righteousness in society by following the path of the warrior (Dharma). The problem comes in when the noble goal changes to greed and egoism, which lead to corruption of the ethics and the conquest and destruction of others as well as one s own conscience. Armies and police can be used as enforcers of dictatorships and slavery and that is most unrighteous. This is the corruption of law enforcement and the degradation of society due to a deviation from the path of righteousness. That deviation occurs when the leadership and the populace are ignorant of the true nature of all human beings, seeing them as separate entities and as lower beings than themselves. Evil political leaders (lack of ethics {due to spiritual ignorance} causing the personality to be controlled by desires) use that ignorance to goad people through fear and anger to commit unspeakable acts of cruelty and violence. All of that leads the soul to hell while on earth, and then also after death. In Indian legend, that is the path of the Kauravas. In the Ancient Egyptian heritage, that is the path of Set and his fiends. In Indian culture, righteousness, order, truth and peace are the path of the Pandavas. In Ancient Egyptian culture, righteousness, order, truth and peace are the path of Heru and the followers of Heru. The path of Heru is

the goal of all spiritual aspirants; it is called 𓅓𓏤𓋴𓅱𓀀 *Shemsu Heru* - Followers of Heru Shemsu Heru.

Peace and Blessings!
Sebai MAA

Question: Should we not fight back against those white people who perpetrated violence against blacks and latinos?

Greetings,

We have seen violence perpetrated by white people against blacks and latinos and police killings such as the one which occurred recently in Oakland California. Shouldn t even we the followers of Ancient Egyptian Religion with it s non violent teaching fight back? Even our philosophy that says we are all human beings white or black does not demand some action or are we to just say the soul is immortal so it does not matter? I know we are supposed to discover we are more than the race identity but I still hold onto my blackness. So if I cling to my Blackness, is it not because it is my path to enlightenment?

Answer #1 by Sba Dja

I felt that the sentence (below) sums up the essence of your letter, so this will be my focus. *So if I cling to my Blackness, is it not because it is my path to enlightenment?*

Our teachings tell us the following:

"It is not possible to give one's Self to the body and the bodiless,

things perishable and things divine.

The one who has the will to choose is left the choice of one or other;

for it can never be the two should meet.

And in those Souls to whom the choice is left,

the waning of the one causes the other's growth to show itself."

250

You may recall that part of our teaching relates to the Anrutef, the special level of consciousness to be reached by an evolved personality, how it is devoid of sex, beer, lovemaking, etc. In other words, the experience of the Anrutef, the state of being one with the Divine, is devoid of ALL attachments/ clingings. So, the response to your statement, *So if I cling to my Blackness, is it not because it is my path to enlightenment?,* is yes, and no.

While your external RELATIVE realities are your path to enlightenment (gender, ethnicity, etc.), they are not equated with Enlightenment, which transcends ALL RELATIVE realities (sex, ethnicity, etc.). Your blackness is only your path to enlightenment to the extent it is Shedy (study and penetration of the mysteries), because Shedy is your path to enlightenment. Thus, the aspects of your blackness that is your path to enlightenment is precisely letting go of any attachments to that blackness, which means letting go of your attachment to the whiteness of people you refer to as "white" people also.

The path of enlightenment is one of letting go of ALL attachments/clingings.

So the issue is not one s skin color, but one s ATTACHMENT to that skin color or equally and conversely, one s hatred for the skin color of others. Attachment and hatred are two sides of the same coin (liking this means disliking that) and this coin is not conducive and must be overcome to attain enlightenment, if not in this lifetime, in another one. In reference to child rearing, you have probably heard that a parent should never tell a child that the child is bad, but only that her/his behavior is bad, so that the child can separate herself/himself from her/his behavior, and thus, have an opportunity to change her/his behavior.

Similarly, the bad behavior of some/many white persons in this culture does not mean that the souls of those white persons (being of the Divine) are bad, but that their behaviors are bad..

What makes anyone's behavior bad, according to OUR RELIGIOUS teachings?

Egoism, correct?

And what is egoism?

Identification with oneself as an individual being, separate from everyone else, and with one s body and or mind, correct?

What is the source of egoism, according to OUR RELIGIOUS teachings?

Ignorance of the Divine, correct?

Thus, the source of egoism **is not** the whiteness of one s skin (or any other skin color). So, the negative actions of white people are not because of the color of their skin, but because of their ignorance of their Divine essence. But this is also true for non- white people. Therefore, spiritual teachers, in leading aspirants to discover their true essence, are the greatest activists and promoters of Maat, because ONLY *Nehast* (spiritual awakening, enlightenment) will allow people to be free of egoism/injustice.

Thus, according to OUR RELIGIOUS BELIEFS, Egoism is the biggest threat to justice, correct?

Therefore, it would follow if one truly wants to promote justice, then one must work to get rid of egoism, the true culprit, correct? But consider that it is difficult to get rid of one s own egoism, even with one s intensity of Shedy practice, correct? Even sages can t get rid of the egoism of aspirants, even as aspirants are sitting listening to the teachings at their feet.

"One cannot force another to grow beyond their capacity."

Thus, do you think then that you will be able to rid every egoistic person in the world of their egoism? Especially considering that most are not practicing an authentic religion in an authentic way (myth, ritual, mystical)? Of course not! How will aspirants learn to become sages if there is no egoism/injustice in the world? How would they be challenged? Thus, the world is not THE reality. It s a relative reality, a training ground for souls, and laden with traps traps of ego-identification with body and mind which bring forth suffering and misery and the events and history of the world are not to be held as absolute realities and different souls have been playing different parts during the course of this human history, sometimes playing opposite

252

parts, one lifetime as a slave, the next as a slave holder, the next as a white supremacist, and the next as a black subjugated by Jim Crow laws, etc. etc.

Again, these are OUR RELIGIOUS BELIEFS. This is what OUR RELIGION of Shetaut Neter teaches us.

So, yes, promote what is just and right, Maat, but realize that the greatest likelihood for success lies with you overcoming your own egoism, so that you do not remain a conduit for egoism/injustice.

"It takes a strong disciple to rule over the mountainous thoughts and constantly go to the essence of the meaning; as mental complexity increases, thus will the depth of your decadence and challenge both be revealed."

So, yes, fight injustice, but do so in yourself as well, by working to overcome egoism (including attachment to the soul s clothing {i.e., skin with its color}) and not let it, egoism, express under the disguise, appearing as Maat but in reality being unrighteousness.

"He who is wrong fights against himself. "

And yes, on the path, you may promote Maat to the best of your ability, but realize that this is not the highest Maat that you are promoting. To the extent you are still tainted with egoism, your Maat will be tainted with injustice (egoism). As Sebai Maa once said in a very profound and sober tone to an aspirant in distress, THIS IS OUR RELIGION AND THIS IS OUR PHILOSOPHY that we rely on, and this is what we lean on and practice in times of struggle, and it will carry us through. Thus, as practitioners of our religion of Shetaut Neter, THESE are our beliefs and practices. We are not practitioners of Christianity, or of Islam, or of Judaism. We are Neterians! And we must assert OUR beliefs.

"It is very hard, to leave the things we have grown used to, which meet our gaze on every side. Appearances delight us, whereas things which appear not, make their believing hard. Evils are the more apparent things, whereas the Good can never show Itself unto the eyes, for It hath neither form nor figure."

Thus, someone who is identified with their blackness or whiteness or maleness or femaleness has to let that attachment go along the path, and identify oneself as a soul, and then leave the individual soul concept behind, and ultimately, discover one s true essence as the Universal Ba/Soul, the Divine Self. So, yes, in your black skin, the clothing your soul chose for this incarnation in this lifetime, it is to be your path to enlightenment, but in discovering that you are not that black skin, that the essence of YOU is one with all creation, including those souls cloaked in white skin. (And by the same token, consider that the same can be said of the white skin of so-called white people, that their white skin is their path to enlightenment).

"Doth not the sun harden the clay?

Doth it not also soften the wax?

As is one sun that worketh both, even so it is <u>one</u> Soul that willeth contrarieties."

Because from the perspective of the soul, one is NOT one s physical body, clinging to one s skin color relative to one s soul (and asserting the same about other souls), is like clinging to a piece of clothing, relative to one s body, and identifying with the color of the clothing as the color of one s body. The soul puts on a piece of skin color for a particular lifetime to give soul s experiences. It is not something to become attached to. If that happens, it is an error, and this is what leads to egoism.

So, yes, you may advocate for justice along the path, but you may not promote that ONLY black people can promote justice or be just. Yes, you can acknowledge the historical legacy of the injustice of some white people in this culture, insofar as you also acknowledge that there were also white people who fought against injustice and assisted black people. Thus, you must acknowledge that the aspect of you who is fighting for justice is not your black skin, but your soul is devoid of skin (and thus color), which is of Maat, and you must acknowledge other souls cloaked in other skin colors who are doing the same, fighting for justice and upholding Maat.

"Strive to see with the inner eye, the heart.

It sees the reality not subject to emotional or personal error; it sees the essence.

Intuition then is the most important quality to develop."

As a priest of Neterianism pointed out, the highest offering to give the Divine is that of Maat, and the highest Maat is to become Maakheru (Enlightened). So by practicing Shedy, by striving to become enlightened, and to overcome your identification of yourself with your blackness by transitioning to identification with your soul that is devoid of ethnicity (race), and which happens, in this lifetime, to be cloaked in black skin, and in striving to see with your inner eye and see white people also as souls, devoid of race who happen to be cloaked in white skin, you are promoting Maat.

This means that the egoism and the fetters of Set are neither the sole experiences of souls cloaked in white bodies nor souls cloaked in black bodies, but of souls cloaked on bodies of all the various ethnicities that identify themselves only with their physical bodies as being who they are. The extent to which this identification occurs is the extent to which egoism is expressed (anger, hatred, envy, jealousy, etc.). Maakheru is the highest practice of Maat   to become true of speech, and this is done by attaining Nehast. Promoting Maat also means an aspirant must learn to:

(8)"Be free from resentment under experience of wrong,"

And being in a black body in this lifetime under the particular circumstances you discussed, certainly gives an aspirant wanting to attain Nehast lots of opportunities to practice and perfect this. Otherwise, if resentment and anger and hatred is not overcome within oneself, then what one promotes as justice (Maat) is just a perpetuation of egoism, and not Maat, and one is actually engendering egoism in one s self, as well as others, which will create negative ari for oneself and for them to have to suffer through and overcome later in life, because to get to enlightenment, the lessons of all are the same.

"Mastery of the passions allows divine thought and action."

"Truth has the force of emotion BEHIND it."

Sebai Maa tells a story of a Samurai warrior (Note: this story gives an example, but by sharing it I am not promoting that the Samurai is an enlightening code). He was ordered to execute various persons as his duty to the king. One day, a woman whom he was sent to kill spit in his face, and it caused him anger; he walked away without killing her. When asked why, he explained that it was the Samurai code that he was not allowed to kill if he experienced any emotionalism (anger, hatred, etc.) towards whom he was killing.

"Virtues fail that are frustrated by passion at every turn."

So, yes, while your incarnation into a black body is indeed PART of your path to enlightenment, it is not all in the way you may currently believe or understand it to be.

Consider a story told of Buddha. He was walking and talking with someone. Along the way, he was interrupted three times, by three different people, and asked the same question, is the world real. First, it was a neophyte aspirant. His answer was yes, the world is real. Secondly, it was by an advancing, but still immature aspirant, and his answer was well, it s both real and unreal. The 3rd aspirant was highly advanced, and Buddha answered, the world is unreal. The person walking beside Buddha was perplexed and asked how come he answered all 3 questions differently. Buddha explained that for the neophyte, she/he needed to advance more before the teaching of the unreality of the world was explained, otherwise, she/he would run away from their responsibilities, saying it s all unreal, etc. The point is that teachings that are appropriate for one level of advancement on the spiritual path must be let go to advance to the next higher level. Recall that the teachings are like soap, being used to wash off the grosser impurities, but then too the soap is an impurity that must be washed off.

So, it s okay to cling to your blackness as long as it is helping you to identify with the black African ancestors that have put forth the profound teachings of Shetaut Neter that you say is **YOUR RELIGION**. But then also, in reverence to those same ancestors, you must be willing to apply their teachings and philosophy and to grow in the teachings eventually to get to the point of letting go of that very idea of blackness that brought you to the teachings, to attain what they have worked so hard to leave a legacy for you to attain, *Nehast,* the spiritual awakening, enlightenment, freedom from the lower self.

HTP, Seba Dja

Answer #2 by Sba Dja

From Seba Dja:

Udja,

HTP & DUA! Peace and Blessings!

Please know that the challenges you are experiencing with the teachings as presented through the Sema Institute, Temple of Aset, which is based upon the teachings of the KMT sages, is quite understandable.

Even the sages described the difficulty and the challenge of attaining Nehast:

> **"It is very hard, to leave the things we have grown used to,**
> **which meet our gaze on every side.**
> **Appearances delight us,**
> **whereas things which appear not, make their believing hard.**
> **Evils are the more apparent things,**
> **whereas the Good can never show Itself unto the eyes,**
> **for It hath neither form nor figure."**

> **"The path of immortality is hard, and only a few find it.**
> **The rest await the Great Day when the wheels of the universe**
> **shall be stopped and the immortal sparks shall escape from the**
> **sheathes of substance.**
> **Woe unto those who wait, for they must return again,**
> **unconscious and unknowing, to the seed-ground of stars, and**
> **await a new beginning."**

You are not the first and will not be the last aspirant to face the challenges of the teachings.

And teaching over the internet is far from being ideal, so let us keep this in mind, as we work to handle very delicate issues. It s like trying to do delicate surgery, cross country, over the internet. And although communicating via internet sort of provides a sense of community and knumt nefer, good association, it is not the same as having the association of direct contact and communication. These limitations just add to the difficulty of the already difficult challenge.

But our religious teachings tell us:

**"Those who gave thee a body, furnished it with weakness;
but The ALL who gave thee Soul, armed thee with resolution.
Employ it, and thou art wise; be wise and thou art happy."**

**(4)"Have faith in your master's ability to lead you along the path
of truth,"**

(5)"Have faith in your own ability to accept the truth,"

(6)"Have faith in your ability to act with wisdom,"

So, know that this is something that, with time, patience, perseverance, you can grow beyond.

You are not the only aspirant who is challenged by the circumstances you have detailed in your letter. There are other aspirants who are equally challenged, some that have been working through it for sometime who are less challenged, but still find it difficult, and others who have worked through these issues and are no longer challenged.

So do not feel that you are alone or take the silence of other aspirants to mean that they don t care. Rather, many are touched, and some have even responded by bringing forth the letter I wrote to another aspirant on this topic and urging you to read and reflect on it.[92] But sometimes, when the *ari* [karma] is very strong, this is not possible or not enough. They are touched because they too at one point have felt as you do. But their **silence** is also there in part because they know that there is little they can say to ease the situation, that has not already been said; they know this from their own experience. They know what is needed is more study, reflection, meditation on the teachings, and yes,   humility.

If a child thinks that the moon is made of cheese, and keeps insisting that this is true, and does not want to listen when someone older attempts to tell her/him that this is not the case and to share the truth about the moon, what can anyone say to the child?

---

[92] presented earlier in this book as the previous essay by Sba Dja entitled: *Question: Does Neterian religion & philosophy promote forgiveness of enemies – Part 1?*

One cannot agree with the child, and so when disagreeing with the child only results in more arguments on the child s part, what is there to do but to be silent towards the child s comments. So, hence the silence. Know that the silence is not there because of anger towards you, but rather, is filled with understanding and compassion.

And this compassion is not a looking down upon, but rather, an understanding of the situation. Just as in the example above of the child, every one older than that child went through what that child is going through due to immaturity; because all were that child at one time in their own development. They also know that with continued growth and maturity, the child will mature, get some insight that the moon is not cheese, and desire to learn and accept the truth about the moon. Similarly, with continued perseverance, patience, study, reflection and meditation and humility, you too will move beyond this in time if you want to and choose to.

Take a moment to reflect on the path of spiritual growth. It s not all or nothing. It s not (except for rare cases where a foundation was laid in a previous life) one day waking up and one has attained Enlightenment because someone gave one a bit of enlightening wisdom. Hence the Sema-Yoga of Wisdom, which is not only listening or studying the teachings, but also reflecting and meditating on them.

And consider how many years the sagely ancestors in KMT spent engaging in these processes/practices/Shedy disciplines. So, it is not to be expected that an aspirant will read anything that is written by anyone and all of a sudden have an immediate change of heart. This can occur, but only when enough prior work has been done. For most, it s a process of being exposed to the teachings and the challenging circumstances over and over again, and each time applying the teachings to the best of one s capacity (and in the very beginning this can even take the form of expressing the teachings with sarcasm, anger and frustration). So, don t expect that the teachings will make these situations go away, or the intense feelings go away anytime soon. Enlightenment is a gradual process, occurring in degrees.

But with continued and diligent practice, and application of the teachings, no matter how difficult or how ineffective the application may seem, take heart to know that changes are occurring at the deeper level of the unconscious mind, and at some point, the positive ari of the teachings will overpower the negative old ari.

So, first is to try to stop building up new ari. Even though you may not want to accept the teachings, at least, out of reverence for the ancestors, acknowledge their wisdom and power:

From the precepts of the Initiate:
(1)"Control your thoughts,"
(2)"Control your actions,"
(5)"Have faith in your own ability to accept the truth,"
(6)"Have faith in your ability to act with wisdom,"

Unless one has worked in a past life and laid a basis, or has worked intensively in this lifetime, to change one s ari (mental impressions) in a particular area, these will not go away overnight. Rather, they will continue to emerge from the unconscious mind and make their way into one s conscious thoughts, and actions, at times in quite forceful ways, and sometimes, if it s a strong impression/ari, one may not have enough control to stop them; however, one should still exert one s self effort in this direction, to one s best capacity, however limited.

If one does as Sebai Maa says, and relies and leans on Shetaut Neter (our religion and our philosophy), it will carry one through these difficult times (Sebai Maa: **"THIS IS OUR RELIGION AND THIS IS OUR PHILOSOPHY that we rely on, and this is what we lean on and practice in times of struggle, and it will carry us through.)**

As I reminded aspirants at the recent conference, and remind the newly initiated every year, *yes, on the path, one is asking to be purified and cleansed by desiring to attain Nehast.* How is a piece of dirty cloth cleaned, especially in olden times? It was rubbed very hard, and sometimes beaten with wood or lashed against a piece of rock. In today s world, the washing machine swirls it around and around, tossing it and turning it upside down, and spins it around and around all in the process of getting it cleaned. Think of how that piece of cloth feels. At some point in the process, it likely felt, just leave me alone, this is too much abuse, just let me stay dirty. However, when the process is over and it emerges clean, then it feels wonderful, and that it was all worth it.

So too, the process of spiritual growth can be most challenging and painful; your fellow aspirants who have experienced the washing of their negative ari can tell you.

Some aspirants do not make it through this process. Some fight with the teachings and with the teacher. Some leave the teachings and the teacher. But others persist and make it through.

"Mastery of self consists not in abnormal dreams, visions and fantastic imaginings or living, <u>but in using the higher FORCES against the lower thus escaping the pains of the lower by vibrating on the higher."</u>

Sebai Maa has a little joke where he says that the world and spiritual teachers are partners, working hand in hand   aspirants who are unable to follow the words of their preceptors leave and go into the world, only to discover the same lesson the preceptor was trying to teach them, and usually in a more painful way. As our grandparents and parents used to tell us, if you don t listen, you feel.

So those who are not spiritually mature enough to be sensitive to the words of the spiritual preceptor must go through the actual experience, which tends to be more painful and complicated. But as I tell aspirants, this is part of the growth process too. Sensitivity comes from being a self-willed aspirant, that is an aspirant who wants to follow their own path because they know best, then encountering the same challenges, seeing the truth in the teachings & the teachers words, and finally settling on the teachings, sometimes returning to the same teacher or studying with another teacher found during their departure from the teachings and or teacher. It s no different than the process of growing up, where a child ignores the good advice of the parent and wants to experience it for her/himself. Then after some pain, the child acknowledges and heeds the words of the parent more.

Hence the initiatic precept that says:

(4)"Have faith in your master's ability to lead you along the path of truth,"

If one is able to act with humility towards the teachings and teacher, then one will be able to avoid some missteps. But either way, a spiritual teacher will not compel an aspirant to remain as her/his student, or force them to do this or that, because it is not possible and will not facilitate the student to grow. A teacher knows that a student who is sincere will be led to what they need for their growth through their various life experiences, even through other spiritual teachers, but ultimately, the lessons are the same, and what must be learned is the same; perhaps after some time of maturation through their life experiences, they will be more ready and able to do so.

And especially for those of African descent here in America, especially those who grew up here with the legacy of chattel slavery and the mental and intuitional slavery that has followed, it is understandably very difficult to transform the *ari* that has developed as a result of reacting to many of the atrocities. And especially in those times, for many, it was their identification with their blackness that carried them through; the era of Black Pride was important to the very survival of blacks, and contributed to many of the freedoms that African Americans benefit from today.

The teachings are not telling one to forget about the past. But rather, to strive to see with the inner eye, the evils of intense egoism what atrocities it is capable of, whether in relation to the African Holocaust (slavery) or the Jewish Holocaust, or the ongoing Palestinian Holocaust, or the ongoing Darfur genocide, etc. etc. See it in a bigger picture, beyond black or white, which is just a superficial layer of the whole mess. Deeper layers will reveal racism and hatred. Deeper layers will reveal egoism. Deeper layers will reveal ignorance of the Self. This is why the word Shedy means to dig or to penetrate the mysteries. One has to dig deep to get to the essence of the meaning.

And what makes it more challenging is that even as an enlightened sage, one does not lose awareness of their skin color in a practical way. Recall that practical realities are still upheld in the relative world by the enlightened. So, an enlightened sage in America who is black won t necessarily walk into a KKK meeting and expect that he or she will somehow be able to wow that group with talk of the oneness of all humanity, and won t end up being killed or at the very least injured. No just like you would not expect to walk into a kinder garden class and teach the little children calculus and expect them to learn it.

And yes, it s even harder to try to let go of the anger and frustration when one is continuing, on a personal level, to experience racism, hatred, etc, against one. And yes, this is also experienced by spiritual preceptors and teachers in black skin. Becoming enlightened does not enlighten others around you; granted you draw more spiritually sensitive people, but you will still encounter people from all levels of spiritual maturity and immaturity.

So, yes, following the teachings are extremely difficult at times, and sometimes, seemingly impossible. But yet, enlightened sages of past and present stand before you as testaments to the fact that it can be done. At some point in one s spiritual growth, it actually becomes possible to get beyond one s initial reaction and to practice the highest teachings during these challenging times:

(7)"Be free from resentment under the experience of persecution,"

(8)"Be free from resentment under experience of wrong,"

And this world currently gives one lots of opportunities to do so   to perfect these spiritual practices!

Egoistic behaviors such as hatred, greed, etc. are signs of spiritual immaturity. Although these souls perpetrating these atrocities may inhabit the bodies of grown up human beings in this lifetime, from a soul perspective, they are immature souls   like children. So yes, currently we are in a time where (spiritual) children, for the most part, are in charge of the running of things in the world. Therefore, what is needed to counter this are spiritually mature persons emerging in large numbers.

"To destroy an undesirable rate of mental vibration, concentrate on the opposite vibration to the one to be suppressed."

Hence the diligent work of Sebai Maa to put forth the teachings and disciplines that will develop such spiritually mature human beings. Hence Sebai Maa s current efforts to put forth the Glorious Light Meditation System into the mainstream society. The efforts of the Sema Institute is joining with the efforts of other authentic spiritual organizations and persons in this direction, hence the rise in new age spirituality.

So, again, what can you do? Work to attain your own spiritual maturity, to attain Nehast, so that the balance in the world CAN be shifted. Support authentic spiritual organizations that are working to develop spiritually mature persons. When there are enough enlightened or spiritually advanced souls in the world, then there will be real change.

So, yes, Neterians should heed your call to act   but to act in a way to counter the madness of the world, not to enhance it. Thus, Meditate,

Engage in Selfless Service, Engage in Righteous Actions, Sing and Chant Devotional Hymns to the Divine, Practice seeing and serving the Divine Self in all .and attain Nehast! Become spiritual warriors!!! Become Heru the warrior!

As our teachings put it, fight the **"fight of piety-to Know God."**

Allow your reverence towards the African ancestors to allow you to revere the spiritual system that they put in place as their answer to dealing with the ills of humanity.

Their goal was to engender spiritually mature people, people, that have experienced Nehast, and therefore, can contribute to society in a truly positive and meaningful way to defeat Set, ignorance of the Divine manifesting as the ills of human behavior.

So consider the power that they must have discovered in the spiritual practices that we term Shedy. Recall that it was a turning away from these practices and Maat that helped lead to the downfall of KMT. Therefore, to rebuild KMT, what is needed is adherence and promotion of these practices.

Consider the proverb below.

"HUMILITY is a greater virtue than defying death; it triumphs over vanity and conceit; conquer them in yourself first!"

Attaining the virtue of humility, according to their teachings, is GREATER than defying death. Think about that for a moment. Humility is greater than defying death. Certainly, this is contrary to the thinking of this current society where killing others to protect one s ego triumphs over humility.

And think of the injunction to   **conquer them in yourself first!"**

There are aspects of the teachings that just won t be understood until one reaches a certain level of maturity. This is nothing particular to you   this is something that we/all sages, all aspirants have and must go through. We have all been in your position at some time in our spiritual growth, so take heart that with your continued practice, with humility, with patience, you will be able to get past this point   but it will not be easy, because as the proverb says, it s hard to let go what one has become used to, and this includes certain ways of thinking and the feelings they engender.

So, know that you have the compassion and prayers and Mer (love) of the Neterian community, and do not hesitate to call for counseling or communion on a one on one basis.

Consider the length of time students spent studying the Mysteries in ancient times. So, being in the teachings 1 year or 2 years or 5 years in our current times is little, and especially consider if one is not receiving direct tutelage from a more spiritually advanced person, as did occur back in the temple system in KMT. Hence you see why Sebai Maa works diligently to support the Conference and programs that aspirants put together. Though it is not optimal, it is the best that our group is capable of at this time.

But in the meantime, have patience with yourself. I close here with some statements from the Kemetic sages

"Perils, and misfortunes, and want, and pain, and injury, are more or less the certain lot of everyone that cometh into the world.
It behooveth thee, therefore, O child of calamity! early to fortify thy mind with courage and patience that thou mayest support,
with a becoming resolution, thy allotted portion of human evil."

So, again,
"Those who gave thee a body, furnished it with weakness; but The ALL who gave thee Soul, armed thee with resolution. Employ it, and thou art wise; be wise and thou art happy."

(4)"Have faith in your master's ability to lead you along the path
of truth,"
(5)"Have faith in your own ability to accept the truth,"
(6)"Have faith in your ability to act with wisdom,"
MER & HTP & DUA, Divine Love, Peace and Blessings,

Seba Dja

Answer to the same question by Sebai MAA

Udja-Greetings,

I have monitored this thread, of the recent issues relating to the video of the incident in Oakland and the related issue of relations between peoples of different ethnicities. It is gratifying to know that this has stirred thoughts that you felt free to share in this forum as the purpose is to bring issues to the fore in order to discover enlightening ways of understanding and higher ways for practicing Shetaut Neter and thereby bring greater light to the world also. It is commendable that many of you have expressed heartfelt feelings and the desire to assist others. This is a sign of your virtuous tendency and is auspicious. So I thank you for the opportunity to confer with you on such great and important matters.

In all regards it is incumbent upon all who express themselves in this forum to observe respect for the teaching, of the sages and the Divine, for without those the enlightenment will not come forth and the troubling issues of life will consume the personality leading to no solutions, a deepening abyss of suffering for humanity, a worsening human predicament and greater sufferings for the soul. In discussing such issues of strong and deep emotional and ethical import it in this forum it is necessary always to remember the difference between the practical and the transcendental and how to apply these at the appropriate times. Then the proper course becomes clearer and the path to maintaining equanimity and dynamic action is possible.

In fact, when the proper understanding is applied it is actually possible to be more effective in resolving any problem.

The problem of the inhumanity of man and woman against man and woman is a longstanding human predicament which is indeed in need of some action to be worked out and that is the responsibility of the government backed up by enlightened leaders and righteous citizenry. But that struggle does not mean that the degraded humanity should disallow an individual human being from rising above the mayhem of human life into the expansion of inner life. For regardless of the era there is always an issue, if not these then something else and human existence remains troubled and will remain so even after our physical deaths. That said, it is important to know the reason for the mayhem and manner in which it should be thought of and approached. Otherwise the purported solution will not resolve the issue but rather compound and extend and even exacerbate it.

We have received two wonderful elucidations by Sba Dja about the philosophical insights into this issue and a proper exhortation by one of the senior initiates for reflection and further study before raising other questions or making other comments. So I need not repeat those. And furthermore, the elucidations of Sba Dja so expertly expounded the wisdom of the proverbs that they seamlessly interweave the teaching with it s proper understanding for our time and rightly, her exposition should be given as much weight as the proverbs themselves, treated as wise commentary on our sacred scriptures, studied methodically and intensively and reflected upon deeply before further questions or comments by aspirants and should not be hastily passed over. You have also been given insight into this issue in the book Conversation with God and in previous lectures.

My message here is one of initiatic instruction. It is understandable and expected that many of us may have feelings of anger but our own teaching admonishes against that for it is a form of self-destruction not unlike the hatred which persists in individuals or in some quarters of all ethnic groups and can be transferred, through socialization, to succeeding generations. So that anger is not to be allowed to grow to hate for what part of ourselves can we hate for are we not all human beings and part of the same matrix of DNA? If we are to uphold the teaching of Akhenaton that God is the same creator of all peoples and with the Pyramid texts and with the teaching of Aset that the body and soul are separate and that the sufferings of the world are due to a soul s ari then there is no further questioning the point and even though one might not be able to shake the feelings initially, the teaching is to be upheld as an ideal until that time and the actions must flow from that wisdom and not from the egoistic feelings this is the pathway to freedom from the world there is no other.

What remains to be worked out is how that wisdom is to be applied in the world of time and space, to be seen as eternal ethnic conflicts or as something more profound? For, how do we account for some members of all ethnicities who are wise regardless of the amount of their melanin? Or the fact that in ancient times the Africans were treated, BY ALL, with awe and respect not for ethnicity but for wisdom? even though their ethnicity was acknowledged and accepted as equal to any other. If that is correct then what does that mean about the current situation? About our times? About the philosophy of racism? It means it is defunct an illusory. This does not mean it is not a reality but it is not the truth! This idea is important because if one follows realities as if they were truths one is enslaved by them. Following truth leads to freedom from relative realities.

The truth about human degradation is that it is universal, depending on the wisdom or ignorance a person may have, regardless of their ethnicity or race. Yes, therefore, neither melanated nor unmelanated persons are worthy of our allegiance on that basis for that is illusory. Both black and white societies have produce elevated art, literature, music, science and other aspects of culture but both have also manifested degradations that should give us pause before accepting notions of racial superiority or inferiority. Many people are fond of the idea that being white is better than being black ; that blackness holds something degrading for human beings. If that is so then why is it that the ancient Greeks, Persians, Mesopotamians and other peoples revered the culture and civilization of the black Ancient Egyptians and even adopted it to build up their own societies? If blackness was so bad why did Arab and European slave owners constantly rape black and brown [Native American] women; why not repudiate and stay away from them? If blackness is so bad and whiteness is so good why is it that we do not find conquerors and megalomaniacs among the black or brown societies and yet we do among the white ones? If they are so civilized and cultured, why have white people committed atrocities against people of their own race [wars in Europe wars between white ethnic groups]; why have they killed people of their own religion [Crusades, World War 2]? Why have white people set up systems of government and economics that promote empires and tyrannical oligarchies that cause untold pain and suffering to masses of human beings the world over? And why is it that we do not see these kinds of social manifestations in black or brown societies prior to major social disruptions such as colonialism, slavery, war with Europeans and or Arabs? These few examples of contradictions allow us to dismiss the notions of white superiority as bogus. However, what about black superiority?

Many people are fond of the idea that those with more melanin in their skin are somehow higher or more evolved beings and that melanin is a substance that allows the personality to perceive higher consciousness and or that it automatically makes a person more in tune with nature and or that it makes a person more suited for life on earth. If that were so, how do we explain the incidences of black on black crime and atrocities amongst black people committed by other black people? Some may say, well, African Americans are not good examples of the power of melanin because their melanin was diluted by mating with white people and that has compromised the power of their melanin. Even if we look at the darkest people such as Africans who have not mated with Europeans or others, people whose skin is blue-black because it has so much melanin, even in these populations we see the same possibility of degradation we can see in any other group of human beings on earth! One example is the genocide of Rwanda. Some may try to explain this by saying that those people in Africa who engage in ethnic wars or tyrannical governments and who kill their populations or commit other atrocities were tainted by Europeans or Arabs or other disruptive groups that caused those people to become degraded. Well, if that is the case then we would be forced to conclude that melanin is in reality so weak that it can be overcome by the culture of others; it is so weak that it can be scrambled by slavery and colonialism, political destabilization, economic depression, etc. Additionally, the incidence of cancer and other diseases has not been lower for black people who live in Western countries, who moved away from a mostly vegetarian diet when they moved to western countries or who adopted the western diet even as they continue to live in Africa. Melanin has not protected black people from the negative effects of living in the temperate zones or the standard western diet; in fact they suffer more diseases. So let us therefore roundly dispense with the illusoriness of ignorant rhetoric, the foolish ideals of melanin superiority. All human beings, including white people, have some degree of melanin, depending on where their body developed on earth. Let us look at the true sources of human degradation, which affect ALL humans, ignorance of the knowledge of Self and the social, political, economic and cultural practices, traditions, and institutions that perpetuate the ignorance! Then we may create a society that is righteous, in which people of any race can live, contribute and cooperate to produce a culture and institutions that support humanity as a whole instead of the power elite, the rich, the powerful, at the expense of the ignorant masses. Our allegiance as aspirants is to truth alone! All human beings are to be respected as potential expressions of the Higher Self. Human beings are also to be viewed with understanding and compassion if degraded and ill (ignorant of the knowledge of Self). Human beings may be revered for their attainment of that conscious realization of their own higher nature. This is the truly worthy attainment to be looked up to. Reverence for other aspects of humanity is regard for what is illusory. It needs to be clearly understood that human beings [black , white or otherwise] do not come into the world with innate superior powers or consciousness. Higher consciousness, virtue, wisdom, etc. need to be learned, cultivated and protected in order to be developed, perpetuated and propagated to the next generation and the rest of humanity. But if there is a disruption in that process the culture, be it black , white or otherwise, can become degraded. So the duty of protecting and perpetuating truth is the most important role in society.

If one takes action based on egoism and feelings based on realities that action will be tainted even though it may be a righteous action   so before taking action ideally there should be clarity of maatian ethical conscience. If that is not possible then there should be following of directives given by those who are ethically conscious. While this protocol does not guarantee success in the world of time and space, due to many other factors, such as the *ari* of other human beings and the *ari* of the world, it is the intent towards the righteous path that counts towards enlightening the personality regardless of the outcome.

There are two main goals, to promote righteousness in society and enlightenment in individual spiritual life. How is this done? The heart is to be transformed by promoting wisdom and its understanding and purifying the inner vessel from the fetters of Set. Then it follows that suitable laws [Maat] and their proper enforcement will be effective in society. For, impure humans will not apply laws equitably and ignorant humans will not release their egoism, cooperate and build powerful institutions that can have a real positive effect in society. Those who instead remain independent and speaking out or as activists while not accomplishing the deeper and powerful work of self-transformation often become burnt out and disappointed and miss out on inner peace and power which in the end could have been more effective in changing lives and social orders than any protest or complaint. This is a hard lesson learned by many of the activists and protesters of the 60 s and 70 s.

Therefore, the task of an avid aspirant is to work through those quandaries and holding on to the truths that set free, working to cleanse the heart so that the deeper power within will emerge and produce the greater benefit that is what all in reality desire.

An avid aspirant must remember that there is a difference between realities and truth. Different realities abound in human life and they change with the times and in accordance with the level of ignorance or wisdom of societies and their peoples. The realities have practical implications that need to be handled but not with degraded minds but with minds born of wisdom; wisdom that follows a transcendental truth. Realities are transitory and illusory and can easily trap ignorant human beings. And then of course there is the issue of our own complicity in creating, contributing to and upholding the ignorance of ourselves and of society. Should we not also blame ourselves as we blame the world? Or should we heal ourselves and heal the world? If we are also to blame should we forgive ourselves or make ourselves suffer forever? If we are to forgive ourselves are we not also to forgive the world? For forgiving self and not the world is a contradiction leading to confusion and inner conflict.

A truth is transcendental, immutable, universal and inviolable and the beacon for the wise, that leads them to freedom and peace.

It may seem insurmountable, to beginning aspirants, to entertain the prospect of growing beyond the hate or the feelings of hurt, the resentments and misgivings; yet wisdom that understands and forgiveness that releases entanglement are the paths. Mind you, understanding, and forgiveness do not mean allowing lawbreaking with impunity but should mean ideally, impartial and indifferent law; law that applies to all and is free of egoistic taint, such as is applied by the wise. For if we were to remove ignorance that led to a transgression do we still need to punish? If not then a punishment except for ignorance is injustice and punishment that is unjust is egoism that will produce more injustice and egoism in self and other, a vicious cycle. In fact such justice that does not work to redress the cause of transgression is itself unrighteous, from a higher point of view, because it exacts an egoistic desire for societal revenge and not rehabilitation, an expression of forgiveness and love for others an expression of the higher truth of the deeper oneness in Spirit. So, for an initiate of the high wisdom teaching, understanding what goes on in the world and how to feel about it and how to take action in the world in such a way as to not get lost and degraded with the world but to handle the world in such a way as to become enlightened is not a simple matter and should be considered carefully so as to avoid taint and bondage. For the simple minded the winds of desire and ignorance blow them hither and thither and the teaching is not for them yet. They may hold whatever beliefs and the world will teach them through the painful path of disappointments and frustrations.

An avid Africentrist, now turned wise, who was born in the days of segregation, was discriminated against and harassed by police, whose mother came from a country colonized by the European and American Empires and whose father was denied the education to achieve his desired career because of his skin color, and whose father s father got his name from a slave owner and whose father s mother was the daughter of a woman who was the product of a slave and slave owner mating -once said I learned to hate them and that gave me hate, I learned to understand them and that gave me understanding and peace, I learned to attain enlightenment and that freed me, and now I am the light for all because I realized it is not a thing of color but a thing of ignorance.

It is ignorance and not color that is the problem of such people so we should not allow ourselves to become infected with the mental disease of ignorance, egoism and hatred. For one who is infected but who has discovered the higher truth, though not yet being able to experience it, is to follow these instructions so as to lead to that end.

Neither this letter nor any words of the moment or of the morrow can eradicate the issue instantly but, if accepted, with faith, can soothe the heart and open the way. In fact the only true way of eradication is the definitive experience of the higher truth first hand, which is the goal of the teaching. Until then an aspirant needs faith in the teacher, faith in the teaching and faith in her/himself and *udja shems,* that is, diligent following of the teachings, disciplines and wisdom.

For those aspirants who want to attain supreme wisdom, deep understanding, it is imperative that they do as is explained in Chapter 31/64 of the Pert M Heru, to *tek n neter - Come to, to enter, the Divinity.* Coming close is not possible through retaining egoistic notions or ignorant desires and is not accomplished by remaining alone or in the company of the lesser evolved, thinking one is virtuous by remaining with them to help them and not seeking the company of the wise. Coming to, to enter, the Divinity is availing oneself of every opportunity to partake in powerful ritual and instructional experiences in the teaching, participating with the teacher and the temple and other members so as to, through these interactions, allow the fire of the sun, Hetheru, the light of the teaching, to burn away the iniquities of the mind; and this cannot be accomplished from afar. The failure to come close, to humble oneself, to admit ignorance, to think that there is some issue or another that is more important than the study of the teachings under qualified preceptorship and instead thinking they can work things out on their own, by working in the community and reading books or attending cultural lectures or religious talks by exuberant pundits or by imbibing the teachings of varied teachers, picking and choosing what to follow in accordance with personal considerations, like a salad bar is the great failure of many spiritual aspirants. For, only the very few are capable of such practice and only when advanced.

For those who have accepted the initiatic path, such as that laid out by the Temple of Shetaut Neter, there should be only one main teacher and one main teaching being followed and even if aspirants read other texts or listen to others, the main teacher should be allowed to trump all others; otherwise there will be confusion and quandary. The world is one such teacher, teaching that life is about progeny, wealth accumulation, or power, or ethnic supremacy, or about helping others, fighting for your rights or promoting justice in the form of punishments for misdeeds. The only question is after a life of following these things what is it all worth on the day of entering Neterchert? For those whose *ari* demands this kind of life, so be it, for it will work out such issues, to some degree, and hopefully unburden them next time . For those who can see beyond, that there is more to life, as they fight the good fight of the world also fight the battle of the two great warriors; for there is a battle of human life and a battle for the throne of Kemet. If one affirms the former and neglects the latter one may attain the heights of worldly glory only to lose it and become a destitute beggar again and again. In the battle for the throne, mastery of life, it is impossible to win with impurities and iniquities and those will also taint the worldly work, no matter how enlightened it may seem to be. So we are returned again to the teaching

For, we cannot harbor ill feelings and at the same time become sane, whole and enlightened   and the more we heal the more whole we become until the truth is revealed   and in the mean time the world is also healed as we are healed. Assuredly, after death, the soul has no use for segregated cemeteries just as it does not know ethnicity in the anrutf! But an ignorant mind does carry the soul to more sufferings after death and more worldly realities after that suffering. Is that not the greater tragedy than that which is experienced in a single lifetime?   that after suffering the life of conflict and mayhem that it is to be repeated again and again?   perhaps the next time in the role of the perpetrator instead of the victim?   all due to ignorance

Let these words be that opening, through deep reflection, concentration and silence. We can be sure that the current conditions of the world will offer many more opportunities to confront this theme and if faced properly, the challenge can promote positive spiritual evolution and also constructive solutions for the world s problems. So for now let us table this thread and reflect on what has been said and we will continue the work of enlightenment and empowerment thus   by and by.

HTP

SMAA

INDEX

📖

Other Books From The Sema Institute
P.O.Box 570459
Miami, Florida, 33257
(305) 378-6253 Fax: (305) 378-6253

This book is part of a series on the study and practice of Ancient Egyptian Yoga and Mystical Spirituality based on the writings of Dr. Muata Abhaya Ashby. They are also part of the Egyptian Yoga Course provided by the Sema Institute of Yoga. Below you will find a listing of the other books in this series. For more information send for the Egyptian Yoga Book-Audio-Video Catalog or the Egyptian Yoga Course Catalog.

Now you can study the teachings of Egyptian and Indian Yoga wisdom and Spirituality with the Egyptian Yoga Mystical Spirituality Series. The Egyptian Yoga Series takes you through the Initiation process and lead you to understand the mysteries of the soul and the Divine and to attain the highest goal of life: ENLIGHTENMENT. The *Egyptian Yoga Series*, takes you on an in depth study of Ancient Egyptian mythology and their inner mystical meaning. Each Book is prepared for the serious student of the mystical sciences and provides a study of the teachings along with exercises, assignments and projects to make the teachings understood and effective in real life. The Series is part of the Egyptian Yoga course but may be purchased even if you are not taking the course. The series is ideal for study groups.

Prices subject to change.

1. *EGYPTIAN YOGA: THE PHILOSOPHY OF ENLIGHTENMENT* An original, fully illustrated work, including hieroglyphs, detailing the meaning of the Egyptian mysteries, tantric yoga, psycho-spiritual and physical exercises. Egyptian Yoga is a guide to the practice of the highest spiritual philosophy which leads to absolute freedom from human misery and to immortality. It is well known by scholars that Egyptian philosophy is the basis of Western and Middle Eastern religious philosophies such as *Christianity, Islam, Judaism,* the *Kabala*, and Greek philosophy, but what about Indian philosophy, Yoga and Taoism? What were the original teachings? How can they be practiced today? What is the source of pain and suffering in the world and what is the solution? Discover the deepest mysteries of the mind and

universe within and outside of your self. 8.5 X 11 ISBN: 1-884564-01-1 Soft $19.95

2. *EGYPTIAN YOGA: African Religion Volume 2-* Theban Theology U.S. In this long awaited sequel to *Egyptian Yoga: The Philosophy of Enlightenment* you will take a fascinating and enlightening journey back in time and discover the teachings which constituted the epitome of Ancient Egyptian spiritual wisdom. What are the disciplines which lead to the fulfillment of all desires? Delve into the three states of consciousness (waking, dream and deep sleep) and the fourth state which transcends them all, Neberdjer, The Absolute. These teachings of the city of Waset (Thebes) were the crowning achievement of the Sages of Ancient Egypt. They establish the standard mystical keys for understanding the profound mystical symbolism of the Triad of human consciousness. ISBN 1-884564-39-9 $23.95

3. *THE KEMETIC DIET: GUIDE TO HEALTH, DIET AND FASTING* Health issues have always been important to human beings since the beginning of time. The earliest records of history show that the art of healing was held in high esteem since the time of Ancient Egypt. In the early 20th century, medical doctors had almost attained the status of sainthood by the promotion of the idea that they alone were scientists while other healing modalities and traditional healers who did not follow the scientific method were nothing but superstitious, ignorant charlatans who at best would take the money of their clients and at worst kill them with the unscientific snake oils and irrational theories . In the late 20th century, the failure of the modern medical establishment s ability to lead the general public to good health, promoted the move by many in society towards alternative medicine . Alternative medicine disciplines are those healing modalities which do not adhere to the philosophy of allopathic medicine. Allopathic medicine is what medical doctors practice by an large. It is the theory that disease is caused by agencies outside the body such as bacteria, viruses or physical means which affect the body. These can therefore be treated by medicines and therapies The natural healing method began in the absence of extensive technologies with the idea that all the answers for health may be found in nature or rather, the deviation from nature. Therefore, the health of the body can be restored by

correcting the aberration and thereby restoring balance. This is the area that will be covered in this volume. Allopathic techniques have their place in the art of healing. However, we should not forget that the body is a grand achievement of the spirit and built into it is the capacity to maintain itself and heal itself. Ashby, Muata ISBN: 1-884564-49-6 $28.95

4.   INITIATION INTO EGYPTIAN YOGA Shedy: Spiritual discipline or program, to go deeply into the mysteries, to study the mystery teachings and literature profoundly, to penetrate the mysteries. You will learn about the mysteries of initiation into the teachings and practice of Yoga and how to become an Initiate of the mystical sciences. This insightful manual is the first in a series which introduces you to the goals of daily spiritual and yoga practices: Meditation, Diet, Words of Power and the ancient wisdom teachings. 8.5 X 11 ISBN 1-884564-02-X Soft Cover $24.95 U.S.

5.   *THE AFRICAN ORIGINS OF CIVILIZATION, RELIGION AND YOGA SPIRITUALITY AND ETHICS PHILOSOPHY* HARD COVER EDITION Part 1, Part 2, Part 3 in one volume 683 Pages Hard Cover First Edition Three volumes in one. Over the past several years I have been asked to put together in one volume the most important evidences showing the correlations and common teachings between Kamitan (Ancient Egyptian) culture and religion and that of India. The questions of the history of Ancient Egypt, and the latest archeological evidences showing civilization and culture in Ancient Egypt and its spread to other countries, has intrigued many scholars as well as mystics over the years. Also, the possibility that Ancient Egyptian Priests and Priestesses migrated to Greece, India and other countries to carry on the traditions of the Ancient Egyptian Mysteries, has been speculated over the years as well. In chapter 1 of the book *Egyptian Yoga The Philosophy of Enlightenment,* 1995, I first introduced the deepest comparison between Ancient Egypt and India that had been brought forth up to that time. Now, in the year 2001 this new book, *THE AFRICAN ORIGINS OF CIVILIZATION, MYSTICAL RELIGION AND YOGA PHILOSOPHY,* more fully explores the motifs, symbols and philosophical correlations between Ancient Egyptian and Indian mysticism and clearly shows not only that Ancient Egypt and India were connected culturally but also

spiritually. How does this knowledge help the spiritual aspirant? This discovery has great importance for the Yogis and mystics who follow the philosophy of Ancient Egypt and the mysticism of India. It means that India has a longer history and heritage than was previously understood. It shows that the mysteries of Ancient Egypt were essentially a yoga tradition which did not die but rather developed into the modern day systems of Yoga technology of India. It further shows that African culture developed Yoga Mysticism earlier than any other civilization in history. All of this expands our understanding of the unity of culture and the deep legacy of Yoga, which stretches into the distant past, beyond the Indus Valley civilization, the earliest known high culture in India as well as the Vedic tradition of Aryan culture. Therefore, Yoga culture and mysticism is the oldest known tradition of spiritual development and Indian mysticism is an extension of the Ancient Egyptian mysticism. By understanding the legacy which Ancient Egypt gave to India the mysticism of India is better understood and by comprehending the heritage of Indian Yoga, which is rooted in Ancient Egypt the Mysticism of Ancient Egypt is also better understood. This expanded understanding allows us to prove the underlying kinship of humanity, through the common symbols, motifs and philosophies which are not disparate and confusing teachings but in reality expressions of the same study of truth through metaphysics and mystical realization of Self. (HARD COVER) ISBN: 1-884564-50-X $45.00 U.S.   81/2 X 11

6.   *AFRICAN ORIGINS BOOK 1 PART 1* African Origins of African Civilization, Religion, Yoga Mysticism and Ethics Philosophy-Soft Cover $24.95 ISBN: 1-884564-55-0

7.   *AFRICAN ORIGINS BOOK 2 PART 2* African Origins of Western Civilization, Religion and Philosophy (Soft) -Soft Cover $24.95 ISBN: 1-884564-56-9

8.   *EGYPT AND INDIA AFRICAN ORIGINS OF Eastern Civilization, Religion, Yoga Mysticism and Philosophy*-Soft Cover In chapter 1 of the book *Egyptian Yoga The Philosophy of Enlightenment,* 1995, I first introduced the comparison between spiritual teachings and symbols of Ancient Egypt and India that had been brought forth up to that time. Now, this book, *EGYPT AND INDIA,* more fully explores the

motifs, symbols and philosophical correlations between Ancient Egyptian and Indian mysticism and clearly shows not only that Ancient Egypt and India were connected culturally but also spiritually. This book presents evidences like the discovery of the "OM" symbol in Ancient Egyptian texts. How does this knowledge help the spiritual aspirant? This discovery has great importance for the Yogis and mystics who follow the philosophy of Ancient Egypt and the mysticism of India. It means that India has a longer history and heritage than was previously understood. It shows that the mysteries of Ancient Egypt were essentially a yoga tradition which did not die but rather developed into the modern day systems of Yoga technology of India. It further shows that African culture developed Yoga Mysticism earlier than any other civilization in history. All of this expands our understanding of the unity of culture and the deep legacy of Yoga, which stretches into the distant past, beyond the Indus Valley civilization, the earliest known high culture in India as well as the Vedic tradition of Aryan culture. Therefore, Yoga culture and mysticism is the oldest known tradition of spiritual development and Indian mysticism is an extension of the Ancient Egyptian mysticism. By understanding the legacy which Ancient Egypt gave to India the mysticism of India is better understood and by comprehending the heritage of Indian Yoga, which is rooted in Ancient Egypt the Mysticism of Ancient Egypt is also better understood. This expanded understanding allows us to prove the underlying kinship of humanity, through the common symbols, motifs and philosophies which are not disparate and confusing teachings but in reality expressions of the same study of truth through metaphysics and mystical realization of Self. **$29.95 (Soft) ISBN: 1-884564-57-7**

9. *THE MYSTERIES OF ISIS: **The Ancient Egyptian Philosophy of Self-Realization*** - There are several paths to discover the Divine and the mysteries of the higher Self. This volume details the mystery teachings of the goddess Aset (Isis) from Ancient Egypt- the path of wisdom. It includes the teachings of her temple and the disciplines that are enjoined for the initiates of the temple of Aset as they were given in ancient times. Also, this book includes the teachings of the main myths of Aset that lead a human being to spiritual enlightenment and immortality. Through the study of ancient myth and the illumination of

initiatic understanding the idea of God is expanded from the mythological comprehension to the metaphysical. Then this metaphysical understanding is related to you, the student, so as to begin understanding your true divine nature. ISBN 1-884564-24-0 $22.99

10.   *EGYPTIAN PROVERBS:* collection of Ancient Egyptian Proverbs and Wisdom Teachings -How to live according to MAAT Philosophy. Beginning Meditation. All proverbs are indexed for easy searches. For the first time in one volume, Ancient Egyptian Proverbs, wisdom teachings and meditations, fully illustrated with hieroglyphic text and symbols. EGYPTIAN PROVERBS is a unique collection of knowledge and wisdom which you can put into practice today and transform your life. $14.95 U.S   ISBN: 1-884564-00-3

11.   *GOD OF LOVE: THE PATH OF DIVINE LOVE The Process of Mystical Transformation and The Path of Divine Love*   This Volume focuses on the ancient wisdom teachings of Neter Merri the Ancient Egyptian philosophy of Divine Love and how to use them in a scientific process for self-transformation. Love is one of the most powerful human emotions. It is also the source of Divine feeling that unifies God and the individual human being. When love is fragmented and diminished by egoism the Divine connection is lost. The Ancient tradition of Neter Merri leads human beings back to their Divine connection, allowing them to discover their innate glorious self that is actually Divine and immortal. This volume will detail the process of transformation from ordinary consciousness to cosmic consciousness through the integrated practice of the teachings and the path of Devotional Love toward the Divine. 5.5"x 8.5" ISBN 1-884564-11-9 $22.95

12.   *INTRODUCTION TO MAAT PHILOSOPHY: Spiritual Enlightenment Through the Path of Virtue*   Known commonly as Karma in India, the teachings of MAAT contain an extensive philosophy based on *ariu* (deeds) and their fructification in the form of shai and renenet (fortune and destiny, leading to Meskhenet (fate in a future birth) for living virtuously and with orderly wisdom are explained and the student is to begin practicing the precepts of Maat in daily life so as to promote the process of purification of the heart in preparation for the judgment of the soul. This

judgment will be understood not as an event that will occur at the time of death but as an event that occurs continuously, at every moment in the life of the individual. The student will learn how to become allied with the forces of the Higher Self and to thereby begin cleansing the mind (heart) of impurities so as to attain a higher vision of reality. ISBN 1-884564-20-8 $22.99

13.   *MEDITATION The Ancient Egyptian Path to Enlightenment*   Many people do not know about the rich history of meditation practice in Ancient Egypt. This volume outlines the theory of meditation and presents the Ancient Egyptian Hieroglyphic text which give instruction as to the nature of the mind and its three modes of expression. It also presents the texts which give instruction on the practice of meditation for spiritual Enlightenment and unity with the Divine. This volume allows the reader to begin practicing meditation by explaining, in easy to understand terms, the simplest form of meditation and working up to the most advanced form which was practiced in ancient times and which is still practiced by yogis around the world in modern times. ISBN 1-884564-27-7 $22.99

14.   *THE GLORIOUS LIGHT MEDITATION* TECHNIQUE OF ANCIENT EGYPT New for the year 2000. This volume is based on the earliest known instruction in history given for the practice of formal meditation. Discovered by Dr. Muata Ashby, it is inscribed on the walls of the Tomb of Seti I in Thebes Egypt. This volume details the philosophy and practice of this unique system of meditation originated in Ancient Egypt and the earliest practice of meditation known in the world which occurred in the most advanced African Culture. ISBN: 1-884564-15-1 $16.95 (PB)

15.   *THE SERPENT POWER: The Ancient Egyptian Mystical Wisdom of the Inner Life Force.*   This Volume specifically deals with the latent life Force energy of the universe and in the human body, its control and sublimation. How to develop the Life Force energy of the subtle body. This Volume will introduce the esoteric wisdom of the science of how virtuous living acts in a subtle and mysterious way to cleanse the latent psychic energy conduits and vortices of the spiritual body. ISBN 1-884564-19-4 $22.95

16.   *EGYPTIAN YOGA The Postures of The Gods and Goddesses* Discover the physical postures and exercises practiced thousands of years ago in Ancient Egypt which are today known as Yoga exercises. Discover the history of the postures and how they were transferred from Ancient Egypt in Africa to India through Buddhist Tantrism. Then practice the postures as you discover the mythic teaching that originally gave birth to the postures and was practiced by the Ancient Egyptian priests and priestesses. This work is based on the pictures and teachings from the Creation story of Ra, The Asarian Resurrection Myth and the carvings and reliefs from various Temples in Ancient Egypt 8.5 X 11   ISBN 1-884564-10-0   Soft Cover $21.95   Exercise video $20

17.   *SACRED SEXUALITY: EGYPTIAN TANTRA YOGA: The Art of Sex* Sublimation and Universal Consciousness This Volume will expand on the male and female principles within the human body and in the universe and further detail the sublimation of sexual energy into spiritual energy. The student will study the deities Min and Hathor, Asar and Aset, Geb and Nut and discover the mystical implications for a practical spiritual discipline. This Volume will also focus on the Tantric aspects of Ancient Egyptian and Indian mysticism, the purpose of sex and the mystical teachings of sexual sublimation which lead to self-knowledge and Enlightenment. 5.5"x 8.5"   ISBN 1-884564-03-8 $24.95

18.   *AFRICAN RELIGION Volume 4: ASARIAN THEOLOGY: RESURRECTING OSIRIS* The path of Mystical Awakening and the Keys to Immortality NEW REVISED AND EXPANDED EDITION! The Ancient Sages created stories based on human and superhuman beings whose struggles, aspirations, needs and desires ultimately lead them to discover their true Self. The myth of Aset, Asar and Heru is no exception in this area. While there is no one source where the entire story may be found, pieces of it are inscribed in various ancient Temples walls, tombs, steles and papyri. For the first time available, the complete myth of Asar, Aset and Heru has been compiled from original Ancient Egyptian, Greek and Coptic Texts. This epic myth has been richly illustrated with reliefs from the Temple of Heru at Edfu, the Temple of Aset at Philae, the Temple of Asar at Abydos, the

GROWING BEYOND HATE

Temple of Hathor at Denderah and various papyri, inscriptions
and reliefs. Discover the myth which inspired the teachings of
the *Shetaut Neter* (Egyptian Mystery System - Egyptian Yoga) and
the Egyptian Book of Coming Forth By Day. Also, discover the
three levels of Ancient Egyptian Religion, how to understand the
mysteries of the Duat or Astral World and how to discover the
abode of the Supreme in the Amenta, *The Other World* The
ancient religion of Asar, Aset and Heru, if properly understood,
contains all of the elements necessary to lead the sincere aspirant
to attain immortality through inner self-discovery. This volume
presents the entire myth and explores the main mystical themes
and rituals associated with the myth for understating human
existence, creation and the way to achieve spiritual emancipation
- *Resurrection.* The Asarian myth is so powerful that it influenced
and is still having an effect on the major world religions.
Discover the origins and mystical meaning of the Christian
Trinity, the Eucharist ritual and the ancient origin of the birthday
of Jesus Christ. Soft Cover ISBN: 1-884564-27-5 $24.95

19.   *THE EGYPTIAN BOOK OF THE DEAD MYSTICISM OF THE PERT EM
HERU* " I Know myself, I know myself, I am One With God!
From the Pert Em Heru The Ru Pert em Heru or Ancient
Egyptian Book of The Dead, or Book of Coming Forth By
Day as it is more popularly known, has fascinated the world
since the successful translation of Ancient Egyptian hieroglyphic
scripture over 150 years ago. The astonishing writings in it
reveal that the Ancient Egyptians believed in life after death and
in an ultimate destiny to discover the Divine. The elegance and
aesthetic beauty of the hieroglyphic text itself has inspired many
see it as an art form in and of itself. But is there more to it than
that? Did the Ancient Egyptian wisdom contain more than just
aphorisms and hopes of eternal life beyond death? In this volume
Dr. Muata Ashby, the author of over 25 books on Ancient
Egyptian Yoga Philosophy has produced a new translation of the
original texts which uncovers a mystical teaching underlying the
sayings and rituals instituted by the Ancient Egyptian Sages and
Saints. Once the philosophy of Ancient Egypt is understood as
a mystical tradition instead of as a religion or primitive
mythology, it reveals its secrets which if practiced today will
lead anyone to discover the glory of spiritual self-discovery. The
Pert em Heru is in every way comparable to the Indian

Upanishads or the Tibetan Book of the Dead. ☐ $28.95
ISBN# 1-884564-28-3 Size: 8 " X 11

20. *African Religion VOL. 1- ANUNIAN THEOLOGY THE MYSTERIES OF RA*
The Philosophy of Anu and The Mystical Teachings of The
Ancient Egyptian Creation Myth Discover the mystical
teachings contained in the Creation Myth and the gods and
goddesses who brought creation and human beings into
existence. The Creation myth of Anu is the source of Anunian
Theology but also of the other main theological systems of
Ancient Egypt that also influenced other world religions
including Christianity, Hinduism and Buddhism. The Creation
Myth holds the key to understanding the universe and for
attaining spiritual Enlightenment. ISBN: 1-884564-38-0 $19.95

21. *African Religion VOL 3: Memphite Theology: MYSTERIES OF MIND*
Mystical Psychology & Mental Health for Enlightenment and
Immortality based on the Ancient Egyptian Philosophy of
Menefer -Mysticism of Ptah, Egyptian Physics and Yoga
Metaphysics and the Hidden properties of Matter. This volume
uncovers the mystical psychology of the Ancient Egyptian
wisdom teachings centering on the philosophy of the Ancient
Egyptian city of Menefer (Memphite Theology). How to
understand the mind and how to control the senses and lead the
mind to health, clarity and mystical self-discovery. This Volume
will also go deeper into the philosophy of God as creation and
will explore the concepts of modern science and how they
correlate with ancient teachings. This Volume will lay the
ground work for the understanding of the philosophy of
universal consciousness and the initiatic/Sema-Yogic insight into
who or what is God? ISBN 1-884564-07-0 $22.95

22. *AFRICAN RELIGION VOLUME 5: THE GODDESS AND THE EGYPTIAN
MYSTERIESTHE PATH OF THE GODDESS THE GODDESS PATH* The
Secret Forms of the Goddess and the Rituals of Resurrection The
Supreme Being may be worshipped as father or as mother. *Ushet
Rekhat* or *Mother Worship*, is the spiritual process of worshipping the
Divine in the form of the Divine Goddess. It celebrates the most
important forms of the Goddess including *Nathor, Maat, Aset, Arat,
Amentet and Hathor* and explores their mystical meaning as well as
the rising of *Sirius,* the star of Aset (Aset) and the new birth of

Hor (Heru). The end of the year is a time of reckoning, reflection and engendering a new or renewed positive movement toward attaining spiritual Enlightenment. The Mother Worship devotional meditation ritual, performed on five days during the month of December and on New Year s Eve, is based on the Ushet Rekhit. During the ceremony, the cosmic forces, symbolized by Sirius - and the constellation of Orion ---, are harnessed through the understanding and devotional attitude of the participant. This propitiation draws the light of wisdom and health to all those who share in the ritual, leading to prosperity and wisdom. $14.95 ISBN 1-884564-18-6

23.   *THE MYSTICAL JOURNEY FROM JESUS TO CHRIST* Discover the ancient Egyptian origins of Christianity before the Catholic Church and learn the mystical teachings given by Jesus to assist all humanity in becoming Christlike. Discover the secret meaning of the Gospels that were discovered in Egypt. Also discover how and why so many Christian churches came into being. Discover that the Bible still holds the keys to mystical realization even though its original writings were changed by the church. Discover how to practice the original teachings of Christianity which leads to the Kingdom of Heaven. $24.95 ISBN# 1-884564-05-4 size: 8   " X 11"

24.   *THE STORY OF ASAR, ASET AND HERU:* An Ancient Egyptian Legend (For Children)   Now for the first time, the most ancient myth of Ancient Egypt comes alive for children. Inspired by the books *The Asarian Resurrection: The Ancient Egyptian Bible* and *The Mystical Teachings of The Asarian Resurrection, The Story of Asar, Aset and Heru* is an easy to understand and thrilling tale which inspired the children of Ancient Egypt to aspire to greatness and righteousness.   If you and your child have enjoyed stories like *The Lion King* and *Star Wars you will love The Story of Asar, Aset and Heru.* Also, if you know the story of Jesus and Krishna you will discover than Ancient Egypt had a similar myth and that this myth carries important spiritual teachings for living a fruitful and fulfilling life. This book may be used along with *The Parents Guide To The Asarian Resurrection Myth: How to Teach Yourself and Your Child the Principles of Universal Mystical Religion.* The guide provides some background to the Asarian Resurrection myth and it also gives insight into the mystical teachings contained in it which you may

introduce to your child. It is designed for parents who wish to grow spiritually with their children and it serves as an introduction for those who would like to study the Asarian Resurrection Myth in depth and to practice its teachings. 8.5" X 11"   ISBN: 1-884564-31-3 $12.95

25.   *THE PARENTS GUIDE TO THE ASARIAN RESURRECTION MYTH:* How to Teach Yourself and Your Child the Principles of Universal Mystical Religion.   This insightful manual brings for the timeless wisdom of the ancient through the Ancient Egyptian myth of Asar, Aset and Heru and the mystical teachings contained in it for parents who want to guide their children to understand and practice the teachings of mystical spirituality. This manual may be used with the children's storybook *The Story of Asar, Aset and Heru* by Dr. Muata Abhaya Ashby.   ISBN: 1-884564-30-5 $16.95

26.   *HEALING THE CRIMINAL HEART.* Introduction to Maat Philosophy, Yoga and Spiritual Redemption Through the Path of Virtue Who is a criminal? Is there such a thing as a criminal heart? What is the source of evil and sinfulness and is there any way to rise above it? Is there redemption for those who have committed sins, even the worst crimes?   Ancient Egyptian mystical psychology holds important answers to these questions. Over ten thousand years ago mystical psychologists, the Sages of Ancient Egypt, studied and charted the human mind and spirit and laid out a path which will lead to spiritual redemption, prosperity and Enlightenment.   This introductory volume brings forth the teachings of the Asarian Resurrection, the most important myth of Ancient Egypt, with relation to the faults of human existence: anger, hatred, greed, lust, animosity, discontent, ignorance, egoism jealousy, bitterness, and a myriad of psycho-spiritual ailments which keep a human being in a state of negativity and adversity   ISBN: 1-884564-17-8 $15.95

27.   *TEMPLE RITUAL OF THE ANCIENT EGYPTIAN MYSTERIES--THEATER & DRAMA OF THE ANCIENT EGYPTIAN MYSTERIES*: Details the practice of the mysteries and ritual program of the temple and the philosophy an practice of the ritual of the mysteries, its purpose and execution. Featuring the Ancient Egyptian stage play-"The Enlightenment of Hathor' Based on an Ancient Egyptian Drama,

The original Theater -Mysticism of the Temple of Hetheru 1-884564-14-3 $19.95 By Dr. Muata Ashby

28. *GUIDE TO PRINT ON DEMAND: SELF-PUBLISH FOR PROFIT,* SPIRITUAL FULFILLMENT AND SERVICE TO HUMANITY Everyone asks us how we produced so many books in such a short time. Here are the secrets to writing and producing books that uplift humanity and how to get them printed for a fraction of the regular cost. Anyone can become an author even if they have limited funds. All that is necessary is the willingness to learn how the printing and book business work and the desire to follow the special instructions given here for preparing your manuscript format. Then you take your work directly to the non-traditional companies who can produce your books for less than the traditional book printer can. ISBN: 1-884564-40-2 $16.95 U. S.

29. *Egyptian Mysteries: Vol. 1,* Shetaut Neter What are the Mysteries? For thousands of years the spiritual tradition of Ancient Egypt, S*hetaut Neter,* The Egyptian Mysteries, The Secret Teachings, have fascinated, tantalized and amazed the world. At one time exalted and recognized as the highest culture of the world, by Africans, Europeans, Asiatics, Hindus, Buddhists and other cultures of the ancient world, in time it was shunned by the emerging orthodox world religions. Its temples desecrated, its philosophy maligned, its tradition spurned, its philosophy dormant in the mystical *Medu Neter,* the mysterious hieroglyphic texts which hold the secret symbolic meaning that has scarcely been discerned up to now. What are the secrets of *Nehast* {spiritual awakening and emancipation, resurrection}. More than just a literal translation, this volume is for awakening to the secret code *Shetitu* of the teaching which was not deciphered by Egyptologists, nor could be understood by ordinary spiritualists. This book is a reinstatement of the original science made available for our times, to the reincarnated followers of Ancient Egyptian culture and the prospect of spiritual freedom to break the bonds of *Khemn,* ignorance, and slavery to evil forces: *Såaa* . ISBN: 1-884564-41-0 $19.99

30. *EGYPTIAN MYSTERIES VOL 2:* Dictionary of Gods and Goddesses This book is about the mystery of neteru, the gods and goddesses of Ancient Egypt (Kamit, Kemet). Neteru means Gods and Goddesses. But the Neterian teaching of Neteru represents more than the usual limited modern day concept of divinities or spirits. The Neteru of Kamit are also metaphors, cosmic principles and vehicles for the enlightening teachings of Shetaut Neter (Ancient Egyptian-African Religion). Actually they are the elements for one of the most advanced systems of spirituality ever conceived in human history. Understanding the concept of neteru provides a firm basis for spiritual evolution and the pathway for viable culture, peace on earth and a healthy human society. Why is it important to have gods and goddesses in our lives? In order for spiritual evolution to be possible, once a human being has accepted that there is existence after death and there is a transcendental being who exists beyond time and space knowledge, human beings need a connection to that which transcends the ordinary experience of human life in time and space and a means to understand the transcendental reality beyond the mundane reality. ISBN: 1-884564-23-2 $21.95

31. *EGYPTIAN MYSTERIES VOL. 3* The Priests and Priestesses of Ancient Egypt This volume details the path of Neterian priesthood, the joys, challenges and rewards of advanced Neterian life, the teachings that allowed the priests and priestesses to manage the most long lived civilization in human history and how that path can be adopted today; for those who want to tread the path of the Clergy of Shetaut Neter. ISBN: 1-884564-53-4 $24.95

32. *The War of Heru and Set:* The Struggle of Good and Evil for Control of the World and The Human Soul This volume contains a novelized version of the Asarian Resurrection myth that is based on the actual scriptures presented in the Book Asarian Religion (old name Resurrecting Osiris). This volume is prepared in the form of a screenplay and can be easily adapted to be used as a stage play. Spiritual seeking is a mythic journey that has many emotional highs and lows, ecstasies and depressions, victories and frustrations. This is the War of Life that is played out in the myth as the struggle of Heru and Set and those are mythic characters that represent the human Higher and Lower self. How

to understand the war and emerge victorious in the journey o life? The ultimate victory and fulfillment can be experienced, which is not changeable or lost in time. The purpose of myth is to convey the wisdom of life through the story of divinities who show the way to overcome the challenges and foibles of life. In this volume the feelings and emotions of the characters of the myth have been highlighted to show the deeply rich texture of the Ancient Egyptian myth. This myth contains deep spiritual teachings and insights into the nature of self, of God and the mysteries of life and the means to discover the true meaning of life and thereby achieve the true purpose of life. To become victorious in the battle of life means to become the King (or Queen) of Egypt.Have you seen movies like The Lion King, Hamlet, The Odyssey, or The Little Buddha? These have been some of the most popular movies in modern times. The Sema Institute of Yoga is dedicated to researching and presenting the wisdom and culture of ancient Africa. The Script is designed to be produced as a motion picture but may be addapted for the theater as well. $21.95   copyright 1998 By Dr. Muata Ashby ISBN 1-8840564-44-5

33. *AFRICAN DIONYSUS: FROM EGYPT TO GREECE:* The Kamitan Origins of Greek Culture and Religion ISBN: 1-884564-47-X FROM EGYPT TO GREECE   This insightful manual is a reference to Ancient Egyptian mythology and philosophy and its correlation to what later became known as Greek and Rome mythology and philosophy. It outlines the basic tenets of the mythologies and shoes the ancient origins of Greek culture in Ancient Egypt. This volume also documents the origins of the Greek alphabet in Egypt as well as Greek religion, myth and philosophy of the gods and goddesses from Egypt from the myth of Atlantis and archaic period with the Minoans to the Classical period. This volume also acts as a resource for Colleges students who would like to set up fraternities and sororities based on the original Ancient Egyptian principles of Sheti and Maat philosophy. ISBN: 1-884564-47-X $22.95 U.S.

34. *THE FORTY TWO   PRECEPTS OF MAAT,   THE PHILOSOPHY OF RIGHTEOUS ACTION AND THE   ANCIENT EGYPTIAN WISDOM TEXTS* ADVANCED STUDIES This manual is designed for use with the 1998 Maat Philosophy Class conducted by Dr. Muata Ashby.

This is a detailed study of Maat Philosophy. It contains a compilation of the 42 laws or precepts of Maat and the corresponding principles which they represent along with the teachings of the ancient Egyptian Sages relating to each. Maat philosophy was the basis of Ancient Egyptian society and government as well as the heart of Ancient Egyptian myth and spirituality. Maat is at once a goddess, a cosmic force and a living social doctrine, which promotes social harmony and thereby paves the way for spiritual evolution in all levels of society. ISBN: 1-884564-48-8 $16.95 U.S.

35.   *THE SECRET LOTUS: Poetry of Enlightenment*
Discover the mystical sentiment of the Kemetic teaching as expressed through the poetry of Sebai Muata Ashby. The teaching of spiritual awakening is uniquely experienced when the poetic sensibility is present. This first volume contains the poems written between 1996 and 2003. 1-884564--16 -X $16.99

36. The Ancient Egyptian Buddha: The Ancient Egyptian Origins of Buddhism

This book is a compilation of several sections of a larger work, a book by the name of African Origins of Civilization, Religion, Yoga Mysticism and Ethics Philosophy. It also contains some additional evidences not contained in the larger work that demonstrate the correlation between Ancient Egyptian Religion and Buddhism. This book is one of several compiled short volumes that has been compiled so as to facilitate access to specific subjects contained in the larger work which is over 680 pages long. These short and small volumes have been specifically designed to cover one subject in a brief and low cost format. This present volume, The Ancient Egyptian Buddha: The Ancient Egyptian Origins of Buddhism, formed one subject in the larger work; actually it was one chapter of the larger work. However, this volume has some new additional evidences and comparisons of Buddhist and Neterian (Ancient Egyptian) philosophies not previously discussed. It was felt that this subject needed to be discussed because even in the early 21st century, the idea persists that Buddhism originated only in India independently. Yet there is ample evidence from ancient writings and perhaps more importantly, iconographical evidences from the Ancient Egyptians and early Buddhists themselves that prove otherwise. This handy volume has been designed to be accessible to young adults and all others who would like to have an easy reference with documentation on this important subject. This is an important subject because the frame of reference with which we look at a culture depends strongly on our conceptions about its origins. in this case, if we look at the Buddhism as an Asiatic religion we would treat it and it's culture in one way. If we id as African [Ancient Egyptian] we not only would see it in a different light but we also must ascribe Africa with a glorious legacy that matches any other culture in human history and gave rise to one of the present day most important religious philosophies. We would also look at the culture and philosophies of the Ancient Egyptians as having African insights that offer us greater depth into the Buddhist philosophies. Those insights inform our knowledge about other African traditions and we can also begin to understand in a deeper way the effect of Ancient Egyptian culture on African culture and also on the Asiatic as well. We would also be able to discover the glorious and wondrous teaching of mystical philosophy that Ancient Egyptian Shetaut Neter religion offers, that is as powerful as any other mystic system of spiritual philosophy in the world today. ISBN: 1-884564-61-5 $28.95

37. The Death of American Empire: Neo-conservatism, Theocracy, Economic Imperialism, Environmental Disaster and the Collapse of Civilization

This work is a collection of essays relating to social and economic, leadership, and ethics, ecological and religious issues that are facing the world today in order to understand the course of history that has led humanity to its present condition and then arrive at positive solutions that will lead to better outcomes for all humanity. It surveys the development and decline of major empires throughout history and focuses on the creation of American Empire along with the social, political and economic policies that led to the prominence of the United States of America as a Superpower including the rise of the political control of the neo-con political philosophy including militarism and the military industrial complex in American politics and the rise of the religious right into and American Theocracy movement. This volume details, through historical and current events, the psychology behind the dominance of western culture in world politics through the "Superpower Syndrome Mandatory Conflict Complex" that drives the Superpower culture to establish itself above all others and then act hubristically to dominate world culture through legitimate influences as well as coercion, media censorship and misinformation leading to international hegemony and world conflict. This volume also details the financial policies that gave rise to American prominence in the global economy, especially after World War II, and promoted American preeminence over the world economy through Globalization as well as the environmental policies, including the oil economy, that are promoting degradation of the world ecology and contribute to the decline of America as an Empire culture. This volume finally explores the factors pointing to the decline of the American Empire economy and imperial power and what to expect in the aftermath of American prominence and how to survive the decline while at the same time promoting policies and social-economic-religious-political changes that are needed in order to promote the emergence of a beneficial and sustainable culture. **$25.95soft** 1-884564-25-9, Hard Cover **$29.95soft** 1-884564-45-3

38. The African Origins of Hatha Yoga: And its Ancient Mystical Teaching

The subject of this present volume, The Ancient Egyptian Origins of Yoga Postures, formed one subject in the larger works, African Origins of Civilization Religion, Yoga Mysticism and Ethics Philosophy and the Book Egypt and India is the section of the book African Origins of Civilization. Those works contain the collection of all correlations between Ancient Egypt and India. This volume also contains some additional information not contained in the previous work. It was felt that this subject needed to be discussed more directly, being treated in one volume, as opposed to being contained in the larger work along with other subjects, because even in the early 21st century, the idea persists that the Yoga and specifically, Yoga Postures, were invented and developed only in India. The Ancient Egyptians were peoples originally from Africa who were, in ancient times, colonists in India. Therefore it is no surprise that many Indian traditions including religious and Sema-Yogic, would be found earlier in Ancient Egypt. Yet there is ample evidence from ancient writings and perhaps more importantly, iconographical evidences from the Ancient Egyptians themselves and the Indians themselves that prove the connection between Ancient Egypt and India as well as the existence of a discipline of Yoga Postures in Ancient Egypt long before its practice in India. This handy volume has been designed to be accessible to young adults and all others who would like to have an easy reference with documentation on this important subject. This is an important subject because the frame of reference with which we look at a culture depends strongly on our conceptions about its origins. In this case, if we look at the Ancient Egyptians as Asiatic peoples we would treat them and their culture in one way. If we see them as Africans we not only see them in a different light but we also must ascribe Africa with a glorious legacy that matches any other culture in human history. We would also look at the culture and philosophies of the

Ancient Egyptians as having African insights instead of Asiatic ones. Those insights inform our knowledge bout other African traditions and we can also begin to understand in a deeper way the effect of Ancient Egyptian culture on African culture and also on the Asiatic as well. When we discover the deeper and more ancient practice of the postures system in Ancient Egypt that was called "Hatha Yoga" in India, we are able to find a new and expanded understanding of the practice that constitutes a discipline of spiritual practice that informs and revitalizes the Indian practices as well as all spiritual disciplines. $19.99 ISBN 1-884564-60-7

39. The Black Ancient Egyptians

This present volume, The Black Ancient Egyptians: The Black African Ancestry of the Ancient Egyptians, formed one subject in the larger work: The African Origins of Civilization, Religion, Yoga Mysticism and Ethics Philosophy. It was felt that this subject needed to be discussed because even in the early 21st century, the idea persists that the Ancient Egyptians were peoples originally from Asia Minor who came into North-East Africa. Yet there is ample evidence from ancient writings and perhaps more importantly, iconographical evidences from the Ancient Egyptians themselves that proves otherwise. This handy volume has been designed to be accessible to young adults and all others who would like to have an easy reference with documentation on this important subject. This is an important subject because the frame of reference with which we look at a culture depends strongly on our conceptions about its origins. in this case, if we look at the Ancient Egyptians as Asiatic peoples we would treat them and their culture in one way. If we see them as Africans we not only see them in a different light but we also must ascribe Africa with a glorious legacy that matches any other culture in human history. We would also look at the culture and philosophies of the Ancient Egyptians as having African insights instead of Asiatic ones. Those insights inform our knowledge bout other African traditions and we can also begin to understand in a deeper way the effect of Ancient Egyptian culture on African culture and also on the Asiatic as well. ISBN 1-884564-21-6 $19.99

40. The Limits of Faith: The Failure of Faith-based Religions and the Solution to the Meaning of Life

Is faith belief in something without proof? And if so is there never to be any proof or discovery? If so what is the need of intellect? If faith is trust in something that is real is that reality historical, literal or metaphorical or philosophical? If knowledge is an essential element in faith why should there by so much emphasis on believing and not on understanding in the modern practice of religion? This volume is a compilation of essays related to the nature of religious faith in the context of its inception in human history as well as its meaning for religious practice and relations between religions in modern times. Faith has come to be regarded as a virtuous goal in life. However, many people have asked how can it be that an endeavor that is supposed to be dedicated to spiritual upliftment has led to more conflict in human history than any other social factor? ISBN 1884564631 SOFT COVER - $19.99, ISBN 1884564623 HARD COVER -$28.95

41. Redemption of The Criminal Heart Through Kemetic Spirituality and Maat Philosophy
Special book dedicated to inmates, their families and members of the Law Enforcement community to promote understanding of the cause of transgressions and how to resolve those issues so that a human being may rediscover their humanity and come back to the family of humanity and also regain the capacity to fully engage in positive spiritual evolution. ISBN: 1-884564-70-4

42. COMPARATIVE MYTHOLOGY
What are Myth and Culture and what is their importance for understanding the development of societies, human evolution and the search for meaning? What is the purpose of culture and how do cultures evolve? What are the elements of a culture and how can those elements be broken down and the constituent parts of a culture understood and compared? How do cultures interact? How does enculturation occur and how do people interact with other cultures? How do the processes of acculturation and cooptation occur and what does this mean for the development of a society? How can the study of myths and the elements of culture help in understanding the meaning of life and the means to promote understanding and peace in the world of human activity? This volume is the exposition of a method for studying and comparing cultures, myths and other social aspects of a society. It is an expansion on the Cultural Category Factor Correlation method for studying and comparing myths, cultures, religions and other aspects of human culture. It was originally introduced in the year 2002. This volume contains an expanded treatment as well as several refinements along with examples of the application of the method. the apparent. I hope you enjoy these art renditions as serene reflections of the mysteries of life. ISBN: 1-884564-72-0
Book price $21.95

43. CONVERSATION WITH GOD: Revelations of the Important Questions of Life

$24.99 U.S.

This volume contains a grouping of some of the questions that have been submitted to Sebai Dr. Muata Ashby. They are efforts by many aspirants to better understand and practice the teachings of mystical spirituality. It is said that when sages are asked spiritual questions they are relaying the wisdom of God, the Goddess, the Higher Self, etc. There is a very special quality about the Q & A process that does not occur during a regular lecture session. Certain points come out that would not come out otherwise due to the nature of the process which ideally occurs after a lecture. Having been to a certain degree enlightened by a lecture certain new questions arise and the answers to these have the effect of elevating the teaching of the lecture to even higher levels. Therefore, enjoy these exchanges and may they lead you to enlightenment, peace and prosperity. ISBN: 1-884564-68-2

44. MYSTIC ART PAINTINGS

(with Full Color images) This book contains a collection of the small number of paintings that I have created over the years. Some were used as early book covers and others were done simply to express certain spiritual feelings; some were created for no purpose except to express the joy of color and the feeling of relaxed freedom. All are to elicit mystical awakening in the viewer. Writing a book on philosophy is like sculpture, the more the work is rewritten the reflections and ideas become honed and take form and become clearer and imbued with intellectual beauty. Mystic music is like meditation, a world of its own that exists about 1 inch above ground wherein the musician does not touch the ground. Mystic Graphic Art is meditation in form, color, image and reflected image which opens the door to the reality behind the apparent. I hope you enjoy these art renditions and my reflections on them as serene reflections of the mysteries of life, as visual renditions of the philosophy I have written about over the years. ISBN 1-884564-69-0 $19.95

45. ANCIENT EGYPTIAN HIEROGLYPHS FOR BEGINNERS

This brief guide was prepared for those inquiring about how to enter into Hieroglyphic studies on their own at home or in study groups. First of all you should know that there are a few institutions around the world which teach how to read the Hieroglyphic text but due to the nature of the study there are perhaps only a handful of people who can read fluently. It is possible for anyone with average intelligence to achieve a high level of proficiency in reading inscriptions on temples and artifacts; however, reading extensive texts is another issue entirely. However, this introduction will give you entry into those texts if assisted by dictionaries and other aids. Most Egyptologists have a basic knowledge and keep dictionaries and notes handy when it comes to dealing with more difficult texts. Medtu Neter or the Ancient Egyptian hieroglyphic language has been considered as a "Dead Language." However, dead languages have always been studied by individuals who for the most part have taught themselves through various means. This book will discuss those means and how to use them most efficiently. ISBN 1884564429 **$28.95**

46. ON THE MYSTERIES: Wisdom of An Ancient Egyptian Sage -with Foreword by Muata Ashby
This volume, On the Mysteries, by Iamblichus (Abamun) is a unique form or scripture out of the Ancient Egyptian religious tradition. It is written in a form that is not usual or which is not usually found in the remnants of Ancient Egyptian scriptures. It is in the form of teacher and disciple, much like the Eastern scriptures such as Bhagavad Gita or the Upanishads. This form of writing may not have been necessary in Ancient times, because the format of teaching in Egypt was different prior to the conquest period by the Persians, Assyrians, Greeks and later the Romans. The question and answer format can be found but such extensive discourses and corrections of misunderstandings within the context of a teacher - disciple relationship is not usual. It therefore provides extensive insights into the times when it was written and the state of practice of Ancient Egyptian and other mystery religions. This has important implications for our times because we are today, as in the Greco-Roman period, also besieged with varied religions and new age philosophies as well as social strife and war. How can we understand our times and also make sense of the forest of spiritual traditions? How can we cut through the cacophony of religious fanaticism, and ignorance as well as misconceptions about the mysteries on the other in order to discover the true purpose of religion and the secret teachings that open up the mysteries of life and the way to enlightenment and immortality? This book, which comes to us from so long ago, offers us transcendental wisdom that applied to the world two thousand years ago as well as our world today. ISBN 1-884564-64-X $25.95

47. The Ancient Egyptian Wisdom Texts -Compiled by Muata Ashby
The Ancient Egyptian Wisdom Texts are a genre of writings from the ancient culture that have survived to the present and provide a vibrant record of the practice of spiritual evolution otherwise known as religion

or yoga philosophy in Ancient Egypt. The principle focus of the Wisdom Texts is the cultivation of understanding, peace, harmony, selfless service, self-control, Inner fulfillment and spiritual realization. When these factors are cultivated in human life, the virtuous qualities in a human being begin to manifest and sinfulness, ignorance and negativity diminish until a person is able to enter into higher consciousness, the coveted goal of all civilizations. It is this virtuous mode of life which opens the door to self-discovery and spiritual enlightenment. Therefore, the Wisdom Texts are important scriptures on the subject of human nature, spiritual psychology and mystical philosophy. The teachings presented in the Wisdom Texts form the foundation of religion as well as the guidelines for conducting the affairs of every area of social interaction including commerce, education, the army, marriage, and especially the legal system. These texts were sources for the famous 42 Precepts of Maat of the Pert M Heru (Book of the Dead), essential regulations of good conduct to develop virtue and purity in order to attain higher consciousness and immortality after death. ISBN1-884564-65-8 $18.95

48. THE KEMETIC TREE OF LIFE
THE KEMETIC TREE OF LIFE: Newly Revealed Ancient Egyptian Cosmology and Metaphysics for Higher Consciousness The Tree of Life is a roadmap of a journey which explains how Creation came into being and how it will end. It also explains what Creation is composed of and also what human beings are and what they are composed of. It also explains the process of Creation, how Creation develops, as well as who created Creation and where that entity may be found. It also explains how a human being may discover that entity and in so doing also discover the secrets of Creation, the meaning of life and the means to break free from the pathetic condition of human limitation and mortality in order to discover the higher realms of being by discovering the principles, the levels of existence that are beyond the simple physical and material aspects of life. This book contains color plates **ISBN: 1-884564-74-7** **$27.95 U.S.**

49. Little Book of Neter a summary of the most important teachings of Shetaut Neter (Ancient Egyptian religion) for all aspirants to have for easy reference **guide to the basic practices and fundamental teachings $3.00 (Soft) ISBN: 1-884564-58-5**

50. Dollar Crisis: The Collapse of Society and Redemption Through Ancient Egyptian Monetary Policy (Paperback)

by Muata Ashby   This book is about the problems of the US economy and the imminent collapse of the U.S. Dollar and its dire consequences for the US economy and the world. It is also about the corruption in government, economics and social order that led to this point. Also it is about survival, how to make it through this perhaps most trying period in the history of the United States. Also it is about the ancient wisdom of life that allowed an ancient civilization to grow beyond the destructive corruptions of ignorance and power so that the people of today may gain insight into the nature of their condition, how they got there and what needs to be done in order to salvage what is left and rebuild a society that is sustainable, beneficial and an example for all humanity. $18.99 u.s.

- **ISBN-10:** 1884564763
- **ISBN-13:** 978-1884564765

Music Based on the Prt M Hru and other Kemetic Texts

Available on Compact Disc $14.99 and Audio Cassette $9.99

Adorations to the Goddess

Music for Worship of the Goddess

NEW Egyptian Yoga Music CD
by Sehu Maa
Ancient Egyptian Music CD
Instrumental Music played on reproductions of Ancient Egyptian Instruments
Ideal for <u>meditation</u> and
reflection on the Divine and for the practice of spiritual programs and <u>Yoga</u>
<u>exercise sessions.</u>

1999 By Muata Ashby
CD $14.99

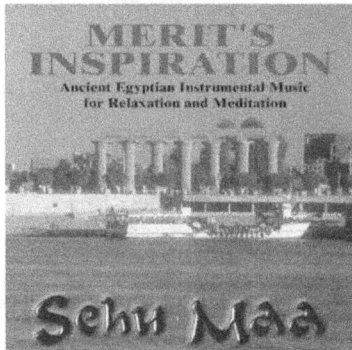

MERIT'S INSPIRATION
NEW Egyptian Yoga Music CD

311

by Sehu Maa
Ancient Egyptian Music CD
Instrumental Music played on
reproductions of Ancient Egyptian Instruments Ideal for <u>meditation</u> and
reflection on the Divine and for the practice of spiritual programs and <u>Yoga
exercise sessions.</u>
1999 By
Muata Ashby
CD $14.99
UPC# 761527100429

ANORATIONS TO RA AND HETHERU
NEW Egyptian Yoga Music CD
By Sehu Maa (Muata Ashby)
Based on the Words of Power of Ra and HetHeru
played on reproductions of Ancient Egyptian Instruments **Ancient Egyptian
Instruments used: Voice, Clapping, Nefer Lute, Tar Drum, Sistrums,
Cymbals**   The Chants, Devotions, Rhythms and Festive Songs Of the Neteru
– Ideal for meditation, and devotional singing and dancing.
1999 By Muata Ashby
CD $14.99
UPC# 761527100221

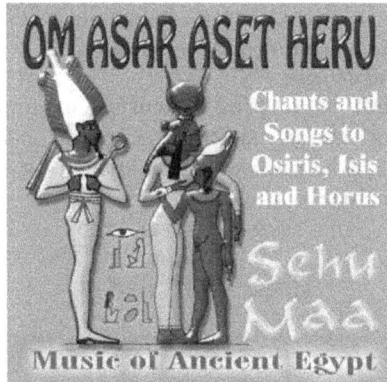

SONGS TO ASAR ASET AND HERU
NEW
Egyptian Yoga Music CD
By Sehu Maa
played on reproductions of Ancient Egyptian Instruments   The Chants,
Devotions, Rhythms and
Festive Songs Of the Neteru - Ideal for meditation, and devotional singing and dancing.
Based on the Words of Power of Asar (Asar), Aset (Aset) and Heru (Heru)
Om Asar Aset Heru is the third in a series of musical explorations of the
Kemetic (Ancient Egyptian) tradition of music. Its ideas are based on the
Ancient Egyptian Religion of Asar, Aset and Heru and it is designed for
listening, meditation and worship.   1999 By Muata Ashby
CD $14.99
UPC# 761527100122

HAARI OM: ANCIENT EGYPT MEETS INDIA IN MUSIC
NEW Music CD
By Sehu Maa

The Chants, Devotions, Rhythms and

313

Festive Songs Of the Ancient Egypt and India, harmonized and played on reproductions of ancient instruments along with modern instruments and beats. Ideal for meditation, and devotional singing and dancing.

Haari Om is the fourth in a series of musical explorations of the Kemetic (Ancient Egyptian) and Indian traditions of music, chanting and devotional spiritual practice. Its ideas are based on the Ancient Egyptian Yoga spirituality and Indian Yoga spirituality.

1999 By Muata Ashby
CD $14.99
UPC# 761527100528

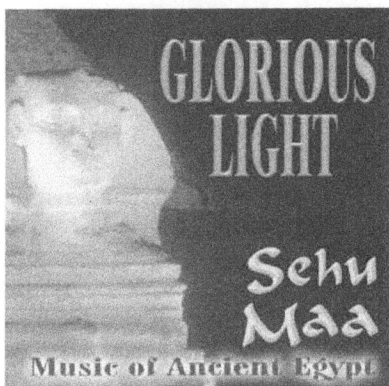

RA AKHU: THE GLORIOUS LIGHT
NEW
Egyptian Yoga Music CD
By Sehu Maa

The fifth collection of original music compositions based on the Teachings and Words of The Trinity, the God Asar and the Goddess Nebethet, the Divinity Aten, the God Heru, and the Special Meditation Hekau or Words of Power of Ra from the Ancient Egyptian Tomb of Seti I and more...

played on reproductions of Ancient Egyptian Instruments and modern instruments - **Ancient Egyptian Instruments used: Voice, Clapping, Nefer Lute, Tar Drum, Sistrums, Cymbals**

The Chants, Devotions, Rhythms and Festive Songs Of the Neteru – Ideal for meditation, and devotional singing and dancing.

1999 By Muata Ashby
CD $14.99
UPC# 761527100825

GLORIES OF THE DIVINE MOTHER
Based on the hieroglyphic text of the worship of Goddess Net.
The Glories of The Great Mother
2000 Muata Ashby
CD $14.99 UPC# 761527101129`

GROWING BEYOND HATE

Order Form

Telephone orders: Call Toll Free: 1(305) 378-6253. Have your AMEX, Optima, Visa or MasterCard ready.

Fax orders: 1-(305) 378-6253   E-MAIL ADDRESS:
Semayoga@aol.com

Postal Orders: Sema Institute of Yoga, P.O. Box 570459, Miami, Fl. 33257. USA.

Please send the following books and / or tapes.

ITEM

_____Cost $_____

_____Cost $_____

_____Cost $_____

_____Cost $_____

_____Cost $_____

Total $_____

Name:_____

Physical Address:_____

City:_____ State:_____ Zip:_____

Sales tax: Please add 6.5% for books shipped to Florida addresses
_____Shipping: $6.50 for first book and .50   for each additional
_____Shipping: Outside US $5.00 for first book and $3.00 for each additional

_____Payment:_____
_____Check -Include Driver License #:

_____

_____Credit card: _____ Visa, _____ MasterCard, _____ Optima,
_____ AMEX.

Card number:_____
Name on card:_____ Exp. date:_____/_____

Copyright 1995-2009 Dr. R. Muata Abhaya Ashby
Sema Institute of Yoga
P.O.Box 570459, Miami, Florida, 33257
(305) 378-6253 Fax: (305) 378-6253

www.ingramcontent.com/pod-product-compliance
Lightning Source LLC
Chambersburg PA
CBHW072052020426
42334CB00017B/1477